Copyright © 2016 by Lani Sharp
All rights reserved. This book or any portion thereof
may not be reproduced or used in any manner whatsoever
without the express written permission of the publisher
except for the use of brief quotations in a book review.

Printed in Australia

First Printing, 2016

ISBN 978-0-9945051-7-0

White Light Publishing House
6 Lincoln Way
Melton West, VIC, Australia 3337

www.whitelightpublishingau.com

❧ DEDICATIONS ☙

This book is dedicated to Eleanor, my daughter's precious Nana. Thank you for your wisdom, dedication, devotion, gentleness, deep sense of kinship, and for being such a special part of our journey.

ABOUT THE AUTHOR

☾ ★ ☽

Lani Sharp is a Natural Born Rebel who just also happens to be an Aquarian, who shunned 'conventional' astrology courses to pursue her own path in the wondrous, inspiring and ever-evolving field of cosmic forces and stellar influences. After failing to find a course or tutor that suited her needs, Lani set out on her own starry Magic Carpet adventure across the skies, partly to discover her own 'truths' about this ancient system, but mostly to prove that one can achieve absolutely anything, including and above all, their dream careers (or lifestyle), if they put their hearts and souls into it. A self-taught astrologer who takes the esoteric and spiritual approach to this much-loved popular art, she has been studying and effectively practising astrology since she was eight years old. When she is not writing about, channelling, practising or teaching astrology, she can be found living her dream life alternating somewhere between her home in Australia's stunning Tropical North or her second home in Victoria's beautiful Dandenong Ranges, enjoying tea parties with her highly imaginative Cancerian daughter, Allira, and their gnome and fairy friends, crystal-wishing, day-dreaming, believing in gnomes, pixies, angels, fairies, magic and miracles, honing her magickal * witchcraft skills, Moon-gazing, Sun-worshipping, Venus-channelling, Jupiter-drawing, assisting others to discover, unravel and follow their true spiritual paths … or of course walking across rainbows!

* Not a mistake. Magick is a Wiccan variation of the word 'magic'.

★

ACKNOWLEDGEMENTS, CREDITS & GRATITUDE BLESSINGS

★

I would love to thank the following people and entities for their amazing contributions, interest, support and faith in me as I wrote the manuscripts for each of the twelve astrological Sun signs. Firstly, the biggest thank you goes to my Mum, Sandra, and my stepdad, Barry, for their unending support, love, advice, daily Skype conversations, acceptance of our geographical distance, and above all, their inner knowing that everything always comes together in the end. Your support of me and my dreams is appreciated beyond words. Secondly, gratitude to my wonderful partner, Travis, for his patience (no mean feat for a Gemini!), for supporting me every step of the way, and for his acceptance of my 'mad scientist' Aquarian mindset by never trying to break down the invisible 'laboratory' walls I built around myself while writing the books. I would also like to extend my enormous gratitude to the following: Allira, my little Cancerian 'crab' daughter, a soul in a billion, who also had to tolerate and operate within the bounds of her nutty professor mother's antics and focus throughout the writing of the books. Thank you to Nicola, my wonderful Facebook friend, for recommending White Light Publishing House, and of course to White Light Publishing House themselves, for pouring their faith and passion into my project from the very beginning - and an even bigger thank you to the wonderful people behind the company for publishing my work, Christie and Jess! Gratitude also goes out to my dear friends, both near and far, who have inspired in me so many ideas through simply being themselves - especially Amanda and Carlie. Amanda, you have always been my 'astrology buddy' and I have always enjoyed - and learned so much through - our discussions on all things astrology and star signs: the good, the bad and the ugly! Having someone like you off which to bounce thoughts and share ideas with, has always been immensely helpful and appreciated. I have saved my final thank you for The Universe, who always delivers to me exactly what I have asked for, without exception. The Universe is my ultimate *higher power*, my guiding light, my powerful driving force, my spiritual helper, my guardian angel, my eternal friend, my inner motivator, my sympathetic listener, my inspirational teacher, and the fulfiller of all my dreams, including this one, having my very first book(s) published, a long-held dream that stretches way back through the years to my days of being a mini dreamer, inquisitor and stargazer. The Universe has always believed in me, but perhaps more importantly, I have always believed in *IT*.

So to all of the above, I wish to say:

Thank you, thank you, thank you!

"We were born at a given moment, in a given place, and like vintage years of wine, we have the qualities of the year and of the season in which we are born"

Carl G. Jung

"There was a star danced,
and under that I was born"

William Shakespeare

INSPIRED BY ALL THE SIGNS

Aries imparted courage and boldness
And helped me dance away the pain
Taurus gave me hugs and comfort
And shelter from the rain
Gemini provided me with laughter
And taught me again how to have fun
Cancer nurtured and sustained me
By reflecting back my Sun
Leo reminded me there was joy
From within myself and above
Virgo awakened my healthy glow
By teaching me how to love
Libra gave me gentle hugs
And judged me not for a thing
Scorpio lent me some of his power
And took away the sting
Sagittarius showered me with gifts
Of words so wise and true
As Capricorn led the way up the mountain
My resolve and strength grew
Aquarius gave me the gift of friendship
And carried me as his brother
And Pisces swam with me to the depths
With a compassion like no other.

Special Note

Throughout the text of this book, and indeed the whole Lucky Astrology book series, I have capitalised the first letter of the word 'Universe'. This is because, quite simply, I feel it is a very special title for the higher power that I personally choose to be guided by, and have accordingly highlighted it as such.

You may also notice that I use the words 'he' or 'she', and 'his' or 'her', when referring to your own Sun sign and other zodiac signs, and never 'he or she' or 'his or her' together. The reason for this is for simplicity, for I don't wish the sentences to be too wordy and therefore the messages within them to be lost. As a general rule, I refer to all six 'masculine' zodiac signs as 'he', and all six 'feminine' signs as 'she', and this remains a consistent rule throughout this book and the whole series.

Your Sun sign, Capricorn, is a feminine sign and will thus be referred to accordingly.

CONTENTS

	Page
ASTROLOGY	15
THE ZODIAC & YOUR PLACE IN THE SUN	22
CAPRICORN THE GOAT	31
QUOTES BY CAPRICORNIANS	38
THE CAPRICORN CONSTELLATION	44
THE CAPRICORN SYMBOL	46
THE RUNDOWN & LESSONS ★	
THE ESSENCE OF CAPRICORN	50
THE THREE DECANS OF CAPRICORN	62
YOUR ELEMENT ★ EARTH	66
YOUR MODE ★ CARDINAL	88
YOUR RULING PLANET ★ SATURN	90
YOUR HOUSE IN THE HOROSCOPE ★	
THE TENTH HOUSE	115
YOUR OPPOSITE SIGN ★ CANCER	120
MAGIC, DRAWING, ATTRACTION, SPELLS,	
RITUALS, WISHING & POWER	129
ASTROLOGY & MAGIC	134
PLANETS ★ DAYS OF THE WEEK	
& THEIR POWERS	140
YOUR NATAL MOON PHASE	144
SPELLS, MAGIC & WISHING WITH MOON PHASES	147
THE MOON ★ WHAT T REPRESENTS IN THE	
HUMAN PSYCHE & NATAL CHART	154
YOUR MOON SIGN	157
YOUR BODY & HEALTH	166
THE CELL SALTS ★ ASTROLOGICAL TONICS	172

~ - 11 - ~

	Page
EARTH SIGN CAPRICORN & THE MELANCHOLIC HUMOUR	175
MONEY ATTRIBUTES	178
COLOURS ★ YOUR LUCKY COLOURS	181
LUCKY CAREER TIPS	193
LUCKY PLACES	197
GEMS & CRYSTALS	198
CAPRICORNIAN POWER CRYSTALS	207
YOUR LUCKY NUMBERS	226
YOUR LUCKY MAGIC HOURS OR TIME UNITS	234
YOUR LUCKY DAY ★ SATURDAY	239
YOUR LUCKY CHARM / TALISMANS	243
YOUR LUCKY ANIMALS & BIRDS	246
YOUR METALS	258
PLANTS, HERBS, SPICES, TREES, SHRUBS, FLOWERS, SCENTS & INCENSE	262
YOUR FOODS	268
YOUR LUCKY WOOD & CELTIC TREE ★ EBONY & BIRCH	271
THE POWER OF LOVE	277
LUCKY IN LOVE? CAPRICORN COMPATIBILITY	289
YOUR TAROT CARDS	307
LUCKY 13 TIPS	323
HAVE YOU PACKED YOUR MAGICAL BAG FOR THE JOURNEY?	326
A FINAL WORD ★ TAPPING INTO THE MAGIC OF CAPRICORN	327

LUCKY ASTROLOGY

By Lani Sharp

CAPRICORN

*Tapping into the Powers of Your Sun Sign for Greater
Luck, Happiness, Health, Abundance & Love*

"That which is above is like to that which is below, and that which is below is like to that which is above, to accomplish the miracles of one thing ... the Father thereof is the Sun, the mother the Moon."

The Emerald Tablet, Hermes Trismegistus (circa 3000 BC)

★ ASTROLOGY ★

Astrology: "Divination through the correlation of earthly events with celestial patterns"
'Real Magic', I. Bonewits, 1971

A BRIEF HISTORY

Astrology can be defined as the calculation and meaningful interpretation of the positions and motions of the heavenly bodies, and their correlation with human experiences. Its central concept is based upon this interconnectedness or correspondence between the stars and ourselves.

The word astrology is derived from the Greek word astron, meaning 'star' and logos which means 'word'. Astrology, therefore, literally means language of the stars. It is based on the ancient law known as 'As Above, So Below', otherwise known as the Law of the Macrocosm and Microcosm. The Macrocosm is the Universe, symbolised by the sky, the starry dome that we can see from the Earth; the Microcosm is us - humans, and all other life on Earth. 'As Above, So Below' is a well-known and deeply impressing maxim of Hermetic origin, inscribed upon the famed Emerald Tablet among cryptic wording by enigmatic figure, Hermes Trismegistus, around 5,000 years ago. These four powerful words are adopted by astrologers and believers in magic to explain, in very succinct wording, the meaning behind the art and science of celestial influences upon our Earthly affairs.

Astrology and many other magical and occult studies, propose that we are not separate from the Universe, we are part of it. The Sun, Moon and planets all follow exact patterns of movement and their motions can be measured precisely by astronomers. The basic idea of astrology is that all individual parts of the Universe, from plants to animals, cooperate with each other and work together in harmony.

Anyone can apply astrological knowledge in their daily lives, but it hasn't always been like that. At one time, astrology was reserved only for Kings and nations, and only the court astrologer/astronomer could cast and interpret horoscopes. Ancient astrology and astronomy used to be one and the same. To be an astrologer, you first had to be able to interpret the stars in some systematic way, and then track the movement of the Moon and the planets against the background of the constellations.

Astrology, the knowledge and language of the cosmos, goes back to the ancient kingdom of Babylonia and was adapted by the Mesopotamians, Greeks, Egyptians and Romans to incorporate their own deities (as indicated in mythology). It is upon a combination of Greek and Egyptian interpretations of astrology that our present knowledge is based.

In the ancient Mesopotamian world, as far back as 800 BC, people lived precariously beneath the open skies. The skies and the stars which filled them, were the real founders of astrology. Today we are aware that the Sun and Moon exert a profound influence upon our Earthly affairs, but for our primitive ancestors, the heavens, the stars and the planets must have been a matter of great and mysterious significance. Early humankind, its senses influenced by natural processes of ebbs, flows, growth, decay and cycles, tended naturally towards a physical explanation of the Universe. At first, the movements of the planets - and all celestial occurrences - were observed as omens affecting the Ruler and his nation; it was only in Egypt in the fifth century AD that the casting of horoscopes for individual people and the calculation of the planetary positions at the time of birth became widespread.

The first astrologers, the Chaldeans, mapped the stars and later passed this knowledge and wisdom on to the ancient Greeks, who, during the third century BC, developed astrology into a science with the use of mathematical aids and instruments to measure planetary movements. The Greeks were the first to cast individual horoscopes. And it was the Greeks who associated the four elements with the signs of the zodiac. The word "zodiac" can be translated from Greek to mean the "circle or path of the animals." The Greeks not only had names for the twelve Solar phases but had symbols for each, and many correspond with the ones we use today.

The Greeks passed on much of their knowledge to the Romans. During the second century BC, Roman astrologers were primarily forecasters who were consulted frequently by rulers of the church and state. By the early third century AD, astrology co-existed with early Christianity. This harmonious co-existence was possible because it was considered that celestial bodies could foretell events, but did not determine the future - indeed, the stars seen by the shepherds at the time of Christ's birth were only predictors of his arrival. After the fourth century AD, Christianity strengthened and the popularity of astrology declined as Christian reluctance to support 'pagan' or 'superstitious' beliefs became more prominent. The Middle Ages saw a revival in astrology, with courses being taught in universities and other educational establishments, and connections were made between the zodiac, alchemy, herbs and medicine. Astrology was once again able to exist alongside the Church, although many remained suspicious of astrologers.

Around the beginning of the fifteenth century, academics of the Renaissance movement examined the past for knowledge, and ancient philosophies, including astrology, flourished; this coincided with arts and science movements developing. The famous prophet and astrologer Nostradamus lived during this period. Leonardo da Vinci depicted aspects of astrology combined with geometry in his art. Writers and poets of the time, including Shakespeare, alluded to zodiacal influences in their work.

During this period, astrology had numerous practical applications. Agricultural calendars were introduced, indicating favourable planting times according to the phases of the Moon; health and illness were linked with movements of celestial bodies; and emotional states and mental health afflictions correlated with the planetary positions.

Eventually, new ways of thinking led to a split between astronomy and astrology, and by the seventeenth century, the realm of science had developed to such a degree that astrology was no longer taken seriously.

The study of the sky above us has been charted for more than 5,000 years. This fact is known because ancient 'horoscopes' imprinted on clay tablets have been unearthed, dating back almost 5,400 years ago. However, no one knows for certain just how, when and where astrology first began, although it is known that it flourished in ancient Chaldea, Mesopotamia, Babylon and Egypt.

Astrology is a science which has spanned many centuries and still remains extraordinarily popular, and its truths have the potential to speak to and *through* all of us. Long before today's interest in it, men of great vision such as Ptolemy, Hippocrates, Plato, Galileo, Jefferson, Franklin, Newton, Columbus and Jung respected its inherent truths, mythology and eternal knowledge. Furthermore, astrology predates many other 'sciences' - for out of it grew religion, medicine and astronomy, not the other way around.

The discipline of astrology is ultimately a study of the interlocking and interrelated forces of the twelve zodiacal forces, or constellations, that grace the heavens, as they pour their energies into the Earthly kingdoms below. As these various energies circulate throughout the etheric realm of our Solar system, these zodiacal entities and archetypes imprint their vibrational frequencies and harmonic resonances upon our bodies, minds, souls and spirits.

ASTROLOGY & THE INDIVIDUAL

Since the earliest period of the history of humankind, people studied the starry vaults of the heavens and conceived that their presence, movements and positions endowed planet Earth's inhabitants with Divine influence. There is much evidence that positions and movements of the planets as seen from Earth at the time of a birth are linked to personality characteristics of individuals. Human energy and emotional cycles are governed by the forces and networks of magnetic impulses from all the planets. Of all the heavenly bodies, the Moon's effects and power are the most marked and visible due to its close proximity to Earth. But the Sun, Venus, Mars, Mercury, Jupiter, Saturn, Uranus, Neptune and Pluto exercise their influences just as surely. In fact, scientists are aware that plants and animals are affected by natural cycles which are governed by forces such as fluctuations in barometric pressure, the gravitational field and electricity in the air. These Earthly dynamics are originally triggered by magnetic vibrations from the atmosphere, or outer space, from where the planets send forth their unseen waves. No living organism or mineral on Earth escapes these immense, if unseen, influences.

The geomagnetic field seems to affect life on Earth in certain observed ways, and these influences appear to correlate with planetary positions. It has been suggested that the fluctuations of the Earth's magnetic field are picked up by the nervous system of the in utero infant, which acts like an antenna, and these synchronise the internal biological clocks of the foetus which control the moment of birth. The foetal magnetic antenna therefore, is sensitive enough to sense these planetary vibrations and fields, and through a combination of inherited genetics and the positions of the planets at birth, they are imprinted with certain basic inherited and 'absorbed' personality characteristics.

Carl Jung, the Swiss psychiatrist and psychological theorist, suggested that the inherent disposition of the individual is present at birth, and is reflected in the patterns of his or her natal chart. Further, he theorised that there is a 'priori factor' in all human activities, namely the inborn, preconscious and unconscious individual structure of the psyche. The preconscious psyche, for example that of a newborn baby, is not simply an empty vessel into which practically anything can be poured, but rather it is this preconscious psyche that gives us the free will to become what we are instead of what others or our environment makes us. The child is not merely a receptacle for the psychic life of those around him or her, albeit sensitive and susceptible to the surrounding unconscious forces in childhood; for he/she also brings something of his own to his experience of them.

Further, Dr Harold S. Burr, who was a Professor of Anatomy at the Yale University School of Medicine, and author of *The Nature of Man and the Meaning of Existence* (1962), asserted that there is order in the Universe, unity in the organism and man is endowed with a soul. He stated that a complex magnetic field not only establishes the pattern of the human brain at birth, but continues to regulate and control it through life, and that the human central nervous system is a superb receptor of electro-magnetic energies, indeed the finest in nature. He contended that the electro-dynamic fields of all living things, which may be measured and mapped with standard voltmeters, mould and control each organism's development, health and mood, and named these fields 'fields of life'.

It can therefore be suggested that astrological and planetary influences endow us with the majority of our characteristics at birth, characteristics bestowed upon us according to our Sun sign and other planetary forces. Other parts of the chart are also highly significant and need to be integrated for a 'whole' picture to form, however the Sun sign is an excellent starting point.

The ancients taught that astrology was one of the keys to the many enigmas that plague humans in their unceasing quest to determine what the meaning of life is, and what their role and place in the Universe is - and this quest still persists today. Astrology, which dates back over 5,000 years, is indeed one such key to unlocking the many secrets of the Universe - and ultimately, the individual self.

"KNOW THYSELF"

"Man, know thyself. All wisdom centres on this."
Carl Jung

Before the temple of the Oracle at Delphi, the ancient Greeks imparted a special piece of advice that was carved onto one of the portals: "Know Thyself."

These two powerful words are easy enough to understand, but much more difficult to apply. Throughout life's inner and outer journey, astrology can provide us with an inner navigational system by which we can be guided towards our highest potential, and closer towards the eternal quest of 'knowing thyself'. It provides the hope that this higher spiritual plane exists and that if we can 'read' and therefore be guided by the unique inner blueprint that our individual birth chart has stamped upon us at the moment we take our very first breath, indeed we can reach this higher spiritual plane and realise our innate potential.

Always remember that astrology is not fatalistic. The stars may incline, but they do not compel. Astrology simply provides us with an inner guide, a blueprint, for our journey through life and the finding of our true selves - and what we do with the resulting knowledge is entirely up to us.

Good luck on your journey!

THE ZODIAC & YOUR PLACE IN THE SUN

The zodiac is a circle of 360 degrees, consisting of equal segments of 30 degrees each. These represent the twelve houses of the twelve astrological signs. This zodiac is how the early astrologers imagined the Solar system to be, a perfect circle with the Earth at its centre, around which the Sun, Moon and the planets revolved. Each sign of the zodiac corresponds to one of the twelve segments, following a chronological order and established according to the rhythm of the seasons and cycles of the Sun and the Moon. But the zodiac itself, or the band of constellations which comprise it, has shifted over the millennia, creating division between astronomical and astrological schools of thought. It has been said that due to this shift over time, one who once considered themselves as an Aquarian, is actually a Capricorn, the sign before it, and a Leo is actually a Cancerian, its preceding sign. This is the result of misunderstandings and differences in perspectives, and explanations around it are beyond the scope of this book, but can be researched further should you wish to delve a little deeper. From the astronomical point of view, it is true that the zodiac to which we refer today is not situated where it 'should' be, but indeed, nothing is fixed under the celestial vault. And so the starting point of the ancient zodiac does not correspond exactly to the one we can observe today. But for the purposes of increasing your power and luck, let's keep things simple and enjoy the ride; after all, astrology - while based upon many scientific theories, mysteries, scepticism, superstitions, facts, measurable patterns, ambiguities, correlations, paradoxes, contradictions, links, stigmatisms and observations that seek to support, refute, prove and disprove this ancient art time and again - is ultimately meant to be *fun* too!

THE SUN

Earth's Luminary ★ *Our Brightest Shining Star*

Our Centre, Core Self, Identity & Inner Guiding Light

"Perfect is what I have said of the work of the Sun."
Hermes Trismegistus, *The Emerald Tablet*

The Sun is our essence, centre, source, ego strength, power, life force, will, vitality, creative expression, purpose, life's direction, our sense of identity, and who we really *are*. Our brightest star is the core of our individuality, our inner guiding light. The Sun is externalising, and represents totality, infinity, eternity, the striving toward and ultimate reaching of one's personal destiny, and *completion* in all areas. It is the creative energising giver of life and the 'father' of the zodiac. It endows us with our inherent creative potential and personal identity - our urge to *create* and to *be*. The Sun is our core self, conscious purpose, our sense of creating something out of our own being. It is the integrated personality and represents the *present*, our greatest Gift. The Sun rules the heart and is thus symbolically the centre of self. Indeed, the Sun *is* the heart and the most commanding presence in our birth chart; the luminary Ruler who governs our essential self and wants to be noticed and appreciated, and above all, to *shine*.

★ KEY WORDS ★

Identity, core self, spirit, life force, power, essence, creativity, higher self, the Father, ego, vitality, pride, individuality, leadership, majesty, inner authority, will, expression, willpower, purpose, the journey, the path and the destiny.

THE SUN ★ THE ULTIMATE SOURCE OF LIFE ON EARTH

Throughout the ages, and indeed since life forms began, the electromagnetic waves generated by the Sun have kept planet Earth habitable for humans, animals, plants and minerals. The Sun is, in fact, the only true source of energy on planet Earth. It provides the perfect amount of energy for plants to synthesise all of the products required for growth and reproduction, which is then stored by plants and ingested by humans and animals who, through many complex processes, utilise these various forms of encapsulated Solar energy - and so the cycle continues. Wood, fuel and minerals (crystals included), too, are merely various forms of this encased Sun energy. In fact, all matter is essentially 'frozen' light. Human body cells are bundles of Sun energy; we couldn't conceive or process a single thought without the molecules of Solar-energised oxygen and glucose.

In essence, the Sun supports the growth of all species, including human beings and microscopic life forms, and without it life on Earth would simply not be possible. The mathematical and metaphysical complexity that stands behind a system of organisation and order so infinitely diverse and intricate as planetary life cannot be truly fathomed, but unerringly and miraculously, the Sun instinctively knows what each species, from a tree to a human, intrinsically needs in order to fulfil its evolutionary purpose and cycles.

Ultimately, the electromagnetic waves generated by the Sun come in a variety of lengths, which determine their specific course of action and responsibility. There are gamma rays, x-rays, cosmic rays, various kinds of ultraviolet rays, infrared, short-wave infrared, radio waves, electric waves, and of course the visible light spectrum, consisting of the seven colour rays.

Most of these energy waves are absorbed and used for various processes in the layers of atmosphere that encircle the Earth, and only a small portion of them - the electromagnetic spectrum - reach the surface of our planet. Although the human eye is only able to perceive about one percent of this spectrum, the waves exert a very strong influence upon us. The waves and rays which do affect us so profoundly, allow all life forms to undergo constant cycles of change necessary for growth and renewal. Physically, we can observe this, but on a deeper, more spiritual plane, we can even *feel* it and allow its radiance to permeate our very souls. Such is the might, force and power of that astonishing ball of fire in our sky: the brilliant, ever-shining Sun.

THE SUN ★ WHAT IT REPRESENTS IN THE HUMAN PSYCHE & NATAL CHART

☼

"The Sun is the most powerful of all the stellar bodies. It colours the personality so strongly that an amazingly accurate picture can be given of the individual who was born when it was exercising its power through the known and predicable influences of a certain astrological sign; these electromagnetic vibrations will continue to stamp that person with the characteristics of their Sun sign as they go through life."
Linda Goodman's Sun Signs, **Linda Goodman, Pan Books, 1968**

The Sun is our essence, our core self, conscious purpose and sense of identity, our creative potential, our spirit, the integrated personality that shines outward from within us. It is concerned with the present. It is our centre, source, power, life force, will, vitality, purpose, life's direction, what and who we *really* are.

The Sun represents our basic urge for self-expression. It is the 'Solar energy cell' in a person's character, the Lord and giver of life, and symbolises the way in which an individual will shine out to the world. Our Sun is our personal identity and aspects to it from other components in the chart show the ease or otherwise of assuredness and confidence with which one will project and express one's individuality. The Sun sign will also show how an individual bounces back from setbacks and disappointments, their resilience and their general outward expression of energy.

The Sun is the archetype of the Father and represents the primary masculine principle in the natal chart. It indicates how we express and experience our masculine side, or animus, our conscious self, how we express ourselves creatively, our personal potential, individuality, self-expression and personal power. It has to do with courage, power, generosity, creativity, vitality, self-confidence, nobility, self-worth, dignity and strength of will. It symbolises authority and purpose, the *ruler*, and its potential is the peak of constructive maturity. It signifies self-sufficiency and abundance, containing enough energy to radiate warmth and give life to everything around it.

The sign in which one's Sun is posited, and its placement in the birth chart, strongly indicates the level and type of vitality available to the personality (the sign), and in which area of life this may be most strongly directed (the house).

The Sun in a natal chart is a powerful symbol because everything is filtered, at a conscious level, through it. It tells us what we need to do to feel fully alive, the type of engine 'driving' us, what we need to do to be authentic and to be fully functioning. Listening to the special message of one's Sun sign can provide one with greater direction, and a more dynamic energy and life purpose.

The symbol for the Sun ☉ depicts a circle with a dot or 'seed' at its centre, from which the core self, power, creativity and the first sparks of life can spring. The circle around this 'seed' represents spirit, symbolising wholeness, eternity and the never-ending flow of energy.

While the Moon, the night sky's luminary, represents the *soul*, the Sun, the day sky's luminary, represents our *spirit*.

There is a reason your Sun sign is otherwise known as your Star Sign - it's because, quite simply, the Sun *is* a star; in fact, it's the largest, brightest, shiniest one in Earth's known visible Universe. This book is about your Sun sign and how you can become much larger, glow with far more brilliance, and shine brighter than you ever dreamed possible. I wish you all the magic in the galaxy for your dreams to come true and your deepest wishes to become reality, through tapping into the amazing power and inherent potential of your Sun sign. So get set for a galactical ride through the lucky stars of your constellation - and may a shooting star cross the path in front of you as you go!

CAPRICORN THE GOAT

★ Cardinal Earth, Negative, Feminine, Sensate ★

"With discipline the peak is reached and experienced"

Body & Health
Knees, Joints, Bones, Skin, Hair, Teeth, Gall Bladder

How Capricorn Emanates its Life Force / Energy
Methodically, Purposefully, Ambitiously, Dutifully

Is Concerned With
★ Practicality ★ Reality ★ Accomplishment ★
★ Hard Work ★ Planning ★ Persistence ★ Success ★
★ Determination ★ Status, Reputation ★
★ Responsibility ★ Achievement ★ Difficulties ★
★ Hardships ★ Discipline ★ Authority ★
★ Dedication to Long-term Projects ★ ★ Austerity ★
★ Wisdom ★ Loyalty ★ Sensitivity to Beauty ★
★ Frugality ★ Money ★ Material Realm ★
★ Duty ★ Perseverance ★

Spiritual Capricorn

Your Archetypal Universal Qualities
The Purposeful One, Father, Wise Sage

What You Refuse
To be frivolous, do things the easy way or neglect duty

What You Are an Authority On
How to Save, Organise, Work Hard and Live Within Your Means

The Main Senses Through Which You Experience Your Reality
Status, Hardness, Definition, Structure, Ascension, Discipline, Boundaries, Purpose

How You Love
Cautiously, Devotedly, Dutifully, Lovingly

Positive Characteristics
★ Excellent Organisational Skills ★
★ Cautious ★ Shrewd ★ Realistic ★
★ Has High but Realistic Standards ★ Pragmatic ★
★ Determined and Persevering ★ Consistent ★
★ Respects Authority and Tradition ★ Reliable ★
★ Scrupulous ★ Thorough ★ Hardworking ★
★ Calculated Risk-taker ★ Aims and Climbs High ★
★ Gives Sound Advice ★ Wise ★ Conventional ★
★ Dependable ★ Trustworthy ★ Cool-headed ★

Negative Characteristics
★ Believes Their Way is the Only and Best Way ★
★ Sceptical ★ Unforgiving ★
★ Slave-driver ★ Fatalistic ★
★ Gruff ★ Cynical ★ Materialistic ★

★ Unadventurous ★ Over-ambitious ★ Critical of Others
★ Cold ★ Status-seeking ★ Staid ★ ★ Workaholic ★
Pessimistic ★ Melancholic ★
★ Fearful ★ Anxious ★
★ Inner Fears Dominate ★ Decisions ★
★ Repressed ★ Perfectionist, Never Satisfied ★
★ Doubtful ★

To Bring Out Your Best

Eat out in expensive restaurants; collect antiques; release and share your feelings; go camping in nature; live in natural surroundings; help others to reach the top; use your innate wisdom to guide and encourage others; climb high mountains.

Spiritual Goals

To learn to understand the feelings and needs of others better; to stop stepping on toes to reach the top; learning to sacrifice more discriminately; to not put money and material ambitions ahead of personal relationships; to develop more warmth and less cynicism; and to develop your natural ability to lead, mentor and help others achieve their goals.

CAPRICORN

22 December - 19 January

Cardinal Earth

Ruled by Saturn

"I UTILISE"

Gemstones ◊ Garnet, Turquoise, Smoky Quartz, Jet

★ Rigid, constant, responsible, reliable, stern, loyal, traditional, authoritarian, persevering, persistent, melancholic, brooding, cautious, self-controlled, realistic, hard-working, conservative, assiduous, Uncompromising, industrious, respectful, cool, rejecting, superior, inhibited, serious, shrewd, dependable, steady, wise, ambitious, strict, self-disciplined, consistent, devoted, dedicated, gloomy, avaricious, dignified, composed, sensual ★

"I have a dream that my four little children will one day live in a nation where they will not be judged by the colour of their skin, but by the content of their character"
Dr Martin Luther King Jr

CAPRICORN

♑

★ Reserved ★ Responsible ★ Solid ★
★ Practical ★ Ambitious ★ Shrewd ★
★ Serious ★ Traditional ★

Capricorn is the sign of the Goat, a lone, sturdy, sure-footed climber of mountains to reach the highest peaks. Ambitious, serious, wise, industrious, materialistic, responsible, reserved and conservative are Capricorns' most notable traits. Being a solid Earth sign, your sign is practical, determined and pragmatic, but can lack spontaneity, passion and warmth at times, and can be ruthless in your striving to reach the top in any area of life. Hard-working and disciplined, Capricorn loves to be in control of its endeavours and is easily seduced and tempted by lofty career ideals. The Goat is shrewd and intelligent, making you a great partner in business, although you ultimately prefer to work alone and to your own rigid personal and professional standards. Responsibility is a big thing for the traditional and authoritarian Goat's spirit, and it takes its roles seriously, rarely shunning its duties. Capricorn is cautious, calm and collected in even the most turbulent of situations, and is strong and dependable in a crisis. A cool but sensuous lover, a steadfast and trustworthy friend and an unerring steady climber to the top of life's mountain tops, Capricorn is the tenth sign and solid 'rock' of the zodiac, never faltering in its obligations or deviating from its true path, forever maintaining its focus on the end result - which, without hesitation nor fail, it will reach *every* single time.

KEY CONCEPTS
★ Trustworthy and loyal ★
★ Dependable ★
★ Industrious and hardworking ★
★ Shrewd and resourceful ★
★ Opportunistic ★
★ Miserly and melancholic ★
★ Dictatorial ★
★ Executive and organised ★
★ Spiritually knowing ★
★ Grounded and pragmatic ★
★ Prudent and self-sacrificing ★
★ Caring and deeply aware of others' needs ★

SOME CORRESPONDENCES THAT ARE ASSOCIATED WITH CAPRICORN

Bricks, engineers, mines, farms, age, falls, coal, pottery, rocks, archaeology, clocks, quarries, architecture, bricklayers, perseverance, the metal lead, economists, knees, chiropractors, builders, ice, responsibility, cold, sculptors, politics, masonry, farming, dark places, bones, old ruins, contraction, decay, pessimism, underground places and passages, excavators, caves, leather work, mines, long-term projects, monuments, the past, dryness, plasterers, concrete, granite, crystals, limitations, civil, underground vaults, osteopathy, industrial and mining engineers, government and officials, endurance, refrigeration, time and the skeletal system. Take your pick and enjoy the ride!

QUOTES BY CAPRICORNIANS

"Take the first step in faith. You don't have to see the whole staircase; just take the first step" - Martin Luther King (15 January 1929)

"Behind every great man is a woman rolling her eyes" - Jim Carrey (17 January 1962)

"I don't know anything about music. In my line you don't have to" - Elvis Presley (8 January 1935)

"I am like any other man. All I do is supply a demand" - Al Capone (17 January 1899)

"I was an optimist, a great champion of the human spirit. And I lost that for a time. I feel like I've regained a bit of that ... but there was a period of my life in which I had a very low opinion of people in general" - Jude Law (29 December 1972)

"I want to be what I've always wanted to be: dominant" - Tiger Woods (30 December 1975)

"It is better to risk starving to death than surrender. If you give up on your dreams, what's left?" - Jim Carrey

"Science knows no country, because knowledge belongs to humanity, and is the torch which illuminates the world" - Louis Pasteur (27 December 1822)

"Everyone wants to be Cary Grant. Even I want to be Cary Grant" - Cary Grant (18 January 1904)

"What I like my music to do is awaken the ghosts inside of me. Not the demons, you understand, but the ghosts" - David Bowie (8 January 1947)

"I am an example of what is possible when girls from the very beginning of their lives are loved and nurtured by people around them. I was surrounded by extraordinary women in my life who taught me about quiet strength and dignity" - Michelle Obama (17 January 1964)

"Capitalism is the legitimate racket of the ruling class" - Al Capone

"No one can give wiser advice than yourself" - Marcus Tullius Cicero (3 January 107 BC)

"I was never the most talented. I was never the biggest. I was never the fastest. I certainly was never the strongest. The only thing I had was my work ethic, and that's been what has gotten me this far" - Tiger Woods

"Insanity runs in my family. It practically gallops" - Cary Grant

"Don't ever empty the bucket of mystery. Never let people define what you do ... it's not about doing something unprecedented and unpredictable. It's just about never being something that is not in the process of transformation" - Marilyn Manson (5 January 1969)

"A woman should be home with the children, building that home and making sure there's a secure family atmosphere" - Mel Gibson (3 January 1956)

"Freedom is just another word for nothing left to lose" - *Me and Bobby McGee*, Janis Joplin (19 January 1943)

"I don't know where I'm going from here, but I promise it won't be boring" - David Bowie

"To understand the heart and mind of a person, look not at what he has already achieved, but at what he aspires to do" - Kahlil Gibran (6 January 1883)

"On stage, I make love to 25,000 different people, then I go home alone" - Janis Joplin

"It's hard to be humble, when you're as great as I am" - Muhammad Ali (17 January 1942)

"I'm politically incorrect, that's true. Political correctness to me is just intellectual terrorism" - Mel Gibson

"If you have a garden and a library, you have everything you need" - Marcus Tullius Cicero

"Look up at the stars and not at your feet. Try to make sense of what you see, and wonder what makes the Universe exist. Be curious" - Stephen Hawking (8 January 1942)

"I think the main reason my marriages failed is that I always loved too well but never wisely" - Ava Gardner (24 December 1922)

"Gratitude is not only the greatest of virtues, but the parent of all others" - Marcus Tullius Cicero

"I am not afraid; I was born to do this" - Joan of Arc (6 January 1412)

"Ever has it been that love knows not its own depth until the hour of separation" - Kahlil Gibran

"I can calculate the motion of heavenly bodies, but not the madness of people" - Isaac Newton (4 January 1643)

"I hated every minute of training, but I said, 'Don't quit. Suffer now and live the rest of your life as a champion'." - Muhammad Ali

"The ninety and nine are with dreams, content, but the hope of the world made new, is the hundredth man who is grimly bent on making those dreams come true" - Edgar Allan Poe (19 January 1809)

"Science is not only a disciple of passion, but, also, one of romance and passion" - Stephen Hawking
"Sometimes our light goes out but is blown into flame by an encounter with another human being.

Each of us owes the deepest thanks to those who have rekindled this inner light." - Albert Schweitzer (14 January 1875)

"It isn't the mountains ahead to climb that wear you out; it's the pebble in your shoe" - Muhammad Ali

"Time travel used to be just thought of as science fiction, but Einstein's general theory of relativity allows for the possibility that we could warp space-time so much that you could go off in a rocket and return before you set out" - Stephen Hawking

"There are years that ask questions and years that answer" - Zora Neale Hurston (7 January 1891)

"Astrology is one of the most ancient sciences, held in high esteem of old, by the Wise and the Great. Formerly, no Prince would make war or peace, nor any General fight in battle; in short, no important affair was undertaken without first consulting an Astrologer" - Benjamin Franklin (17 January 1706)

"If I have been able to see further than others, it was because I stood on the shoulders of giants" - Sir Isaac Newton

"If you want something done, ask a busy person" - Benjamin Franklin

"No, I do not weep at the world. I'm too busy sharpening my oyster knife" - Zora Neale Hurston

THE CAPRICORN CONSTELLATION

The signs of the zodiac are the twelve symbolic features that ancient people imagined while observing the heavens. They saw shapes, patterns, faces, and natural and supernatural beings in the stars, from which they established, over centuries, a kind of celestial hierarchy and system based upon their observations. Groupings of stars became constellations, and twelve of these constellations make up the zodiac, a Greek word meaning 'circle of animals', that we know today.

Star constellations are not really self-contained groups but are particularly bright stars that give the appearance of being close together and form distinctive patterns. These are the patterns that over the ages have been identified as animals, deities or mythological figures and heroes. The stars are the living past. We receive their light long after it has left the star itself and so they are a good focus for escaping from the parameters of time. Their stellar influence is analogous with the aura, the bio/psychic energy field surrounding humans, animals, plants, crystals and even places. These individual energy systems interact with the energy waves emanated by other people, and even the cosmic rays emitted by planetary bodies, for psychic energies are not limited by time or distance.

The cluster of stars we know as Capricornus, the Sea-Goat, is dim, its only discernible pattern that of a rough, faint triangle. After its polar opposite, Cancer,

Capricorn is the most inconspicuous constellation of the zodiac. However, it contains two objects of astronomical interest. The first is a global cluster, which can be viewed through a good pair of binoculars; the second, a phenomenon called the Capricornids, consists of a shower of long, bright, slow-moving meteors which occurs each year in late July.

WISHING UPON YOUR STAR

The practice of wishing upon a star is familiar to most of us, and is a mystical superstition that is ingrained in many of us from childhood. As a night-time ritual, you can wish upon your own sign's constellation or that of the sign whose energies you wish to call forth; indeed, you can wish upon any constellation you feel an affinity with. If you can't see a particular constellation in your night sky, you can always meditate on it in your mind, or you can use the traditional technique of wishing upon the first star you see, while reciting the popular rhyme: *Star light, star bright, first star I see tonight, I wish I may, I wish I might, have the wish I make this night!* Any one of the three rituals will hold power for your own special wish. Good luck!

THE CAPRICORNIAN SYMBOL ♑

Astrology uses symbols or 'glyphs' to represent the planets and signs. The glyph is made up of shapes representing the energy and physical matter of which the Universe is composed, and how these shapes are used in each symbol provide hints as to the properties of the sign or planet it represents.

The ancient view was that there were five elements: Fire, Water, Air, Earth and Ether (or Spirit). Ether is invisible energy, while the four tangible elements are known as 'matter'. Ether, as pure energy, cannot be influenced by any of the physical/matter elements, although it surrounds them and indeed fuels them. The Greek philosopher and scientist Aristotle regarded this idea as a circle (Ether/Spirit) with a cross (matter) in the centre. This glyph is used in astrology as a symbol for Earth, and the cycle of life. All the symbols used in astrology represent the relationship between energy and the 'matter' elements.

Capricorn is the only zodiac glyph to incorporate the straight line, crescent *and* circle, meaning that it embodies all three principles. Its glyph suggests the curve of the goat's horns and is said to represent the serpent power of the body aroused.

The symbol of the Mountain Goat with the dolphin's tail, shows that the destiny of this sign is to rise to perfection through experience on all levels, from the lowest depths of the sea to the heights of the mountain, where the sure-footed goat comes into his own, carrying himself with sturdy independence and living off very little. The stylised curve of the mythical Sea-Goat, combined with the line of intellect symbolises the realm of realism and matter which has the potential to rise, and at its highest level, forms the circle of spirit. Astrologically, Capricorn is associated with the act of climbing, ascending, reaching heights. Symbolically, the Goat, the animal which can scramble to heights no other creature dares to attempt, on apparently bare rock faces, to reach the most nourishing or desired vegetation, can be pictured as unswerving in her drive to achieve material success, Spartan in her habits, and a respectable, hardworking soul whom we ought to respect for her solid virtues and unwavering dedication to reach the sustenance she strives toward.

An alternative symbol is the unicorn, the mythical enemy of the lion, contrasting the mobilised with the latent serpent power.

The symbol of Capricorn could also be interpreted as a waterfall, which cascades down from the top of the mountain.

But ultimately it is represented by two variations of the same animal: The Mountain-Goat and the Sea-Goat, its glyph being more symbolic of the Sea-Goat as it implies a curving fishtail.

THE GOAT ANIMAL

Goats were first domesticated over 10,000 years ago in the mountainous regions of Asia and Europe. Because of the goat's characteristics and behaviour, particularly the male goat, they symbolise virility, lust, destructiveness and cunning, often appearing in myths and legends with a sexual connotation attached to their essence. In Ancient times, there was credence given to the belief that the goat was the Earthly manifestation of the devil, hence the appearance of the devil with goat-like characteristics such as cloven hooves and a small pointed beard (it is interesting to note that the Major Arcana Tarot card The Devil is also connected with Capricorn the Goat).

THE CORNUCOPIA

Capricorn is associated with the cornucopia, the mythical 'horn of plenty' and a symbol of abundance and nourishment. Originally this was one of the horns of the Greek goat-nymph Amaltheia in mythology, who nurtured Zeus as a child when he was hiding from his father's cruelty. Zeus repaid her kind service to him by immortalising her in the cosmos as the sign of Capricorn. He also borrowed one of her horns to give to the nymphs, blessing it with phenomenal powers to refill itself with whatever type of food and drink its owner desired, promising it would always be filled with fruit, nectar and ambrosia. This story symbolises the Earthy, abundant nature of Capricorn, who always ensures that her labours are fruitful, productive and rewarded. Resourceful and appreciative of materialistic comforts, Capricorns are among the most self-sufficient and self-reliant characters of the zodiac, and like the cornucopia, they understand the efforts required to 'miraculously' refill life's containers with material bounty and pleasures.

Being both phallic *and* hollow, the cornucopia symbolises the productive union of male and female.

THE AGE OF CAPRICORN ★ 20,000 - 18,000 BC

The Age of Capricorn was a time of sophisticated development in tools and artistry. Lasting from around 20,000 to 18,000 BC, it was the height of the Ice Age in Europe. Indeed, the harsh environment and conditions placed many limitations on people, reflected in the rulership of Capricorn by Saturn, the planet of boundaries and limitation. During this age, tools became more advanced, suggesting the pragmatic and hardworking nature of this sign. Progress in tools and technology took place on all fronts; cooking was evident during this time by the discovery of the oldest known, primitive but identifiable ovens found in the Ukraine, which date from 20,000 BC. The oldest jewellery items known date from this age also - three fish vertebrae necklaces found in Monaco. Harpoons and spears were developed for hunting, and micro blade technology also emerged. With these new tools, it was possible to create intricate carvings and such works of art which still survive today.

THE RUNDOWN & LESSONS
SOME QUIRKS, ODDITIES, UNIQUE CHARACTERISTICS AND IDIOSYNCRASIES OF CAPRICORN

"He seldom stumbles. His eyes aren't fastened on the stars. He keeps his gaze fastened ahead, and his feet firmly planted on the ground. Jealousy, passion, impulse, anger, frivolity, waste, laziness, carelessness - all are obstacles. Let others trip and fall over them. Not Capricorn."
Linda Goodman

There are two types of thinkers: what I like to call 'right-brainers' and 'left-brainers'. The left hemisphere of the human brain deals with things such as control of speech, verbal functions, logic, mathematics, linear concepts, details, sequences, the intellect and analysis; the right hemisphere is concerned with spatial, music, holistic, artistic concepts, as well as simultaneity and intuition. You could go on to say that the left brain is masculine or yang in quality, and the right brain is feminine or yin in quality. Based upon these very simplistic outlines, it can be further stated that Earth sign Capricorn dwells mainly in the right hemisphere, with a decent amount of left thrown in for good measure.

Known for your perseverance, down-to-Earth pragmatism and patient nature, your sign Capricorn relates most strongly to the material, manifest world. The Earth element and Cardinal quality of Capricorn makes you an old soul with a wise mind, always striving and climbing with steady footing up the highest of mountains. Negative, cool, dry, melancholic and stable, an enterprising (Cardinal), practical and solid (Earth) approach characterises the sign of Capricorn.

Capricorn is the last of the Earth signs and is ruled by the serious but hardworking planet Saturn. People born under this sign are generally reliable, practical, organised, dutiful, efficient and deeply dependable. Since you are an Earth sign, you are concerned with material wealth. Those influenced strongly by this vibration won't use money as Taurus does - to keep them in comfort - but rather, to acquire power and prestige. Capricorn is driven by a need for emotional and financial security, and is oriented to business and career success through self-discipline, a quiet confidence, consistent effort, and hard work. You assess overall life achievements and the ultimate value of sacrifices made along the way.

The driving force of Cardinality, the materialism and practicality of the Earth element, and the conservatism of Saturn, all combine to make the Goat a character who works hard for what she wants and wastes no time or emotion in hoping for easy options. Concealed behind your reserved exterior lies an unequalled ambition and you will use whatever means you have at your disposal in order to reach your goal: success in your chosen endeavour, whether it be on the career, family or romance front. 'Good things come to those who wait', is your motto and so you work slowly and steadily onwards - and upwards. Status and prominence are important to you, but they must be earned, not inherited. You constantly seek to improve yourself and earn respect for your achievements. Seldom do you desire 'flash in the pan' success though, for you need the security of firm foundations, concrete form, workable strategies and long-term growth and performance. Much the same considerations apply to your personal life. You see your commitment of marriage as a responsible step, never to be taken lightly. But your partner must be a fitting one, a true complement. You may even marry to improve your standing or stature, or for dynastic reasons. In any case, falling in love is not an easy, light-hearted matter for Capricorn. Your cool nature tends to inhibit your emotions and you can be painfully shy, unable to risk declaring your feelings and stiffly unable to expose your deepest inner needs. Often you fail to acknowledge your true emotions, even to yourself. The repressive nature of your ruling planet cannot be too greatly emphasised. Saturn may also account for your tendency towards pessimism and cynicism, traits which, oddly enough, can manifest themselves in your character as dry, and sometimes bitter, black humour. But mostly, even your sarcastic or cynical humour cracks others up when it is delivered with the crackling wit and perfect timing you are known and loved for.

Inside anyone who has a strong Capricorn influence in their natal chart, is someone who is a hard-working slave-driver - most often of themselves. Virgo is the outward self-critic of the zodiac, but Capricorns are likely to keep any contempt deeply hidden in case others uncover their 'secret' and their reputation suffers as a result. You may also constantly worry about security - financial, physical, social and emotional. Although you would love to occasionally let your serious façade dissolve and let go of yourself from time to time, Capricorns are very conscious of what others are thinking, and a sense of duty or fear of looking foolish will usually hold you back. Even when you are looking determined and confident to reach the top, you sometimes doubt your own sure-footedness. Security of finances, success and the self are your biggest drivers, so much so that you often feel more insecure and downright frightened of losing your footing than other people care or dare to realise. Capricorns are also secretively romantic and crave love and perseveration in their lives.

Of the four major 'turning points' of the year, the winter solstice is arguably the most significant. Here, at the moment of greatest darkness in the Northern Hemisphere, the Sun 'turns back' once again. Having reached its greatest southerly deviation on the eastern horizon, it can be seen to rise a bit further north as the days gradually begin to lengthen. This can be said to symbolise the journey of individual consciousness being completed, collective wisdom assimilated and the self-becoming the Self, that transcendent personality which is symbolically born at the winter solstice.

Control, or more precisely, self-mastery, is what Capricorn is really about, for when we arrive at this final stage of Earth in the astrological mandala, we are expected to have gained some mastery over this Earthly realm, and this includes our physical appetites. Humans in their social aspect reach the point of maturation in Capricorn. On a collective level, Capricorn embodies the striving toward the power of the state and the authority of the monarch.

The Capricorn individual exudes the behaviour and moral fortitude worthy of this final stage of the Earth element. A traditionalist who devotes tremendous energy to ambition, duty and responsibility, the mature years are usually the happiest time of life for Capricorns. It is only after you have proven yourself to the material world, through achieving success, status or a stable family, that your softer qualities can emerge. It is at this point that you may experience a strong pull towards exploring the spiritual realm or helping wider society. Indeed, rarely satisfied with any empire you build, personal or professional, and bound so strongly by material chains, you can often suppress your creative urges and free expression, which can manifest as your two most threatening demons: depression and worry. But there is much hope in the Capricorn essence, for as you grow older life will become richer. It is later in life that your true wisdom emerges, from the seeds of self-discipline, hard work and true mastery of life's lessons.

Throughout life, the Goat has many associates yet few friends. Your friends will have had their loyalty tested over the years and they have proven themselves, and to this close circle of loved ones, you are generous, warm and sacrificing. You will take on many burdens on their behalf, and deprive yourself rather than see them suffer. The cool streak of the Capricorn is faint at the very least in these situations. But in most other situations, you can be aloof and uninvolved. This detachment helps you to cultivate your famed executive frame of mind, and is a state in which you can order others about with efficiency and impunity, a state in which individual concerns matter little to you, as long as the situation at hand stays together and grows stronger. Indeed, you can be likened to the teacher who mercilessly gives her students too much homework and yet, produces the most A-grade students of all the signs. You are the CEO of the company who may cause your immediate charges to suffer hardships and austerity, but in doing so will allow the next three generations to live in wealth, comfort and status. Money itself is rarely your passion, it is the power and status that it generates that is of highest regard in all your decisions. Money is more of a Taurean concern; Taurus likes to have, whereas you like to *use*. Resources never go to waste in a Capricorn's capable hands.

Most Capricorns know no bounds for their aspirations. Your soaring ambitions, relentless manipulation of resources, shrewd mind and ways of understanding the true value of things usually bring you some position of authority in your lifetime. You are an avenue for mastery and power over others, and you may frequently use this quality, and - depending on where you are on the personal evolutionary scale - will use it for the betterment of others, or purely for self-interest reasons. If you use your power for self-aggrandisement at the expense of others, you can be a great force of destruction - and object of intense dislike. But if you use it for the purposes of improving the lot of others, you can be a supreme example of and role model for great healing and leadership.

You are not the carefree party type, although you are a social climber as well as a mountain climber; you are quite picky about who you mix with, and most Goats secretly prefer to be in the company of, or at least dream about being in the company of, those of an upper income level. You court success, respect authority and honour tradition, and while others may label you as snobbish or stuffy, you are usually too wise and dignified to make unnecessary enemies or arguments by indulging in such lowly self-defence.

To many, your oft impenetrable coolness and calm, focused demeanour may seem cold and calculating, but to the Capricorn it's sensible. And as astrologer Linda Goodman so aptly put it, opportunity never has to knock twice at the Goat's door, for she'll hear the first knock. In fact, she's been leaning against the door, listening and waiting for it. And call it crafty, cunning or clever if you will, but you have a shrewd way of submerging your ego to gain what your ego truly desires - success, mastery, control, power and leadership.

Although Capricorn is a feminine sign, its ruler, Saturn is considered androgynous. Sagittarius tends to bypass Capricorn as a rite of passage on its journey through the zodiac, instead moving straight towards Aquarius and Pisces. The reason for this may lie in Capricorn's inherent Earthiness, which brings an almost staid practicality, rigidity and over-caution. Its Cardinality, however, presents initiative and out-going activity. Ultimately, Capricorn makes ideas real and gives them form.

Sensual but naturally guarded, trust can be an issue and suspicion of others' motives an ever-present danger. Discerning and outwardly unemotional, underneath you possess immense reserves of sensitivity and concern for others, although not on a deeply personal level. Capricorn rarely does anything without a purpose, goal or reason, and without goals you can slide into a depression. Goals also give you a fulfilling sense of duty and identity. Overall, you possess an enormous strength of will, self-understanding, determination, tenacity and inherent wisdom, as long as you have something or someone to work towards.

In childhood Capricorn can prove to be a difficult energy, as there is a certain aloneness and separateness about them; they are also usually beyond their tender years in maturity and responsibility, and can therefore be overly serious and misunderstood by others. There is a steadfast patience about Capricorn, and a quiet knowledge that achievement will come about in the fullness of time. Nothing will deter you from a goal and you always complete what you begin, rarely changing direction. You emanate strength, permanence and solidity, but there is often an underlying sadness and a vague sense of guilt for the people and things around you, for you feel responsible for and often take on the burdens of others. Your enormous capacity for self-sacrifice can prove to be a double-edged sword however, as you find out sooner or later.

Capricorn will always 'reality test' things before applying them for practical use and you are striving continually to bring solidity into manifestation. But you often feel alone once you reach the pinnacle, and your need to control, often rooted in insecurity, is ever present. Capricorn will always be involved with the material world; financial success, wealth and status are important and usually achieved. However, an overemphasis on materialism can lead to the pathway behind you being covered with the weeds of seriousness, rigidity and a cold, detached tenacity. Spontaneity and joy can also fall by the wayside under the weight of the heavy mantle of duty and responsibility.

Intellectually, you have a strong, shrewd, goal-oriented mind that has the ability to formulate long-term strategies and solutions. Although you rarely think outside the square, you are capable of mapping out the most detailed, efficient path right into the future, and your innate wisdom combined with your practicality, seems to achieve whatever ends you seek using whatever means you have at your disposal.

But although you are resourceful, intelligent and accomplished in most areas, underneath your façade of confidence, you often suffer inferiority complexes, control issues (over yourself or others), nagging doubts, irrational fears and a loneliness that you can't seem to shake. This sense of isolation is only made worse by your inability to break out and express overt warmth and affection with ease. Your tendency to take life too seriously is softened by a dry, sardonic sense of humour, but your eroding pessimism seems to be ever waiting in the shadows. More than any other zodiac sign, Capricorn will inevitably experience a period of depression or melancholy at least once in their lives; expressing feelings more openly would help alleviate any symptoms, but many Goats fail to recognise this link between their thoughts and their frequent bouts of sadness.

Capricorn's relationship to her family dynamics can be either her greatest strength or her biggest downfall. Many Capricorns carry the wound of not getting what they needed from their parent or parents. This wound seems to afflict most Goats, and in turn they worry so much about their own offspring that they try too hard to control them and lose them just the same. While Cancer, your polar opposite, concerns itself with the emotional bonds of the family, you represent a more public image involving your family, and strive hard to keep the status quo, if for nothing else than that your family has enough food on the table, enjoys a sound education that can lead to a worthwhile career, and is able to wear good quality clothes - all things which you may have been deprived of yourself. When you yourself, or a close family member, has achieved the pinnacle of (your idea of) success by attaining the topmost positions in life, you will feel that your Solar destiny has been fulfilled.

In Capricorn, the Solar wheel is turned for the fourth and final time. Capricorn endows us with a certain mastery of self, whether that involves an inner, spiritually-directed mastery or an outer, publicly-governed mastery over others, and it is here in this sign that we have reached the top of the mountain in the astrological mandala (and the literal top of the wheel astrologically). It is at this point where we usually feel compelled, through duty, discipline and sacrifice, to turn our attention to the needs of the collective, a process furthered and completed by the following two, and final signs, Aquarius and Pisces.

Saturn, your ruler, is Father Time and an appropriate governor for your slow, steady nature. Your innate practicality, cool efficiency and organisational capabilities are legendary, but beware of becoming *too* measured, as life has a way of surprising even the most well-prepared of us, and, in the words of Max Ehrmann in the famous 1927 prose poem *Desiderata*, it is always important to 'nurture strength of spirit to shield you in sudden misfortune'. It would do you well to nourish your spiritual side and keep this in mind to help keep the clouds at bay - or at least always parted so that your wonderful inner Sun can shine through.

LESSONS TO BE LEARNED FOR GREATER POWER, ENLIGHTENMENT & LUCK

Capricornian problems and ultimate undoings arise through your driving need for success at all costs, your need to control your surroundings and others, your emphasis on status, your judgement of others based upon their ability to help you climb to the top, your rigidity and your rule-abiding nature. Pessimism, criticism, narrow-mindedness and strictness can lead to inner dissatisfaction and you may overcompensate by becoming cold, unforgiving or working too hard, sacrificing close personal relationships to reach your goals. You also adhere blindly to authority and societal impositions. Your challenge is to find your inner voice and embrace your spiritual side, which can be difficult for a sign who holds the material realm in such high regard and remains fixed in only tangible realities.

Your completely practical realism can be both your greatest strength and greatest weakness. This realism can be the basis of your shrewd organisational and leadership skills. It also keeps you from grabbing at the limelight and from believing that success can occur without hard work or disciplined action. When you combine your practical ambitions with the humility and reverence that comes so naturally to your sign at its best, you will fulfil your goals and gain respect through your service and duty to others. Ambitious but realistic, you respect authority, especially that of your own inner voice, and move steadily towards being in a position of power of some sort. If, however, your practical realism is driven by insecurity, self-righteousness or rigidity, your weaknesses emerge. Then cold-heartedness, emotional withdrawal, abuse of power, controlling behaviours, and selfish domination can rear their ugly heads. On the other hand, the self-respect and moral force you embody when at your strongest, can allow you to achieve mastery over yourself and indeed, your entire Universe.

Ever ready to organise and utilise every element at your command to reach your goals, your stable, responsible and ambitious climb upward makes you the most powerful of the Earth signs. But your steadfast determination can kill all spontaneity - (as well as any doubt) - if you lose sight of life's more intangible mysteries. When you accept the greater spiritual side of life and allow yourself to love more freely, your path to success will be a more joyful one. Whether you can find that balance or set your life in concrete is always up to you.

THE THREE DECANS OF CAPRICORN

Decans are thirty-six groups of stars that rise in a particular order on the horizon throughout each Earth rotation. These decans were developed in Egypt thousands of years ago. The rising of each decan marked the beginning of a new 'decanal hour' of the night for these ancient people, and eventually three decans were assigned to each zodiac sign. Each decan covers ten degrees of the zodiac wheel, and is ruled by different planetary rulers that rule over the other two signs of the same element (and a traditional ruler, when only seven of the planetary bodies were known). Decans continued to be used throughout the Ages, in astrology and in magic, but many modern astrologers, for whatever reasons, tend to disregard them. Following are brief descriptions for each decan of Capricorn. Which one do you belong to? Can you relate to the description and the energies of your decan's ruling planet?

FIRST DECAN CAPRICORN ★
December 22 - 31

Ruler ★ Jupiter (traditional *) / Saturn (modern)

Keyword ★ Organised

First Decan Capricorns' Three Special Tarot Cards ★ The Devil, Queen of Pentacles & Two of Pentacles

Birthdays in this decan range from 22nd December to 31st December. This is the Capricorn decan, ruled by Jupiter * and Saturn. Capricornians born during this decan possess a strong, philosophical slant to their nature. Jupiter is the ruler of this decan, but is unable to express itself fully as it is controlled by the restrictive Saturn, ruler of Capricorn. However, the need for order, method and organisation, intellectual rigour, an analytical mind and tenacity are apparent in those born during this period, together with an underlying ambivalence and swing between optimism and pessimism. You are also sometimes unaffected by both pain and pleasure, and have a quirky way of seeking both equally. Just, idealistic and faithful, you have a robust intelligence, and sound communication and leadership abilities. You are patient, firm and hardworking, but are also endowed with a steady enthusiasm, energy and determination to see anything through to its end. You may be inclined to be temperamental or depressed, but can usually reason with yourself and overcome these tendencies with your cool, effortless demeanour.

SECOND DECAN CAPRICORN ★
January 1 - 10

Ruler ★ Mars (traditional) / Venus (modern)

Keyword ★ Calculated

Second Decan Capricorns' Three Special Tarot Cards ★ The Devil, Queen of Pentacles & Three of Pentacles

Birthdays in this decan range from 1st January to 10th January. This is the Taurus decan, ruled by Mars * and Venus. Capricornians born during this decan possess an ambitious, conservative, strong-willed and materialistic streak, however martyrdom may play a part in your personality. Under the influence of Saturn, the ruler of Capricorn, Mars, ruler of this decan, reveals that those born of during these dates, focus single-mindedly at an aim which they normally reach. Audacious and persistent, you love to acquire beautiful things and extravagant comfort and indulgences, but are normally too uptight or restless to enjoy these bounties. You enjoy both pleasure and profit and most of your focus lies on these two things, which you strive for with enviable determination. You are dedicated to your career, and enjoy work that utilises your charm, imagination and love of mixing with people. Your tenacity, insight and occasional excessive indifference to the feelings of others, can make you frightfully efficient. You usually have most things going on in your favour. When your qualities are channelled properly, you can, like the mountain goat, indeed reach the peak of your field.

THIRD DECAN CAPRICORN ★
January 11 - 19

Ruler ★ Sun (traditional *) / Mercury (modern)

Keyword ★ Courageous

Third Decan Capricorns' Three Special Tarot Cards ★ The Devil, King of Swords & Four of Pentacles

Birthdays in this decan range from 11th January to 19th January. This is the Virgo decan, ruled by the Sun * and Mercury. Capricornians born during this decan possess a strong intellect and mental will that takes them to high places. Saturn, the ruler of Capricorn, combined with Mercury, ruler of this decan, gives you a serious, studious nature and a way with words. It also encourages manual qualities, favouring skilful and crafty work. You may have a dry wit, which could either delight or repel those around you, but either way you are very clever if a little misunderstood. This influence also makes you pragmatic, independent and resolute. Although you are a bit of a taskmaster, you are likely to climb to the top of any ladder you set your sights on, as you are ambitious and eager to get ahead - and stay ahead. Your single-minded determination ensures you are leader of the pack and keep those 'under' you exactly where you wish them to be. Well-disciplined, persistent and generally enthusiastic, your downside is that you may over-think the past and hold grudges, which can hinder your progress.

* The decan's traditional ruler based on the Chaldean order of the planets

YOUR ELEMENT ★ EARTH

According to the *Oxford English Dictionary*, the word *element* has a mysterious origin, and was first found in Greek texts meaning 'complex whole' or 'a single unit made up of many parts'. From the ancient up to medieval times, there were only four elements - Earth, Air, Fire and Water - and the occult-oriented also believed in a fifth: Spirit, or Ether. (Cornelius Agrippa called Spirit the 'quintessence'.)

Alchemy is a tradition of visions and dreams, and images can combine on different levels of reality. Alchemists have long used images in their illustrations to express the enigma and mystery of their art, and to include all dimensions of our experience. The traditional worlds of Earth, Water, Fire and Air symbolise these dimensions very well. Broadly speaking, and in human terms, Earth corresponds to the level of the body and the senses, Water to the flow of thoughts and feelings, Fire to inspiration and energy, and Air to the world of the higher mind and intellect. Each of these worlds has its own realm of imagery. Capricorn belongs to the realm of the Earth element.

★ The Practical Group ★

The path to SERVICE & DUTY

Focused on Materiality and Security

Alchemical Associations ★ The Physical, the Mineral Salt and the Colour Black

Key Attributes ★ Stability, Balance, Patience, Practicality, Realism

Governed by ★ The Physical Body and Sensations

Symbolism ★ Groundedness, stability, structure, protection, solidity, common sense, connection to the material and physical planes, and the five senses

Governed by ★ The Tangible and the Sensory

Earth Characteristics ★ Grounded, Practical, Balanced, Realistic, Materialistic, Solid

★ THE MAGIC OF EARTH ★

Earth is the solid rock on which everything else is grounded. It provides the soil for the roots you need to lay down at some point in your life, and yields the minerals and food you need to survive and thrive. Earth is the provider, the protector, the material aspect of the world and of yourself. If you have forgotten to keep both your feet on the ground, your dreams will carry you away - Earth is needed to provide grounding for them. Earth is supportive and reminds you that everything in life needs to be built on solid, sound, dependable foundations. The element of Earth is indeed life's great anchor.

★ KEYWORDS ★

Cautious, methodical, organised, predictable, substantial, stable, reliable, practical, pragmatic, sensual, patient, enduring, productive, grounded, persevering, dependable, useful, sensible, dutiful.

"Earth is both of this world and the Otherworld, for she is host to all the other Elements besides: Air doth blow upon her face, Fire doth ignite within her belly and spew forth from her mountains, Water flows through her deep valleys, and Spirit marketh upon her skin the sacred pathways of our quest. Earth is our dwelling till we pass beyond into the secret glades of Otherworld, yet whilst we do live in human form then shall we honour and respect the Earth whence we came."

***Merlin's Book of Magick and Enchantment*, Nevill Drury**

Earth is the material substance principle. It gives form and substance to manifest what Fire has inspired and initiated. Earth is associated with the sensation function and its motivating force is material gain and security. Characterised by function, practicality and solidity, Earth seeks straightforward engagement with the physical world, mastery of it through efficient organisation and structure, and attainment of physical and economical comforts, respect, prestige and status. Taurus represents personal development, Virgo represents interpersonal development, and Capricorn represents transpersonal development. They are feminine polarity, introverted in expression.

In ancient legends, the Earth was regarded as maternal and protective, symbolising abundance and fertility. In mythology, Gaia or 'Mother Earth' was one of the first beings to emerge, along with Ouranos 'Father Sky'. They were bound by the ocean which whirled in an endless circle, keeping them together.

Earth is a complex and intriguing element, for when we think of it, we think of two things: the planet Earth, and the actual stuff our planet has as its base: soil, rock, and 'ground'. Earth connection is essential to having a grounded anchor for our magic to manifest; when Earth supports our 'work', we have a solid foundation for lift-off into the stars. Earth is like a home-base, a launching pad, and represents security, groundedness, foundations, practicality, the 'seen', tangible realities, and quite literally everything that has a has a down-to-Earth quality about it. Our desires begin and end with this element, and it is a great leveller; indeed, from it we all emerge and unto it we return.

Earth is the Universal archetype of the Divine feminine. Our planet is affectionately referred to as Mother Earth, the Great Mother, and Gaia, among many other names. Symbolising the inexhaustible spirit of creation, she is associated with abundance. When we work with this element, not only are we calling upon the powers of the mountains, caves, minerals and deserts that comprise its wondrous expanse, but we are also invoking its support and massive strength, for from it emerges abounding hidden treasures, giving us proof that material things can indeed be manifested from the Divine, deep and dark.

Throughout the history of magic, the element of Earth has been associated with a variety of deities, spirits and angels. And from the magical, as well as the esoteric and alchemical viewpoints, Earth has the lowest vibration of the four elements because it is so solidly manifest in our world. Rooted in practical concerns, it governs the primal facets of lie and of physical regeneration. It provides all we need for life, in the form of nourishment and shelter, and also provides material comforts and wealth. The treasures nurtured deep under its surface are testament to this, and have been long been yielded by mining methods and their ownership. Such treasures include gold, silver, other precious minerals, crystals, resources and other materials.

As the element suggests, Earth signs are down to Earth and self-sufficient. Pragmatic and conservative, they need structure and routine to feel safe and secure. Whether a practical Taurus, analytical Virgo or determined Capricorn, Earth signs approach life with caution and careful, methodical planning. Earth signs are not spontaneous by nature and do not like surprises or sudden changes, preferring a predictable and stable life. They tend to be organised, patient, calm, reliable, steadfast and provide a voice of reason, serving as a rock in loved ones' lives; they can indeed be truly relied upon in a crisis. However, their poised and modest nature sometimes makes it difficult for others to gauge how they are feeling or to prompt them to express their emotions.

Although Earth signs have sophisticated tastes and are strongly associated with materialism, they never manifest them in superficial ways, preferring to work hard, set goals and aim high. In essence, they strive to create a life free from money troubles and drama. They are tactile and sensual and though they may not be overly demonstrative (with the exception of Taurus), they are sentimental and affectionate in their own genuine ways.

In Earth we see the great cycles of nature and the effects it has on all the other elements. Though the cycle of the seasons relies upon the Sun, these seasons would become stagnant and motionless if it weren't for the movement of the Earth. For that reason, the mysteries of life, death and rebirth can be associated with this element - and although it is the Water element's inherent nature to explore these things on a deeper, more spiritual plane, Earth is the starting point for this exploration.

The Earth signs are sense-orientated, experiencing the world through a physical body. Concerned with security issues and moulding matter into form, Earth is productive, sensual and fertile. Earth supports, embodies, incarnates, contains, protects and provides a sense of groundedness. It is in the here and now, dealing with the present. Materialistic and sometimes power-hungry and greedy, the Earth element can also lack imagination and spontaneity.

The Earth element is firmly planted, coherent, has a sense of continuity, sustaining, follows things through, is sensory, sensual, resourceful, appreciative of beauty, pleasure-seeking, aesthetically aware, regular, containing, limiting, rigid, makes real, gives form and substance, is predictable, ritualistic, routined, enduring, reliable, committed, passive, conservative, stagnant, and sensitive to fertility and cyclical changes.

Although gravity pulls downward toward the Earth, mountains rise above it, and are associated with the Earth sign Capricorn. The first sign of this element, Taurus, represents the ground or soil, the second Virgo represents what is planted and grown in the soil, and Capricorn represents the high mountainous backdrop.

This energy is heavy, moving downward, symbolically anchoring us to our own personal ground. Earth signs are motivated by the desire to establish financial, physical and emotional security - through a steady job, money in the bank, a stable relationship.

Earth symbols include tortoises, caves, underground tunnels, mines, grottos, soil, rocks, minerals, farms, fields and mountains.

To start connecting with the 'Earth Spirit' realm, you can choose to concentrate on the spirits of the Earth - also known as devas - beginning with trees, flowers, soil, and of course Mother Earth herself. The Earth is an incredible, breathing, pulsating, living, vibrating spirit, majestically supporting all life on our planet. Also known as Gaia, she is the organic Mother of all of us, and becoming sensitive to her energy is to instantly feel physically stronger, securely supported and sustained.

Positive Earth Qualities ★ Earthy types are practical, hard-working, sensible, enduring, efficient, organised, realistic, patient, self-disciplined, conservative, persistent, common-sensical, unpretentious, stable, dependable, and capable of running households or businesses with a cool, pragmatic, unhurried, unfettered efficiency. Other positive traits of Earthy types are the following: Rooted, industrious, strong, determined, calm, goal-oriented, responsible, tenacious, sensual, committed, steady, concrete, cautious, grounded, solid, secure, robust, methodical, achieving, enduring, strong-willed, receptive, retentive, physical and reliable.

Negative Earth Qualities ★ Earthy temperaments can lack vision which may hold them back and they can become narrow, too 'rooted' in the one place, unadventurous, rigid, sluggish, resistant, immovable, and obstinate. They can also express their weaknesses in other not-so-desirable traits: Slow, stodgy, uninspired, unimaginative, petty, excessively conventional, dull, overly-cautious, narrow in perspective, stubborn, lacking in spontaneity, resistant to change, staid, hoarding, ultraconservative, inflexible, wilful, stingy, resistant to change, unoriginal, lethargic, closed-minded, over-reliant on the physical senses, overly conforming, lacking in perspective and spontaneity, selfish, bossy, heavy, bound by routine and rules, plodding, bureaucratic, perfectionism, possessive, dogmatic, controlling, authoritative, fussy, self-indulgent, fearful, suspicious, pessimistic, melancholic, critical, materialistic, greedy and resigned.

THE ARCHANGEL OF EARTH ★ URIEL

An archangel is an angel of greater than ordinary rank. They possess a stronger, more powerful essence than the guardian angels, through overseeing and guiding the other angels who are said to be with us here on Earth. The word 'angel' derives from the Greek word *angelos* meaning 'messenger'. To humans, angels are often seen as bringers as all sorts of messages. Angels in all their forms are believed to bring the message of 'spirit' into matter, carrying the blueprints of creation and the Source from the Divine into the manifest world. Angels are not and never have been human; they, like fairies and nature spirits, are part of a different evolutionary pattern – but they do appear to us in human form (usually with wings) because that is what we understand. An angel can be in many different places at once, and with the same intensity and concentration, and wish for us to be aware of them and benefit from them.

There are said to be three categories of angels in the cosmos, each with three subdivisions *. 'Angel' is the generic term and also relates specifically to those closest to the physical. Similarly, archangel may be taken to mean any of the higher orders, and indeed signifies the order just above ordinary 'angel'. Found in a number of religious traditions, the word 'archangel' itself is usually associated with the Abrahamic religions. The word archangel is of Greek origin, and means literally 'chief angel'. All archangels end with the 'el' suffix, 'el' meaning 'in God' and the first part of the name meaning what each individual Angel specialises in. The archangel who rules your sign will be the one with whom you most resonate. The astrological sign is an energy signature, a matrix of a specific stellar pattern that will subtly affect and influence you. Although there are many associations for the great archangels of the Universe, we must keep in mind there is great overlapping in their duties and guidance. For example, we may say that one is for healing and another for protection, but they can all perform the functions of the others, and each has only areas of greater focus and responsibilities. Four of the multitude of archangelic beings work intimately with the Earth. These are Raphael (Air), Michael (Fire), Gabriel (Water) and Uriel (Earth). Associated with each of these archangels are one of the four elements, specific colours, one of the four directions or quarters of the Earth, three signs of the zodiac, and a variety of other energies and powers. Understanding these associations and considering them in relation to our own paths, can help us determine with which of them we are more likely to resonate. Your sign, being of the Earth element, vibrates to the essence of Uriel.

* The first sphere, the *Heavenly Counsellors*, comprises Seraphim, Cherubim and Thrones. The second sphere, the *Heavenly Governors*, comprises Dominions, Virtues and Powers. The third sphere, the *Heavenly Messengers*, comprises Principalities, Archangels and Angels. Of course, all such classifications are a human construct, a way of placing order upon the unknowable and allowing us to perceive something about which we have no words to express. However, as long as we think of angelic hierarchies as a way of working with celestials, of remembering important attributes, and we are able to imagine and experience these beings, this order of angels will prove useful to those wishing to draw upon their messages and assistance.

★ ARCHANGEL URIEL'S ASSOCIATIONS ★

Element of Earth
The northern quarter of the Earth
The Summer season
The colours white, burnished gold and all earth tones
The crystals tiger's eye and rutilated quartz
The astrological signs of Taurus, Virgo and Capricorn

Uriel, whose name means 'Fire of God', is the archangel who brought alchemy * to humankind. He is said to be the brightest archangel, a pure pillar of Fire, he can bring warmth to the winter and melt the snows with his flaming sword. Uriel is the archangel of alchemy and vision, overseeing healing, magic, nature and manifestation. This being is known as the tallest of the archangels with eyes that can see into and across eternity. Uriel oversees the work of all nature spirits - working with Uriel will open you to the fairy kingdoms - and works to assist humanity by awakening to them and working in harmony with them. Inspiring us to work with angels, Devas and higher spiritual essences, to perfect our vision of Divine realms, and to refine our mystical nature by burning away our deep-seated desire for comfort and blind ignorance, Uriel is the gatekeeper to the Garden of Eden, the gates of which we can only pass through once we have mastered the wisdom we are given to find our own path to enlightenment.

* Alchemy is the sacred art of transmuting base metal into gold by reducing it to the primal black matter and then, by chemico-magical processes, striving to extract and refine

spiritual as well as actual gold, the key to finding the way back to Paradise or Source.

CAPRICORN'S ZODIAC ARCHANGEL ★ HANIEL

Additionally, each sign is associated with a particular archangel. Such knowledge can help you to build up a relationship with these beings, based upon your strengths and needs. However, no link is rigid, and as you work with angels you will come to develop your own affinities. When invoking a specific archangel, a useful ritual to draw them closer is to light a candle in that angel's colour, burn some oil or incense of its scent, and hold the appropriate crystal while focusing on what you are needing guidance on.

YOUR ARCHANGEL ★ Haniel is a protective angel, bringing determination and the energy to understand your life's mission and true purpose. He can assist you with communication, soothes panic, and helps you to overcome deeply ingrained negativity and to receive communication from the higher planes. Haniel's gift is the development of pure individuality, independent of the expectations and pressures of others.

SCENT/OIL ★ Pine

CANDLE COLOUR ★ Turquoise

CRYSTAL ★ Turquoise

THE DEVIC REALMS & EARTH ★ NORTH: REALM OF THE GNOMES

"Through magick we do conjure the Elements, evoking unto us the special properties of the Life-force for our learning and our coming-into-light. And yet are there secret paths of knowledge that have fallen from the minds of men ... For the way of Magick is a path to sacred knowledge, of reverence and humility - and the world is a wondrous place. Yet how many amongst us have fathomed these depths?"
Merlin's Book of Magick and Enchantment, Nevill Drury

Deva is a Sanskrit word that means 'shining one'. Devas are the life force within nature, and there are four devic realms - Fire, Earth, Air and Water - which contain ethereal elemental spirits or sprites. Elementals are the building blocks of nature, and close to being true energy and consciousness. The four elements correspond to four different states of matter: energy/transmutation (Fire), gas (Air), liquid (Water) and solid (Earth), which are linked to the four human states of consciousness: inspiration, thought, feeling and practicality. There are four spirits, or elementals, which reside in the devic realms, associated with each element. People have been painting pictures, telling stories and writing about these devic realms for hundreds of years, albeit sometimes through disguised mediums such as fairy tales or children's fantasy stories like Tolkien's *Lord of the Rings*. The power of the natural world is easily observed and since ancient times primal forces have been ascribed to various spirit beings. Belief in nature spirits is of such ancient origin and is Universal; cultures everywhere have names or words to describe them. In the sixteenth century, a famous Swiss physician, alchemist and mystic called Paracelsus * defined these beings as 'Elementals', classifying them according to the element of nature they inhabit. There are four main levels of elemental beings: Gnomes (Earth), Undines (Water), Sylphs (Air), and Salamanders (Fire). The fifth element of Ether is the element from which came forth the other four, and Ether, or Spirit, has never been defined in any particular category, and encompasses the aspects and beings of all the other elements.

Elementals are usually benevolent guardian beings or spirits that look after nature's secrets and treasures in whatever part of the natural realm they occupy. They can only be seen or 'felt' by those possessing heightened psychic abilities, yet they can be summoned by those practising alchemy, spells and magic in order to harness the forces of nature for their own particular intentions. In our modern lives, it may seem as though this magic doesn't exist, but the truth is that most of us are simply less in touch with it than ever before. The consequence of this is that we are destroying vast areas of land, polluting waters, creating toxic landscapes, and disrespecting the laws of nature, which often whisper their messages softly. It is therefore important for us to look at the beauty that surrounds us with true appreciation and genuine regard, and to open ourselves up to the magic resides within it. The four devic realms can teach us much about nature; they act as custodians for the four elements, and learning to work with them is a way of attuning to all the energies and beings of nature. Elementals are four-dimensional, and have nothing to obstruct their movements. Therefore, they move as easily through matter as we do through air and space. They do require some contact with humans for their own evolution. Helping to direct them is an overseer, traditionally called the King of that element, and an archangel. Each of these elements is affiliated with one of the four directions and each elemental spirit embodies its own special energy. If you wish to re-connect and re-harmonise yourself by working with nature and its messages and lessons, you could begin by learning a little about your element's realm: Your element is Earth, which is connected with the North direction and the realm of the Gnomes.

* Paracelsus is considered the most original medical thinker of the sixteenth century. His belief in supernatural beings, intuition and the invisible causes of illness helped him discover hydrogen and nitrogen. Paracelsus believed that "Elementals are unlike pure spirits for they are mortal, but they are not like man for they have no soul."

★ GNOMES ★

Gnome: *noun* - A legendary dwarfish creature, supposed to guard the Earth's treasures; diminutive spirits or small fey 'humanoids' in Renaissance magic and alchemy, first introduced by Paracelsus in the 16th century, known for their eccentric sense of humour, inquisitiveness, and engineering prowess; are typically said to be small, humanoid creatures who live underground.

Gnomes are a race of small, misshapen, dwarf-like creatures that dwell in the Earth and often protect secret treasures in vast caverns. Their actions are reflected in the presence of mineral deposits and other kinds of geological formations. Gnomes are the beings of craftsmanship. They are needed to build the plants, flowers and trees. It is their task to tint them, to make crystals and gems and to maintain the Earth so that we have a place to grow and evolve. As guardians of the treasures of the Earth, they are attuned to helping humans find the treasures within the Earth or part of it; this can be hidden riches, the energy of crystals and stones, or the finding of gold within one's life. Ultimately, they work with humans through nature. They give each stone its own individuality and essence. Indeed, they do this with every aspect of nature, and thus we can learn from each one, for every tree, rock and flower has something it can teach us.

According to Paracelsus, gnomes cannot stand the light of the Sun, and even one ray would turn them to stone. If you wish to retrieve any treasures that are buried underground or associated with the Earth, you must first appease the gnomes or they will cause you mischief.

The gnomes are the 'knowing ones', from the Greek *gnoma*, meaning 'knowledge'. The gnomes are the guardians of winter, the direction of the north, the physical world, and of fertility and abundance. The north is traditionally known as the gateway to inner wisdom. The Earth provides us with food and beauty in many forms. The gnomes are caretakers of everything that grows, from tiny flowers to towering trees. The King of Earth is Cernunnos or Ghob, its archangel Uriel, its magickal tool the pentacle or disc (which calls down the spirits into form), and its sacred ceremonial stone is the garnet in all its four colours. Perhaps Merlin sums up the gnome realm best: "From time to time, no doubt, these gnomes do make merry with the lives of human folk, having their ways in mischief and making jokes. And yet, for all their pranks and mischief, are these gnomes good and virtuous within their natures, and offer gifts of kindness when hard times come upon our lives."

INVOKING THE EARTH DEVAS

Gnomes are said to be the easiest of the devas to sense since their energy is almost tangible. Earth spirits can be very helpful since they embody practicality and common sense, and have an innate knowledge base around money, the material, and how to grow things. They relate to food, nourishment, health, treasures, fertility, protection, wealth, and all Earth magic.

Gnomes can also assist with the security of your home and are excellent guardians, so it is no accident that many gardens around the world are filled with representations of these powerful beings, as they are said to protect the home they are attached to. Gnomes can also be called upon to bring financial stability to your household, attracting the funds needed to pay a bill or to meet an urgent expense.

If you have a laborious task ahead, have job or financial worries, need to ground your ideals, or are in need of developing a special hands-on skill, ask the earth devas for their help. The easiest way to contact them is to spend some time outdoors around the Earth element and natural features, particularly rocks and thick-trunked trees. You may find it helpful to hold a crystal or stone of resonance when asking the Earth elementals for assistance.

THE NORTH DIRECTION'S CORRESPONDENCES

If you wish to work more with your particular element and direction, the following may help propel your wishes and magical journey:

Time of Day ★ Midnight
Polarity ★ Female, positive
Exhortation ★ To keep silent
Musical Instruments ★ Drums, percussion
Colours ★ Black, deep green
Season ★ Winter
Magical Instrument ★ Pentacle, stone
Altar Symbol ★ Platter
Communion Symbol ★ Bread, salt
Archangel ★ Uriel
Human Sense ★ Touch
Art Forms ★ Sculpture, embroidery
Animals ★ All domestic
Mythical Beast ★ Unicorn
Magical Arts ★ Talismans
Guide Forms ★ Earth, underworld goddess

Meditation ★ Fertile landscapes
Images & Themes ★ Caves, rocks, organic produce, Moon, stars, night, growth and life

HOW YOU CAN GET IN TOUCH WITH YOUR EARTH ENERGY

"The mountain's position is strong only when it rises out of the Earth broad and great, not proud and steep"
I Ching, hexagram 23, ken/k'un

★ Use Earth energy when making wishes around the following: Financial security and stability, material possessions, practical areas of your life, solidity, endurance and stamina, fertility and fertile opportunities, abundance, work and career, home and garden, children, manifesting anything on the physical plane

★ In magical practices, Earth can be represented by soil, salt, crystals and minerals. Earth spells are most powerful when performed outside. A forest, cave or mountain make naturally sacred spaces in which you can attune to the Earth's energy, infusing your work with the forces of nature. Use tools made with materials grown in the Earth, such as clay or stone, salt, herbs, sand, rocks and crystals - and try using a pentagram disc as a base to strengthen the links with your element

★ The best days on which to employ Earth magic are on a Saturday, ruled by the Earthy planet Saturn, or a Friday, ruled by the Norse Earth Goddess Frigg. If possible, choose dawn or dusk when the magical half-light is neither day nor night, a truly mystical time

★ Hike in the mountains

★ Indulge in some hot-stone massage therapy

★ Go camping

★ Spend time outdoors, connecting yourself to the Earth itself - in the form of trees, rocks, mountains and fields

★ Smell a flower, appreciate its fragrance

★ Heal your emotional body with flower essences

★ Red, brown and black-coloured crystals will activate your connection with the element of Earth and will nurture you and enhance healing

★ Exercise regularly, focusing your full attention on your body and its movements

★ Undertake physical activities that enhance your mind/body integration, such as t'ai chi or yoga

★ Learn to love your body

★ Eat Earthy foods and heavy foods which will help ground you, including breads, and rooted fruits or vegetables that grow in soil

★ Aim for greater order and organisation in your life, with regard to time, resources and possessions

★ Cook. Consciously attune yourself to the meals and food you prepare

★ Climb trees

★ Hug trees

★ Lie down in a field of flowers

★ Meditate on the Pentacles suit in the Tarot (the Pentacles suit represents the Earth element)

★ Collect and carry stones, shells, gems and wood, and any other products of the Earth that you find meaningful

★ Study the Earth sciences, such as geology, crystallography or environmental studies

★ Plant, grow and tend your own garden. Flowers, cacti, fruits and root vegetables are ideal

★ Help others learn how to be more realistic, hands-on and practical; as an Earth sign, you are an excellent role model

★ Learn how to make pottery or sculpt using your hands

★ Wear and surround yourself with the colours green, brown and other Earthy tones

★ Cultivate a whole-body sensuality, by giving and receiving massages regularly. You're a natural!

★ Attune yourself to the Earth goddess Gaia

★ Formulate and maintain a regular schedule and routine to help stabilise your energies

★ Devote yourself to finding a home, space or plot of land to call your own, helping to provide you with a foundation and a sense of rootedness in the one place

★ Invest your money in something secure and long-term

★ Surround yourself with friends who are also bodily-oriented and practical; they will help to reinforce and strengthen these facets of yourself

★ When working with the Earth element in magical practice, stand at the North quarter of your magical space, as the North is its domain, and invite its living essence into your 'circle'

★ Earth spirits are also known as fairies, gnomes, tree devas or elves. They provide grounding and attend to emotional healing, so Earth signs would be wise to adopt one (or all) as their very own spirit guide.

YOUR MODE ★ CARDINAL

Each sign belongs to one of the three quadruplicities, Cardinal, Fixed and Mutable. If we closely examine the Earth's yearly cycle, we can form a very accurate picture of the nature of these quadruplicities, for they correspond directly with the manifestation of the seasons. Each season has three months: the first month brings the new phase of the cycle, the second month brings a concentration of the season's energy to its fullest expression, and the third month represents the transition from the current season to the next one. The astrological quadruplicities represent the three basic qualities in all life: creation (Cardinal), perseveration (Fixed) and destruction (Mutable). Every thing that is born, from a period of time to a human being, experiences a life and then dies. In this context, death can be taken to mean that the form of the energy changes; but the energy itself can never be annihilated, for form is mortal, whereas essence is immortal.

The Cardinal mode covers the signs Aries, Cancer, Libra and Capricorn, and is the most initiating and self-motivated group of the three modes, able to instigate and inspire beginnings; in other words, to "get the ball rolling." The Cardinal mode has an initiating action and quality, operating with ambition, enthusiasm, independence and enterprise. Forceful, opportunistic, and at times aggressive, you have the will to accomplish and creatively project yourself onto the world. You charge right in to get the job done - but you can fail just as spectacularly. Although you have a great start-up ability, tenacity and endurance are not your fortes, and you often don't follow things through to the end. If there is no crisis for you to tackle, you may even make one up just to create a challenge for yourself. You find it hard to be held under anyone's thumb and will always find a way to wriggle free to set off on your next quest. Your energies may be directed towards yourself, your home and family, or the wider world of career or society, but in any case it is difficult to divert your attention away from your chosen course. Cardinal signs have great drive, are self-motivated and would rather lead than follow. It is hard to influence you because you make your own firm decisions and believe that you know best. The Cardinal mode signifies beginnings, decision-making, boldness, courage, will, new starts, and initiations. You tend to be dynamic, authoritative, 'bossy', active, restless, involved, busy and energetic, and are determined initiators of goals and new purposes. The Sun's entry into the Cardinal signs indicates the beginning of seasons in the northern hemisphere: the start of Aries marks the Spring Equinox, the beginning of Libra the Autumn Equinox, the start of Cancer the Winter Solstice, and the beginning of Capricorn the Summer Solstice.

Capricorn is the most patient, steady, enduring and persevering of the Cardinal quality; you will almost ruthlessly climb life's ladder without looking down or back. Your persistence and stamina will usually see projects sustained for a lot longer than your Cardinal counterparts Aries, Cancer and Libra.

YOUR RULING PLANET ★ SATURN

The Wise Teacher

Planetary Meditation
I am my Earth (my body),
and my Sky (my transcendence)
I am my Sun (my spirit),
and my Moon (my soul)
I am my Venus (my pleasure),
and my Jupiter (my faith)
I am my Mars (my courage),
and my Saturn (my lessons)
I am my Mercury (my thoughts),
and my Uranus (my truth)
I am my Neptune (my dreams),
and my Pluto (my transformation)

Each planet has its own distinctive and original meaning which, according to its position in the zodiac, combines with the qualities that are inherent in each of the twelve astrological signs. If a planet is your sign's ruler, however, it exerts a significant influence upon your life, regardless of its birth chart or zodiacal position.

"Very often, therefore, in human affairs we are subject to Saturn, through idleness, solitude, or strength, through Theology and more secret philosophical, through superstition, Magic, agriculture, and through sadness."
Marsilio Ficino (1433 - 1499), *The Book of Life*

> "There's always a faint melancholy and seriousness surrounding the Saturn personality. None of them completely escape the Saturnine influence of stern discipline and self-denial. (And) respect for the wisdom of age and experience is ingrained in the Saturnine nature."
> **Linda Goodman**

Malefic ★ Associated with Boundaries, Structure, Control, Limits, Restrictions ★ 29.5 Year Cycle

★ KEY WORDS ★
Practicality, Boundaries, Restrictions, Limitation, Ambition, Control, the Father, Duty, Authority, Obstacles, Reality Checks, Contraction, Rigidity, Solitude, Wisdom, Caution, the Teacher, Discipline, Perseverance, Austerity, Inhibition, Frustration, Thrift, Consolidation, Direction, Denial, Responsibility, the Shadow, Endurance, Patience

★ KEY CONCEPTS ★
★ Time and the Wisdom Gained Through Experience ★
★ Karmic Lessons ★
★ Lord of Time ★
★ Maturity & Old Age ★
★ Self-imposed Limits & Fears ★
★ Lessons to be Learned ★
★ Tradition & Conservatism ★
★ The Father, The Boss, The Authority Figure ★
★ Solidification, Structure, Foundation & Stability ★
★ Ambition, Endurance & Self-Discipline ★
★ Crystallisation & Concretisation ★
★ Satan & the Reality Check ★

Day ★ Saturday

Numbers ★ 4 and 8

Basic Energy & Magic ★ Authority, Banishing, Stabilising

Colours ★ Black, Midnight Blue, Green, Grey, Dark Brown

Gods/Goddesses/Angel ★ Cronos (sometimes spelt 'Kronos'), Saturn, Cassiel

Metals ★ Lead, Iron, Steel

Gems/Minerals ★ Onyx, Jet, Diamond, Green Calcite, Obsidian, Garnet, Deep-hued Sapphires

Trees/Shrubs ★ Cypress, Elm, Buckthorn, Willow, Aspen, Pine

Flowers/Herbs ★ Patchouli, Myrrh

Wood ★ Birch, Ebony, Alder

Animal ★ Crow, Wren

Element ★ Earth

Zodiacal Influences ★ Rules Capricorn *; Exalted in Libra; Detriment Cancer; Fall Aries

* Traditional ruler of Aquarius

Saturn, whose unique and distinctive rings make it one of the most spectacular bodies in our Solar system, is second only to Jupiter in size. It is the farthest planet from the Sun which we can see with the naked eye. Before the discovery of the outer planets Uranus, Neptune and Pluto in more recent times, Saturn was considered to mark the outer edge of our Solar system. The most visually beautiful of all the planets, Saturn's array of colours are astonishing: its equatorial zones appear brilliantly white, its subtropical and temperate zones darker yellow, and the polar caps often look green. The system of rings that surround the planet and its lustrous, contrasting colours can be clearly seen with a telescope, through which is appears as a blue sphere encircled with three yellow rings against the velvety blackness of deep outer space. Saturn has ten known satellites, the largest, Titan, being bigger than Mercury. To guess at Saturn's astrological functions by virtue of its known physical attributes, we would probably draw the conclusion that its influence must be enormous; aside from being massive in size, it is capable of exerting huge pressures, capturing and holding weaker bodies and even using them to create what are apparently impenetrable barriers around itself. On closer inspection, we find that Saturn behaves very eccentrically and its highly unusual orbit makes it remarkably oblate in shape.

If our assumptions are correct, we can see why Saturn has acquired such a fearsome and arguably unlikeable reputation. Perceived and described as dull and malevolent, it has given us the term 'saturnine', which quite literally means sluggish, cold and gloomy in temperament. Relating to lead, its medical connotation, 'afflicted by lead poisoning', derives from medieval alchemy, whose work attributed the force of Saturn with the element lead, or *plumbum*. But Saturn is also one of the least understood energies in the astrological matrix. Although its principles can be seen in part as difficulties, obstacles and limitations, Saturn is also a teacher, and it has been said that when the student is ready the teacher appears. And appear Saturn does, always in a timely manner (although this may not be welcomed or even apparent to the uninitiated).

The astrological glyph of Saturn combines the crescent of consciousness with the cross of the Earth, or matter, in other words, the mastery of the conscious mind in relation to its position and experience of the physical environment.

Associated with boundaries, restrictions, limitations and concretisation, and urge to build structure and stability, Saturn in our birth chart shows where in our lives there are lessons to be learned, or the burdens of duty or responsibility. It teaches us that we need to plan, define and then persevere before we can make any progress; and this lesson, particularly in youth, can be uncomfortable or even painful.

It could be said that each of us has a soul which has chosen to wrestle with the difficulty of expressing spirit through the base material of a human body, and Saturn represents that battlefield. The apparent difficulties experienced on this harsh plane can be transmuted into qualities which can enhance our soul's journey. But to achieve this, Saturn's deeper side needs first to be understood. Cold, hard and stern, Saturn deals with issues of discipline, barriers, focus, maturation, patience, obstacles, inhibitions and frustrations, and shows how we face and deal with limitations, setbacks, authority and restrictions. He points the way along the path of both duty and destiny, and provides firm direction and important lessons along the way. As the way-pointer, Saturn shows us where our soul must dwell in order to fulfil our inner purpose and destiny. Representing rules and lessons on many levels - personal, collective, societal, cosmic and karmic - if we allow it, Saturn can be a great sage-like presence in our lives.

Saturn produces its effect by causing difficulties in the expression of the qualities of its zodiac sign, in the affairs of its house, and in the relationships (or 'aspects') it has with any other planets in the birth chart. The arising discomfort and fear often causes one to shrink away or obliterate the negative feelings with overcompensating behaviours. However, the discomfort cannot be ignored or swept under the carpet; it has to be accepted, confronted, understood and worked with so that the Saturnian energy in the birth chart can be transformed into the fortitude and enlightened understanding it so promises.

The glyph (or symbol) for Saturn implies the cross of matter imposed upon the crescent soul, symbolising the responsibilities and challenges that mortality imposes. Worked with constructively, our natal Saturn can temper our soul with structure, order and discipline.

Saturn is the archetype of the judge. Many approach him with fear and trepidation as a result.

Saturn limits you. Saturn says "No." Saturn punishes you. Saturn is unmoved by your pleadings and protests that life is unfair, as he sagely knows that you always have a choice: to accept responsibility for your actions, or to resist authority and necessary restrictions placed upon you - to your detriment. Saturn knows that you can reclaim your power at any time and stop playing the victim, for you have only imposed this label on yourself and no one else is to blame for the consequences. When you stand respectful and humbled before Saturn as judge, devoid of excuses, you will discover that he is in fact fair and merciful. He may even turn a "No" into a "Yes" - but not before you have learned his education.

Although known as the 'wise teacher', a simple enough concept, Saturn constitutes one of the most complex archetypes in the astrological mandala, in that most of the other planets and luminaries (the Sun and Moon) reveal their problematical sides when combined with Saturn, for Saturn stands for doom, darkness, dis-ease and delay, and he is the archetypal harsh taskmaster of the planetary realm. Saturn has always been associated with the letter of the law rather than the spirit, and as such he does have a dark, ruthless side. However, in astrological tradition his benefits may be greater - or at least more substantial - than those of all the other planets. His lessons may be tough, but they are what we need to learn in order to grow, materialise and manifest through what is learned and applied from these tests.

As a symbol of wisdom (or folly), lessons learned (or not learned) and obstacles overcome (or not overcome), Saturn defines the outline of your personal story, particularly as it unfolds as you age. Someone once said about the natal chart, "Saturn always seems to be in the wrong place!" but if Saturn's influence is problematic, it is most likely because of your own reluctance to deal with his warnings and harsh tests. In this sense, he forces you to examine and analyse yourself sincerely, honestly and solemnly.

Saturn is often regarded as a significator of 'the father' in astrology, alongside the Sun, but in Saturn's context the connection to the father often symbolises problems with him. In order to break free of any restrictive fathering issues we have had, one must consciously develop one of the more positive aspects of Saturn - his role as mentor or positive role model. But Saturn, as the inner teacher, may turn into a tyrant, a grim patriarch obsessed with rules and laws. To seek to transform Saturn into this inner teacher is an oft challenging task because it forces us to deal with some other troublesome Saturnian aspects as well. Occasionally when we attempt to transform him from tyrant to mentor, we are confronted with *all* our limitations, both material and psychological. Modern society does not seem to recognise the spiritual need for a mentor figure or the insights they could impart, but in days of old, a man served alongside his teacher as apprentice, especially in the age of fine craftsmen. This relationship has all but vanished in the modern fast-paced era of social isolation. Very few of us have the opportunity to be initiated into the mysteries of life or career by a genuine mentor figure, with most of us having to cultivate an inner guide or model a figure from history. Saturn in the horoscope is the most suited to playing this mentor role, but first he must be freed from his role as the tyrannical, restrictive parent. In modern life, repressed instincts, disowned feelings, suppressed compulsions, our lurking shadow, the recesses of the soul, may all come up for review under Saturn's scrutiny. And as long as we remain bogged down by limiting attitudes, Saturn cannot function at its best. Subjecting us to delays and restrictions on all planes, Saturn may induce a state of depression, helplessness or melancholia - states of mind in which we feel tightly confined in an endless dark tunnel; it is probably not coincidence that Medieval and Renaissance scholars associated Saturn with one of the four humours of ancient medicines and unsurprisingly linked it with the melancholic humour, which provides as good a metaphor as any for Saturn's depressive influence.

Saturn complexes are indeed common in the human psyche, and once we recognise these energies, whether imposed from external sources or self-imposed, we can learn that the only way up and out is through the assuming of personal responsibility for the undesirable situations or mind states we find ourselves in. Many people who suffer from Saturn's impositions remain in their dark corner of isolation for years because they have not yet taken personal accountability for the predicament in the first place, but rather point the finger at parents, or blame society, authority, or outside circumstances for any continuing misfortune in their lives. Saturn's restrictions are symbolised in various ways. Perhaps the most symbolic of all is that to the ancients this planet was the most distant body of the Solar system, therefore representing the limits or boundaries of the planetary realm. Additionally, in more recent times probes sent to Saturn have convinced scientists that this planet has the most complex set of rings in existence. The force field of these rings may be the reason for Saturn's immense gravitational field. It is not merely a coincidence then, that gravity, staying within boundaries, and setting limits, are all Saturnian concepts.

It is interesting to note that Marcilio Ficino, an influential scholar, priest and humanist philosopher of the early Italian Renaissance, warned his fellow magi of Saturn's gloomy power over scholars and philosophers, asserting that learned men were more likely than other people to suffer from Saturnian afflictions. However, it could also be said that if scholarly gloom was associated with Saturn, so too was scholarly *wisdom*, for Father Time (another label for Saturn) bring serenity as well as doom and melancholy. And indeed, Saturn can impart a great sense of character and resilience when it is functioning effectively.

Time was perhaps a feature in the construction of Saturn's mythology. In centuries past, the completion of the year at the winter solstice marked the time when the tax collectors appeared and all monies owing to the government, debtors or landlords had to be accounted for and paid. Hence Saturn's bad reputation for insisting that accounts should be settled for one to have peace of mind. Also, in Babylon, Saturn was called Ninib, an agricultural deity. At the mythological level, Saturn began life as a simple god of seed and grain, and his festival, the Saturnalia, was held in December, the tenth (*decem*) month of the Roman calendar. In Roman mythology, Saturn ruled over a golden age during which humans lived in peace and prosperity. Saturn's correlation with agriculture suggest the nature of time itself, in that fruits can come to harvest only during the proper season or time, once the groundwork has been done, and fruit cannot be forced to bear before its time. In similar respect, those with a well-placed Saturn in their birth chart possess a good sense of timing: they lay the groundwork carefully, plant seeds at the correct time, then nurture their plants as they patiently await harvest. Saturn's wisdom is of the Earth itself, and it rules the 'golden years' of old age. People with a prominent Saturn will age with dignity and wisdom, returning to the Earth in proper time; Saturn is Old Father Time, the Lord of Death. Saturn is happiest in maturity, when burdens and responsibilities apparently weigh the least. As well, age confers wisdom and the profound knowledge that comes from a life thoroughly examined, other Saturnian domains.

To understand Saturn's functions, we have to associate him with Jupiter. In symbolic astrology, we see many of the workings of the cosmic law of polarity. Jupiter expands; Saturn contracts. All motion, all life, depends on expansion and contraction, drawing in and expelling, inhaling and exhaling, push and pull. Picturing Saturn as a kind of father figure also makes it easier for us to understand his position in our lives. Traditionally, it is the father who metes out conditional love, who controls, instructs and punishes. This, in essence is what Saturn does astrologically. Wherever Saturn appears in our charts there is a lesson to be learned in responsibility and conditions. Ultimately, Jupiter is expansive, Saturn is restrictive. In our charts, they can potentially complement each other to bring out each other's best qualities. It is interesting that Saturn's glyph is composed of the same two symbols as Jupiter's but in Saturn, the two are inverted. Saturn's symbol is the cross imposed over the crescent semi-circle, representing the principle of contraction.

Despite Saturn's reputation as the harsh disciplinarian, his common sense and practicality blend well with the extroverted optimism and enthusiasm of Jupiter, creating a breadth of vision combined with sensible caution. He is also the tester and teacher who shows us that in order to successfully operate as both a Universal and a social being (Saturn is a social planet, along with Jupiter), we must abide by certain cosmic and terrestrial laws, rules, concepts and impositions that govern our behaviour. Saturn can also serve in the role of Satan, the tempter, whose force allows us liberation if we learn our lessons wisely. As the shadow side of Jupiter, Saturn is the reality factor, but in adversity has endless patience, tolerance and guardianship of inner mysteries and secrets that are acquired over years rather than weeks. With him, we can work unafraid with our own shadow, allowing what we have cleared away out of sight to be released and utilised or discarded - whatever is ultimately for our highest good.

Satan tempts us with the illusion of material gain and physical immortality, but no matter how much economic influence or affluence one possesses in one's lifetime, one will inevitably lose out to Saturn, Satan's ally, for we are mortal and Saturn is Father Time, the Old Man, and the Grim Reaper who deals in forces of Light and Dark. Although Saturn can be cruel to mere mortals, he can also play the role of bestower of gifts to the well-behaved and worthy - and the withholder of rewards from the undeserving. And one who passes Saturn's many tests is blessed by being helped along the path to greater illumination and that quality which eludes many - *wisdom*.

But not all teachers or fathers are wise, kind and guiding. And the more often we fail to strike a balance between contraction by expansion, the more we set ourselves up for failure and disappointment. Saturn, while providing a shelter, can just as easily turn into a prison. We can easily feel trapped by his authoritarian, restrictive powers. Saturn can be a tight girdle. Unhappy relationships you can't seem to break off, a job you hate, a home life you long to break free from, a tough problem that persists - all are Saturnian in nature. The trick is to keep both the contracting and expanding energies in check. Saturn will teach you how to do this, if you will listen. Saturn is about control; while we must exercise control in our lives, we need to understand how it works and use discretion. Positive and negative polarities are involved with Saturn as with everything else. Saturn consuming and controlling you with hatred, jealousy, resentment, hostilities and martyrdom is negative; Saturn applied to control all these emotions and divert them into constructive use is positive. And ultimately, contraction has to work in harmonious partnership with partnership, otherwise the see-saw will cause you to sink - like lead.

Saturn tells us of our urges for control, safety, caution, forethought and slow, well-planned and long-term achievements. Saturn is not a personal planet, like the Sun, Moon, Mercury, Mars and Venus, whose expressions are all very individualistic. Saturn is the bridge between material consciousness and the higher consciousness embodied by the three outer, generational planets: Uranus, Neptune, and Pluto. So, despite its reputation as a greater malefic and bringer of sorrows, Saturn *does* allow for personal growth to a spiritual end, but does so only through the fulfilment of one's Earthly obligations, duties and responsibilities. Saturn also forces you to surrender illusions and falsehoods which hold you back from the liberation that can only be granted through a depersonalisation of self. Saturn does not deal in emotions and has little tolerance for feelings; his job is purely to get the job done cleanly and efficiently.

In the birth chart, Saturn reveals the area of life the Hindus call Dharma, which is the duty one has to undertake in order to build and fortify one's character. Saturn will also describe what obstacles you need to overcome to achieve success and satisfaction. But he can just as easily be the one who puts those obstacles right in front of you!

Saturn is the crystallisation/concretisation principle of the birth chart, and informs of our urge to build structure and stability. Saturn builds the foundation upon which the building is put, and will only put another layer of bricks on top when the ones underneath have solidified.

Saturn is our wise inner voice. It is the planet that determines our maturity. The position of Saturn in our birth chart has an important effect on how we listen to and interpret that inner voice. It is all about how far we expand our horizons and how we become aware of our own limitations. We become mature when we become able to collect our thoughts, cultivate the wisdom learned through tough lessons, and master our actions. We can then master the elements of our destiny and take responsibility for the consequences of our desires and actions. We can then discover our *real* motivations. In fact, in essence we become a person in our own right.

Saturn, the Roman deity who devoured all but three of his children, is associated with our ambitions, the way we accept (or don't accept) our responsibilities and authority, and the very structure of our lives. He forces us to take stock of our assets, liabilities, limitations and shortcomings, often through 'reality checks'. Saturn rules structure, boundaries and patience. It brings us obstacles and limitations both internally and externally, forcing us to confront what must be done and thereby teaching the lessons of patience and discipline. Although Saturn presents obstacles and restrictions, its energy is also vital in building solid foundations.

People with a strong Saturn in their chart are enduring, serious, informed choices, conservative, self-reliant, dependable, self-disciplined, resourceful, self-controlled and wise (usually before their time). Saturn makes the rules, sets the limits and brings the consequence of error. He gives form to thought, is about conscience and consequence, and gives us regular and necessary wake-up calls. Significantly, it is the fairest of all the planetary energies, giving us back what we put in. And while it imposes boundaries, its purpose is to keep us safe and realistic.

In essence, Saturn can be a both blessing and a curse. For anyone on a spiritual search, Saturn's burdens can be a blessing, it being the checkpoint where our imperfections are brought to our attention and our personal demons need to be wrestled to the ground. However, too much Saturnian influence can make one rigid, alone, lonely, limited, isolated, emotionally repressed, fearful, over-cautious, pessimistic, cynical, austere, unfeeling, sceptical, and unwilling to accept anything that is new or pushes established boundaries. It is interesting to note that Saturn rules the skin, which is symbolic of a boundary or barrier which keeps us safe from harm; this serves as a good metaphor for Saturn's qualities (Saturn also rules teeth and bones, the building blocks of the human body). Saturn is essentially about structures, and without structure, a skeleton or some kind of framework, nothing would stand up straight. And Saturn can also bless and endow one with noble qualities: truth is solidified under its influence, the mind is strengthened, character is heightened, hypocrisy banished, illusions are shattered, delusions are illuminated, a clearer understanding of material values is bestowed, and true freedom is ultimately rewarded. After all, it has been said that if your barn burns down, you are in a much better position to see the stars. Saturn occasionally builds walls around us, but can also help you tear them down if you are courageous enough to break through them with a firm resolve.

The position of Saturn at the moment of your birth determines your stability, practicality and level of authority (both inner and outer). Saturn's placement also shows your sense of responsibility and where your fears lie. It reflects the restrictions and obstacles in your life and how you climb the ladder of success, as well as the difficulties you will encounter when you get 'there'. Saturn represents where and how you most want to make your mark in society. He teaches the value of patience, maturity, sacrifice and prudence, and brings longevity, commitment and temperance. Serious, reserved and devoted, Saturn teaches you to grow up and take ownership of your life.

The rings of Saturn symbolise the limitations imposed by Saturnian action that operate as a harsh external discipline until we learn to discipline ourselves. This ringed planet of boundaries can indicate areas in your life that you need to be particularly diligent about trying to change, and also symbolises the course of time and patience, tradition and experience. Discipline and duty are important to Saturn, as is any form of order or delay. A strictness of structure and the way in which we conduct our affairs are all ruled by Saturn. It shows what kind of lessons must be learned and what hardships must be conquered to become a mature and wise person.

Overall, Saturn is the Tester (Satan) whose function is to perfect character through constant trials. It represents the principles of concentration, self-preservation, caution, integrity, accountability, stability and endurance. Saturn is the planet of old age, where the life processes are slowed up. It signifies old or serious people, those in responsible positions. Its action is to limit, conserve, test, deepen, perfect, inhibit and restrict.

Saturn is associated with fear, safety, fatigue, Saturday, ancestors, pains, ground, basics, elderly, fate, necessities, deficiencies, beggars, gates, discounts, fasting, shortage, inertia, orthodox, protective paint, builders, fields, economical, black, mud, refrigeration, narrow, shades, houses, clay, farms, melancholy, aches, bodily falls, the past, hermits. foundations, stop, reduction, regrets, scarce, austerity, inferiority, faithful, defeat, granite, perseverance, delay, aged people, concrete, doom, agriculture, adhesives, dull, fossils, inflexible, garbage, bridges, failure, hostages, seriousness, clamps, worry, suspicion, recollections, onyx, patience, bitter, limits, calendars, weights and measures, burdens, stones, fidelity, strict, heavy, mourning, finality, decay, excavations, scavengers, memories, woe, prejudice, blindfolds, dryness, surveyors, cement, leather, glue, senility, estates, obedience, neglect, enduring, wrapping, sceptics, ceramics, old, frustration, inhibitions, blockages, resistance, endings, watches, fences, cold, embargoes, loads, stoic, regularity, obituaries, gaols, mortar, precaution, vaults, holes, formation, paupers, handcuffs, building, sculpture, meditation, subways, compression, relics, insulation, duty, bricks, reservoirs, obsolete, frugal, rubbish dumps, caution, basements, funerals, winter, censors, mines, afflictions, harness, deaf, bereavement, doubt, late, statues, freezing, lonely, quiet, anchors, pavements, anxiety, repentance, bones, destitute, minimum, glaciers, second-hand, fundamental, hardship, apathy, integrity, latches, brakes, permanent, loss, flint, starvation, unlucky, problems, plaster, security, contraction, shrinkage, archaeology, history, architecture, ice, remains, cemeteries, frowning, wrinkles, leanness, thrift, denial, poverty, skeleton, introverted, tragic, gloom, asbestos, chills, misers, despair, coal, responsibility, astringents, selfishness, foreclosure, ballast, property, difficulties, pessimism, quarries, thorough, frameworks, barriers, materialism, tradition, skin, conservative, gravel, synopsis, routine, stale, rubbish, belts, cynical, boredom, prudent, dark, boulders, hunchbacks, slavery, restriction, last, boundaries, think, brief, isolated, bruises, ugly, morgues, tombs, frost, castles, diminishing, junk, recessions, slow, chalk, retirement, sorrow, knees, undertakers, tightness, discipline, land, clocks, masonry, tar, misery, hindrances, humility, dirty, terminations, pottery, slums, impossibilities, conscientious, conservation, cowards, tedious, debility, depression, misfortune, time, fractures, real estate, rickets, quarantine, grave, hesitation, immobility, tenements, hibernation, sadness, invalids, knocks, stability, the metal lead, solitude, politics, monuments, postponement and ancient ruins. I'm sure you get the idea!

This Saturnian energy and influence, throughout your whole life, gives Capricornians the gifts of wisdom, perseverance, stability, structure, realistic application of ideas, tenacity, a sense of duty, sensible caution, patience and lucidity. Too much of this

Saturnian energy can make one cold, unfeeling, controlling, tight, unmoved, harsh, selfish, mistrustful, cynical, indifferent, fatalistic, resentful, sterile, mean, severe and overly authoritarian. It can also indicate enduring periods of hardship, depression, sorrow or chronic ill-health. But the Saturn-ruled Capricornian always knows how to use her best qualities to achieve her ambitions and goals in life; after all, your motto is "I Use," because in your amazingly shrewd, resourceful, direct and no-nonsense way, you *do* use everything you can to your full advantage. And like the mountain goat that represents your sign, you keep putting one hoof patiently in front of the other until you reach the peak. How will *you* use your phenomenally powerful Saturnian influence?

THE ASTROLOGICAL SIGNIFICANCE OF YOUR NATAL 'SATURN RETURN'

Are you about to turn 27 or 28, or are you already between the ages of 27 and 30? If so, you are either going to experience your full natal Saturn return shortly, or are undergoing the enormous shift that the Saturn return represents in one's life. This is a powerful time of potential transformation through often painful lessons more commonly known in everyday simple terms as 'reality checks'. The period of a Saturn return is a time during which you are forced to examine yourself more closely, as a result of a crisis, significant event, an undesirable feeling or state of being that lasts a considerable period of time, a depression or sadness that won't lift, or something, however big or small, occurring in your life that simply motivates you to seek deeper meaning. A question usually asked during this period, is, "What do I need to learn from the pain or mistakes of my past to grow as a person?"

Saturn is connected with the primitive, 'inferior' side of human nature which Carl Jung called the shadow. It can be regarded as a symbol for all that is base, crude and unconscious within us. It pertains to the past, parental images, and to the crystallisation and identification with what has gone before. It may also be seen as perpetually in conflict with itself, unconscious, and ultimately in need of redemption, yet containing within it all the potential seeds of the future, which can provide us with life-giving spirit and alchemical gold.

In its orbit around the Sun, Saturn forms a conjunction (or 'return') with its natal place at around 29 years of age. Each time this planet touches its original birth position is significant. The completion of every such cyclical return indicates that the dark, undifferentiated and unconscious side of the personality is activated and accorded an opportunity to grow through the medium of some situation requiring struggle, strain or pain. At age 29, the culmination of this first Saturn cycle, it is possible for us to face and free ourselves from painful feelings of inadequacy, overcompensation, parental ties, and values from the past that have outlived their usefulness. We can then begin the next 29-year cycle as a developing individual rather than as a product of our familial background, outgrown values, or the manifestations of our deeper shadow self.

An average life span has two Saturn returns, dividing the life into three separate chapters. Each return will provide us with the right timing for a change of plan, structure or level of responsibility, and if these opportunities for change are not taken then frustration can set in. At approximately seven-year intervals, Saturn's square position delivers a personal reminder that freedom has limits, times during which we may encounter jolts to the ego or other testing circumstances that teach us to further learn and grow.

Saturn may present us with limitations and restrictions, but it may also mature us by forcing us to work *within* these boundaries. It may hold us over the shadow of a tyrannical parent, a shadow from which we must learn to emerge and spring to life in our own identity. The accomplishment of all these inner works can lead to a rebirth, a golden age of the spirit which may occur at any time, not only in our later years. The most marked periods for this achievement to manifest come during what are called Saturn returns, something most astrologers and people are familiar with, and often associate with fear and change. At the age of 29, 58, and 87 this occurs, times when individuals may be affected and tested by this stern planet.

The first return, at 29, usually implies a sobering period during which the individual comes to accept that maturity and responsibility must now replace youthful abandon and folly. The second Saturn return, at age 58, can be one of the most illuminating Saturn experiences, especially if the individual has truly achieved the wisdom that Saturn seeks of its subjects. On the other hand, it can also present difficulties, particularly if the individual is not inspired by their work and sees life as drudgery and hard work for little return. Few people live to experience their third Saturn return at 87, but coming on the heels of the Uranus return, it can be undoubtedly profound, instil a deep sense of satisfaction and fulfilment, and be indeed life-affirming.

Saturn is the Tester (Satan) whose function is to perfect character through constant trials. The rings of Saturn symbolise the limitations imposed by Saturnian action that operate as a harsh external discipline until we learn to discipline ourselves. It represents the principles of concentration, self-preservation, caution, pessimism, integrity, responsibility, stability, endurance. Saturn is the planet of old age, where the life processes are slowed up. Its action is to inhibit, conserve, delay, restrict, test, limit, perfect and deepen.

The nature of the Saturnian experience under each return will be suggested by the house, sign and aspects to the planet in your personal natal chart.

The year immediately prior to the first crucial Saturn return, is often one of gradual breaking down, some 'tough' lessons or events that stimulate 'reality checks', as well as a recognition of all that is false, one-sided, dependent and unrealised within the personality. This year may comprise a period of depression and painful self-evaluation, discouragement and challenges - but it need not be so, as it also heralds the true end of psychological childhood, and launches one upon a truer, purer quest into the future. During this period, we may face conflicts and opposition from other people, without realising that it is in fact our *own* darkness that is confronting us and that we have probably outgrown the 'skin' of the past, and it must be shed in order to move on and grow.

Sometimes the Saturn return is accompanied by feelings of helplessness and inferiority and one's self confidence may be more fragile than he or she assumed because old wounds, anxieties, complexes and a searing sense of inadequacy may resurface.

The Saturn return pertains to the area of life where it is found in the birth chart. For some, it may be reality tests and re-shufflings connected with career; for others it may be related to marriage; for others still, it may relate to their spiritual unfoldment.

Handled constructively, the Saturn return can be the catalyst and opportunity for great change, consolidation of long-desired goals, self-realisation or even self-actualisation in more evolved souls, and the planting of seeds which will mature in the second half of life. Badly handled, it can entail a collapse of virtually everything we perhaps once regarded as secure and safe.

The Saturn return will ultimately almost always prove a vehicle which offers you room to grow and develop your own inner strengths for the duration of your life. Saturn usually digs its roots deep, giving its effects a degree of permanence. However, you experience your Saturn return, you cannot make any substantial decisions without being aware of your shadow side, otherwise it will inevitably do the choosing *for you*. For whether it is palatable or not, it is reality and its very essence must be integrated into your life in order for you to evolve and unfold. Saturn knows better than most, that if you're not busy growing then you're instead busy dying. Your Saturn return teaches that the choice is always yours.

YOUR HOUSE IN THE HOROSCOPE ★ THE TENTH HOUSE

MIDHEAVEN - MC - The cusp of the Tenth House. This is the degree of the zodiac directly above us at the moment of birth. It signifies the most public and outer part of ourselves: "How I function in the World."

The Tenth House shows your place in society, your social status, reputation and the regard that others have for your achievements. It relates to your aims and ambitions, to your worldly aspirations and often to your career and professional path. The Tenth House also relates to the father or the conditional parent.

A house is one of the twelve sections dividing the terrestrial globe, viewed from a precise time and geographical place, into sectors from the poles to the horizon. The horoscope, or birth chart, is divided into these twelve sections called houses. Each house governs a different area or 'department' of life, such as relationships, career, leisure and even karma. The reason for this division of the Earth into houses can be understood when we consider that the Sun's rays affect us differently in the morning, at noon and at night, and also in summer and winter, and if we study the cause, we will readily observe that it is the angle at which the ray strikes us or the Earth which produces that difference in effect. Similarly, with the stellar rays, astrologers have observed that a child born at or near midday, when the Sun's rays strike the birthplace from the Tenth House, has an improved chance of public or career advancement in life than one born after sunset. By similar observations and tabulations, it has been found that the other planetary rays affect the various departments of life when their ray is projected through the other houses, and therefore each house is said to 'rule' or govern certain departments of the human life experience.

The Tenth House, ruled by Capricorn, is the house of career, public life, direction in life, social status, ambition and vocation, and the conditional parent. While the opposite Fourth House deals with home and family matters, the Tenth is concerned with what you can achieve in your own right. This house therefore indicates your public role and persona in the world at large, and reveals the way in which your desire for social and existential accomplishment is manifested.

Our authentic vocational purpose, public reputation, social standing and status, motivation, prestige, societal recognition, achievements, senior figures, worldly honour, authority figures, aspirations, professional expression, desire for fame or notoriety, worldly roles, father or father figure *, our choice of profession, our true 'calling', and all matters affecting outward appearances and one's personal image, are all found in this sphere of the horoscope. The Tenth House can also relate to people in positions of power and authority, such as your boss or other superiors.

Ruled by the realm of the Earth element, this is one of the three Houses of Substance, and is an all-important 'angular' House, being the Midheaven, meaning that it forms one of the four significant angles of the birth chart (the other three being the First House or Ascendant, the Fourth House or Imum Coeli, and the Seventh House or Descendent). But where fellow Earth sign Taurus is concerned with substance on a *personal* level and Virgo with substance on an *interpersonal* level, Capricorn and the Tenth House are connected with substance on a *transpersonal*, or wider-reaching level.

The Tenth House is significant for the occupation, the carving out of your niche in the world, your personal power, glory, honour (or dishonour) and social standing. Corresponding to the Midheaven, or the highest point of the horoscope, the Tenth House is concerned with the career and in a general way shows how far you will get in realising your worldly ambitions, the level of success you are likely to achieve, and how high your reputation will grow and stand.

The Sun is at its most powerful when it culminates at midday and is represented by the line of the MC. The term MC stands for Medium Coeli, or Midheaven. It marks the point of culmination of the Sun, where the Sun is at its highest position, and corresponds to noon on your day of birth. The opposite point of this axis is the IC, the Imum Coeli, meaning the 'under sky', and it marks the lower meridian of the birth chart, corresponding to midnight. The MC culmination represents those parts of ourselves which are out in the public spotlight, this 'spotlight' being the very essence of the Tenth House. This is where we enjoy our fifteen minutes of fame and are at our most visible. It is where we make public our ambitions and shows how those aspirations will manifest themselves. The Tenth House, therefore, can be a useful and insightful pointer to your ideal career. It reveals your reputation, authority, profession and status in the community. It shows achievements, the degree of influence you have (which relates to your self-esteem), and the mother or father (whoever was conditional). This house is where we want to receive acknowledgement and credit for what we are and all that we have achieved, the nature of any contributions we make to society, our place in the world, and where we seek applause, respect and validation of our public self. This house is significant for any personal power and glory that comes about as a result of your vocational efforts.

The Tenth House informs to a large degree about the degree of responsibility you have, that is to say your potential capacity to be accountable for your actions, and the importance you place on success and social recognition, which are then perceived as a kind of seal of approval that confirm your independence and fulfilment.

Other exoteric and esoteric keywords for the Tenth House include: Profession, business prestige, public image, life direction, professional qualifications, business and corporate opportunities, position, worldly goals, accomplishment, Masters and hierarchy.

The Tenth House is the gateway to your particular degree of success from the lowest (bottom of the ladder) to the highest. Depending on what planetary influences are playing out on this sector at any given time, it can bring either failure, mild satisfaction, success, recognition, promotion, honour, publicity, and even fame.

The Tenth House is your own Mount Everest, and how far you climb it will be indicated by the planets within it and sign on its cusp - but ultimately, as with anything else, how high you ascend will be up to you.

* Please note that many astrologers link the Tenth house with the mother and the Fourth with the father, but it seems that this rule is variable. Some astrologers say that the parent who has the strongest influence is described in the Tenth house, others say the same sex parent is described in the Tenth house. Classically however, the Fourth house rules the mother (natural ruler Moon) and the Tenth house rules the father (natural ruler Saturn). It is also fitting that father or father figure matters are indicated in the Tenth house, as the father is usually (though not always) the conditional caregiver and Saturn is a conditional planetary energy.

YOUR OPPOSITE SIGN ★ CANCER
WHAT YOU CAN LEARN FROM THE CRAB

If we look at the zodiac, we can see that it can be broadly divided into two hemispheres, this division being based on the natural division of the year by the two equinoxes. Astrologers often refer to the first six signs, the hemisphere in which the day predominates (the days being longer in the spring and summer months), as the Personal Sphere of Experience, and the second six signs, the hemisphere in which nights are longer, as the Social Sphere of Experience. These two halves of the zodiac perfectly balance and complement each other, and each individual 'personal' zodiac sign has something to teach its directly opposite 'social' zodiac sign. To generalise, the signs of the personal sphere tend to experience life through a type of self-projection and self-interest which is often socially uncomplicated, unsophisticated or naïve. Their objective is to learn greater social awareness and thereby integrate themselves with the larger, more Universal human collective. On the other hand, the signs of the social sphere are prone to experience life through the use of their more developed social consciousness. In essence, the personal signs (Aries, Taurus, Gemini, Cancer, Leo, Virgo) usually provide stimulation and new energy to their environment, while the social, more Universal signs (Libra, Scorpio, Sagittarius, Capricorn, Aquarius, Pisces) provide experience, opportunities for wider expression, and give a more broad-minded approach and perspective to their surroundings.

Each sign in a pair seeks and is attracted to the qualities of its complementary opposing sign. Cancer searches for the power and endurance of Capricorn, while Capricorn seeks the softness and understanding of Cancer. Cancer dwells within the realm of the establishment of *personal* security and structure, while Capricorn resides in the realm of the establishment of *social* security and structure.

Although the word 'opposite' conjures up feelings of separateness and differences, the astrological polarities should not be seen as two signs in conflict with each other - their positive expression is to create a natural balance and equilibrium. Each sign has something to learn from its opposite, but also has a contribution to make towards the other sign's more evolved expression. The Fourth (Cancer) and Tenth (Capricorn) House polarity is concerned with the inner world or 'home' versus the outer world or 'vocation'.

The sensitive, fluid, responsible, instinctive, feeling-oriented individual, easily influenced by others and living through them (Cancer) seeks the structure, self-motivation and resourcefulness which is the fruit of individual effort (Capricorn). The disciplined and self-reliant individual, capable of mastering the environment through harnessing of self-propelled energy (Capricorn) seeks the warmth and security of human relationships, the embrace of close others and the intimate exchange of feelings (Cancer).

Cancer's Fourth House represents inward activity and motivational drives resulting from your home life and upbringing, while the Tenth house is the outward manifestation of them, the bringing of them into the public arena. It is with the Fourth House whose cusp indicates the lowest heavens (the I.C.) that we find the foundations of an individual's life. This area represents your environment, background, heritage, where your roots are, and where your personality took shape. Opposite on the axis, is the Tenth House, where an individual must 'earn' her wings; similarly, it could be said that Cancer represents your given, inherited qualities to a large degree, while Capricorn symbolises that which you must work diligently for. The Fourth House contains all the markers you need to grow into yourself, and its opposite is where you must carve out your own mark on the world. It is here, in Capricorn's domain, where you are creating your own markers, to stand out and apart from others as a separate entity in your own right, which is usually expressed through your professional self on a vocational platform. Here is where you will acquire your own moral, social, and of course material independence and earn your freedom and autonomy. But it is also important to remember that to reach this goal with as much serenity and harmony as possible, you must first have strong roots. If your roots are unstable in any way, it can be easy to live through Capricorn's less favourable traits: operating through a superiority complex to mask insecurities, which will force you to rise ever higher, to dominate, rule and conquer both on the social and material front - but at a cost. At the other end, you may never fulfil your ambitions, nor evolve because of a lack of self-confidence, conviction, nerve or courage. How you assert your individuality in the wider world will depend largely on your natural family background and your familial roots. Cancer knows indeed, that having a solid foundation is much more conducive to outer success. Indeed, career, achievement and what the world remembers you for (Tenth House), are all outer expressions of independence and maturity, but they also have a strong link with the early home environment, security and upbringing (Fourth House). These two houses represent the 'parents' who are psychologically and emotionally important to every individual. Planets in these houses and the signs on the cusps, will indicate the importance of your home and career lives, and how you find a balance between the two.

Negative and Cardinal, this Water-Earth polarity compares the fluctuating femininity of the Moon with the rigid structure of Saturn. It concerns the breadwinner versus the homemaker; the father versus the mother; the unconditional parent versus the conditional parent; the disciplinarian versus the nurturer.

Both the Goat and the Crab have the initiating power of Cardinality, but with your negative yin receptivity, both signs are also paradoxical. Cancer knows the emotional value of family, tradition and roots but has a lack of practical ambition. The Cancerian may also be easily influenced, sensitive to others' needs, and may only indirectly achieve her aims. Capricorn demonstrates the attitude needed to succeed in the world and shows how to build something solid and of lasting value, but often this is achieved at the expense of human feeling. Caring, sympathy and kindness can get lost in the discipline and austerity of Capricorn's nature, but Capricorn's structure can be softened by Lunar Cancer's influence, and Cancer can teach Capricorn much about feelings and sensitivity.

Capricorn is controlled, closed, emotionally inhibited, self-disciplined, insensitive, self-sufficient, industrious, determined, grounded, highly conscious, attuned to external realities, success-oriented, ambitious, detached, isolated, 'fathering' and controlling, and sets limits, exercises power and authority, seeks public recognition, concerned with the professional and material, and desires professional security.

From Cancer, you can learn to develop a lifestyle by which you can nourish and nurture others. Cancer can also teach you how to stop judging others so harshly, or based upon their status or reputation, and stop making climbing life's ladder your intense life's mission, by focusing instead on close loved ones and your family. The Crab can also teach the Goat how she can stop pigeon-holing and slotting everyone into an inner hierarchical system, but rather to try tapping into a more intuitive awareness of other people's unique place in the world.

In order to develop your true highest potential and follow your soul's true path, your soul needs to learn how to express greater warmth and let go of any control issues. You have amazing resilience, perseverance and self-discipline to achieve great things, but your softer side needs to come to the fore. Your soul's greatest lesson is to take a step back from your more rational mind and allow your deeply caring, nurturing self to shine through. Family is of great importance to you, but so far on your life's journey you may have found it difficult to really go with the flow in this area of life, perhaps being busy being the disciplinarian or the leader in a family role, or overly strict or rigid with your own children. This softer, more emotional and intuitive side of yourself is needing greater expression.

Being ever stoic and dutiful are other obstacles which may need to be overcome - you push yourself too hard at times and beat yourself up if you haven't lived up to your 'usual' high standards, but that is exactly what your inner self is telling you to do, that is to release the need to always be achieving and striving. Your soul's biggest lesson and true life purpose will become apparent to you once you learn how to nurture your family or domestic life in a way that is mutually satisfying, and letting go of any control or discipline issues you may have, whether they be directed at yourself or others. Instead of always trying to strive for 'status', try to be a little more private, humble, nurturing and protective of yourself. Go into yourself from time to time, hide away and be still and reflective, rather than living from the outside as you tend to do so much with your busy lifestyle. This may be difficult for your hard-working and ever-ambitious nature, but it will serve you well and pay off in the long run

Tender, imaginative, sensitive, emotional, intuitive, instinctive, fluctuating and deeply caring, the Crab is a tender-hearted softie who can melt your icy exterior with her soothing lessons, and teach you how to develop these qualities. While you offer business cards to those who walk through your life's door, the Crab will unwaveringly offer warm, home-baked cookies and a sympathetic ear.

Overall, you are under the influence of your proud temperament, your rigid nature, which grants no concessions, and a fundamental tendency to only rely on yourself and not trust others. Because of your clear-mindedness and excessive pride, you can become pessimistic and aloof, and yet underneath your cool façade, you are sensitive and feeling - you may need the Crab's help to bring these to the surface. As you are naturally reticent and retentive, the Cancerian's fluid nature can assist the Goat's hardnosed character to express itself with a flowing tenderness. You must learn how to express your gentle nature more readily and spontaneously, and with greater affection and outward demonstration. You hide a deep nostalgia for childhood, perhaps one you feel you never had, which can sometimes make you melancholic, and more vulnerable than you appear to be. The Crab teaches you that this vulnerability is fine, and that it is indeed what makes you a functioning human. The paradox with vulnerability is that although you fear the exposure it brings, it can also add a field of protection around you, as it is the very essence upon which successful human relationships are built. In other words, to show your vulnerability is to add a shield to your armour as others will undoubtedly love you more substantially for having been brave enough to show it. The Crab can teach you how to abandon your old self, the one who comes across as a difficult person, who refuses any help, support, comfort or reassurance, and she imparts the inherent wisdom to be found in the art of receptivity and graciousness.

It's okay to put your feet up and relax while someone else takes care of you for a little while. It can get lonely up there on the mountaintop, but not if you have a Cancerian friend baking those cookies and keeping you warm by stoking the home fires. And remember that "charity begins at home," because the Crab, scuttling along in her own, unhurried way, knows this better than anyone other sign. She also knows that home is where the heart and hearth is, and could never be accused of saying, "I wish I'd spent more time in the office" on her deathbed because quite simply, she didn't. And her life is richer for it.

WHAT THE CRAB CAN ULTIMATELY TEACH THE GOAT

Release ★ Rigid structures, harsh judgement, categorising others, pride, refusal to relax or acknowledge weaknesses, coldness, insensitivity

Embrace ★ Nurturing and nourishing others, tenderness, imagination, intuition, softness, sensitivity, expressing emotions, compassion, warmth, affection, flow, reflection, vulnerability, supporting others in a more feeling way

Cancer is moody, emotionally unstable, fluid, sensitive, vulnerable, empathetic, sympathetic, responsive, mothering, smothering, nurturing, protective, pampering, attached, dependent, passive, timid, retreating, private, psychic, hidden, intuitive, attuned to the unconscious, develops roots, seeks personal nourishment, concerned with the personal, family and home-oriented, and above all else, desires domestic security - all of which you can learn from the Crab.

To evolve to your fullest potential, your complementary opposite sign Cancer is telling you that you need to stop worrying about status and prestige and rather to live authentically from yourself; to tap into your spiritual reserves and develop them more fully; allow your inner authority to emerge so that it can be put to work for others; to use your amazing strength, determination and incredible shrewdness to really benefit yourself and others. Your ultimate karmic goal is to develop an inner *and* outer authority.

There is a wonderful hermetic and alchemical 'law' which is the concept "as within, so without" - in all her smothering protectiveness towards family and close loved ones, the Cancerian instinctively intuits her way through life, knowing that her inner fortitude will fuel her onward trip. She cares little for status, reputation and worldly accomplishment, for she knows that all these will take care of themselves only when the self has the strong familiar foundations and roots from which to launch into the wider world.

MAGIC, DRAWING, ATTRACTION, SPELLS, RITUALS, WISHING & POWER

A Note on the Universe

Within each of us resides the merging of the Sun and the Moon, the dance of the constellations, the vibrations of the planets, and the vast microcosm and macrocosm of the entire *Universe*. Uni means 'one' and Verse means 'song'; therefore, the word Universe literally means 'One Song'. If you learn to tune yourself in, you can even hear it!

What is Magic?

Magic is a kind of special energy that is beyond description, and like most kinds of energy it has its own rules and ways of being manipulated. It remains an elusive term, and no definition has ever really found Universal acceptance. Attempts to separate it from superstition, religion and other-worldly phenomena on the one hand, and 'science' on the other, are ridden with difficulties. However slippery the term 'magic' might be, there is a general agreement that most of us wish for more of its presence in our lives and often fall short of achieving this wish.

Those performing spells, 'asking the Universe', wishing, praying, or undertaking rituals, are using this very special energy to draw things to them. Learning to manipulate energy in these ways is never hard (and shouldn't be), but it can be complex and does require knowledge, practice, creativity, patience and above all, imagination. Most of us use simple magic every day, whether by saying little prayers, making wishes, visualising, and exchanging - sending out and receiving - good, positive or hopeful vibes. When you understand that all the forces and magic you need are *within* you, and you learn to *believe* in that power, you are then able to make all manner of changes to your life and, most importantly, yourself.

Magic is an invisible force which connects and permeates everything. Every thought you have and every action you take, will affect the strength of this force, and can be influenced and directed towards a specific purpose by using certain means. The most important of these are your intentions, facing in the direction of your desired outcome, your will and your *belief* that it works. The more you want something to happen, and the clearer you can visualise the desired outcome, the stronger your will and feelings towards it will be, ensuring an avalanche of amazing people, events and circumstances will flow into your experiences, gathering speed, momentum and power as it nears your goal or dream.

The Universe (or whichever higher power you believe in) works for us and through us. Ideas are given to us but they must be carried out *through* us, in the form of asking or acting or performing a ritual or casting a specific spell. The Universe's abundance is your abundance, and it flows through your mind into manifestation. The Universe or Divine Being in which you believe, gives you the necessary ideas and clothes them with all that is needed to bring them into form when we ask *believing*.

Based on ancient human beliefs, systems and superstitions, declaring what you want and acting out your deepest desires can actually help to make things happen. Magical ideas include the notion that thought affects matter and that the trained imagination can alter the physical world, that all aspects of the Universe are interdependent and that we can discover connections and correspondences between everyday occurrences and cosmic, or Divine, energies. A miracle or a wish coming true can suggest something is going on that extends beyond the laws of nature, that something unseen has occurred; but just because we cannot see it or touch it, it doesn't mean it's not there. Magic exists, especially if you truly believe it does, but science is so far incapable of capturing its essence or the rationale behind it. Personally, I prefer to leave that task to the higher powers of the Universe.

To help your dreams come true and to use your inborn power to its full effect, you can employ boosters based on the special energies and qualities of your Sun sign. These 'boosters' are chosen to be in alignment with the purpose of a particular goal, and contain energies of their own which will enhance the strength of your spell, prayer, ritual or 'asking'. Specific magical energies can be invoked by carrying out a spell or ceremony using specific herbs or colours, or on a particular day of the week, according to either your Sun sign (to heighten the power of the asking), and/or that is in sympathy with that for which you are asking (I have included days of the week for other Sun signs and spell types).

Some materials and boosters you can use to increase the power, magic or energy in any area of your life include: candles, wish lists (written on an appropriate piece of paper written with a specially-chosen writing tool), symbols, affirmations, chants, incense, herbs and flowers, locations, colours, days of the week, elements, crystals and gemstones, animal symbols, charms, talismans, amulets, gods and goddesses, essential oils, planetary hours and your Solar totem animals. All are covered, some more briefly than others, for your very special Sun sign to radiate the energy to powerfully draw your wildest dreams towards you!

Overall, it pays to remember that the Universe (or whatever higher power/s or force/s you happen to believe in) creates *through* you that to which you give your attention. What you contemplate becomes the law of your being, and through your pure unwavering belief, is eventually brought through to manifestation on the material plane. What you think about is entirely up to you. But just be mindful that whatever you think about the most becomes your dominant thought, then your main point of attraction, and is ultimately magnified until it becomes your reality or your experience. So choose your thoughts with care. And to quote Ralph Waldo Emerson, "Be careful what you set your heart upon, for it will surely be yours." I carry a copy of this beautiful prophecy in my purse as its words resonate so strongly with me. In other words, be mindful about what you're wishing for, for you will most probably get it, whether it's good or bad - magic, after all, doesn't discriminate. Just make your dominant thoughts good ones, and you will attract everything you set your heart and intentions upon. Good luck!

ASTROLOGY & MAGIC

"Everyone practices magic, whether they realise it or not, for magic is the art of attracting particular influences, events and situations within human life. Magic is a natural phenomenon because the Universe is reflexive, responding to human thoughts, aspirations and desires …"
David Fideler, *Jesus Christ, Sun of God*

Astrology is the most sublime of the occult * sciences, while at the same time it is one of the most practical for everyday application, for it divines the human soul itself. The cosmos, particularly the patterns that formed across it at the exact moment we were born, indicates the road along which our mental and spiritual endowments are likely to impel us, therefore enabling us to prepare in advance for life's battles, pitfalls, milestones, celebrations and of course to make the utmost of opportunities. Such is the magic of the human mind, that it can 'see' into the future and relive the past without having to be physically present in either, and when combined with astrological *knowing*, particularly the knowing that springs from understanding some of the dynamics of our natal chart, however basic, our inner - and outer - magic can be lifted to phenomenal heights.

In ancient times, not only was astrology the ardent study of the most learned and powerful minds, but among the masses of ordinary people its authority and guidance was accepted and followed without question. How this powerful knowledge was used was - and still is - up to the individual, but all who used it applied it to their perceived advantage.

As primitive humans observed the skies, no doubt they gradually realised that certain stars upon which their fate depended accompanied the seasons, or certain times of the year. They may also have reasoned that if governed their fate, they also governed their bodies, and it is therefore conceivable that the skies were associated with Divine influence. Certain celestial influences were believed to emanate from the thirty-six decans of the signs, and the mysterious but apparent effect that they exercised upon humans were thought to be due to a subtle ether shed by the heavenly stars and spheres on the Earth, that affected not only people, but also other animals, plants and minerals. For the ancient mind, linking magic with astrology may have also provided a much needed sense of predictability and patterns.

Early astrologers named and made associations with the imaginary divisions of the twelve signs and the twelve houses, and people born under a certain sign were said to inherit to an extent, its properties and nature. They also believed that the influence of the planets and stars corresponded with the medicinal properties of certain plants and minerals. They therefore asserted that the influence of a star or planetary position would affect the type of medicine or healing they would offer a subject to attain the most beneficial outcome. Throughout the writings of early philosophers and theorists, there is constant reference to this unmistakable mystic connection between the seven known planets and Earthly affairs and ailments. The seven metals were connected with the seven planets, to which the seven colours and the seven transformations were added. So the alchemist came to share the astrological doctrine that each planet ruled some mineral: the Sun ruled gold, the Moon silver, Mars iron, Venus copper, Saturn lead, Jupiter tin, and Mercury quicksilver. Consequently, in alchemical symbolism the same sign came to represent the metal and its corresponding planet.

In subsequent years, astrology became closely related to alchemical knowledge and development, and the alchemist came to be regarded as an authority not only on the transmutation of metals, but also on astrology and magic. This goes some of the way to explaining how magic and divination, which had always been inseparably bound up with astrology, came to be associated with alchemy. In all the occult sciences, the supreme power was believed to be in the stars above, and from their mysterious emanations all the metals, crystals, minerals, plants and herbs derived their special properties over time. Further, as alchemy became ever more spiritual and concerned with more abstract and philosophical concepts, eventually it was considered that the transmutation of lead into gold was simply a metaphor for the transformation of base matter, in this case the human soul, into a much purer and higher state of wisdom and being.

The Sun and Moon were believed to have greater influence over the human body than all the other heavenly bodies, and to exert their influence in various ways whenever they entered a certain sign of the zodiac. And although the Moon was traditionally regarded as the most important factor of a horoscope, the Sun has come into its own in later centuries, with the result that almost everyone knows their Sun sign but only those who have delved deeper are aware of the sign their natal Moon falls in. For this reason, I have chosen to focus this book series on the twelve Sun signs, as this is what the majority of people are most familiar with.

The following pages contain methods, energies, materials and objects which may be used to increase the magic and power of your Sun sign's influence upon you. Precious stones, flowers, colours and so on, are regarded as having a potent effect upon good fortune by attuning your mind to receive harmonious vibrations from the astral forces that surround you.

Finally, a basic working knowledge of basic astronomy and astrology is an asset when working with luck, abundance, wealth and personal power. You can attract more of these things when you align yourself with the workings of the wider Universe, the movement of the Sun, stars, Moon and planets and become aware of the correlations between the outer cycles of the skies and the inner cycles within yourself. Also, for those who are knowledgeable about Moon phases, equinoxes and solstices, a world of lucky possibilities can also magically open up to you. You don't need to know about astrology's deepest complexities to understand how everything interrelates; just learning the basics will give you an edge - and hopefully the following lucky tips will provide you with at least a small glimpse into the insights gleaned from your Sun sign, which I am certain will endow upon you the potential for amazing results to manifest in your life - and maybe even a step up one further rung towards the heavens!

* The word 'occult' comes from the Latin *occultus*, which literally means 'knowledge of the hidden'.

USING COLOURS, CRYSTALS, DEITIES, PLANTS, FOODS & MATERIAL SUBSTANCES FOR INCREASING POWER & MAGNETISING MAGIC

Alchemist, reformer and mystic Henry Cornelius Agrippa, born in 1486, in his principal work, *On Occult Philosophy*, expressed his belief in the doctrines of astrology and in the theory that the spirit of the world exists in the body of the world, just as the human spirit exists in the body of man. He contended that this spirit also abounds in the celestial bodies and descends in the rays of stars, so that the things influenced by their rays become conformable to them. By this spirit every occult property is conveyed into metals, stones, herbs and animals, through the Sun, Moon and planets, and even through the stars beyond and higher than the planets. A firm believer in the efficacy of charms, he stated that they may "be worn on the body bound to any part of it or hung around the neck, changing sickness into health or health into sickness." I believe the same effect could be applied to wishing and the thinking of positive thoughts, to mean, "Changing thoughts and dreams into manifest reality." He also recommended that these charms be worn in the form of finger rings (that have been created using the materials in agreement and harmony with your Sun Sign's magical energy).

Material substances are connected with abstract purposes by a complex but highly usable and accessible system of correspondences. Use these time-honoured connections in your own spells and wishes to magnetise your desires to you. The following pages will give you some materials, energies, forces and ideas you can summon the power of in order to enhance your magic and luck.

PLANETS

The Planetary influence of the day is important when 'asking' for something. If you are wishing for luck, for example, try working with your Sun sign's inherent energies combined with the perfect day of the week for it. So a Capricornian might try using her natural shrewdness and intelligence, to ask for greater luck on a Thursday, which is Jupiter's Day and Jupiter is renowned for being a lucky planet, or better still, ask for luck on a Saturday, which is Saturn's Day, planetary ruler of Capricorn, at the time of day when Jupiter's influence is at its most powerful (information about planetary hours for each day of the week can be found on the Internet or in books on the subject, and can be complex and detailed. It is an art to memorise the correct times, days and energies for the correct spells. If you are determined enough to achieve your dream or goal however, you will be determined enough to put in the research to do it properly!) Here is a very simplified list of the days of the week and their meanings:

DAYS OF THE WEEK & THEIR POWERS

MONDAY ★ Moon
Cancer

The Divine feminine, changes, intuition, emotions, secrets, dealing with women, purity, goodness, perfection, unity, psychic ability, magic, spirituality, invoking a goddess's or angel's guidance, anything that fluctuates, contracts, increases or decreases.

TUESDAY ★ Mars
Aries & Scorpio

Enthusiasm, competition, passion, energy, courage, protection, victory, anything requiring assertiveness, standing up for yourself, or a 'fighting spirit', determination, vitality, sexuality, self-confidence, men's power, men's mysteries, drive, ambition, achievement, triumph, masculinity.

WEDNESDAY ★ Mercury
Gemini & Virgo

Education, travel, exams, study, communication, making connections, thinking, dealing with siblings, writing and speaking, knowledge, learning, adaptability, charm, youth, absorbing information.

THURSDAY ★ Jupiter
Sagittarius & Pisces

Increase and expansion of anything (remember to be careful what you wish for), luck, growth, influence, worldly power, accomplishment, fulfilment, gambling, philosophy, higher education, abundance, optimism.

FRIDAY ★ Venus
Taurus & Libra

Love, luxury, the arts, indulgence, beauty, marriage, money, prosperity, fertility, women's power, women's mysteries, grace, charm, appeal, hope, pleasure, decorating, self-worth, self-esteem, personal values, business partnerships, romance, creativity, sharing, bonding.

SATURDAY ★ Saturn
Capricorn & Aquarius

Long-term goals, career, institutions, establishments, security, investments, karma, reversal, structure, protection, solitude, privacy, determination, ending, blocking, renewing, transforming, anything to do with the public.

SUNDAY ★ Sun
Leo

All-purpose, success, wishes, generosity, happiness, optimism, spirit/essence, recognition, health, vitality, material wealth, invoking a god's aid or guidance, personal empowerment, spirituality, the Divine masculine.

YOUR NATAL MOON PHASE

Although this book is aimed at enhancing your life through the energy of your Sun sign, a bit of Lunar help can give your wishing a boost! As well as using the planetary days and hours system to add a bit of zest to your wish fulfilment, try combining your Sun sign's power periods with your natal Moon phase (your natal Moon phase can be calculated using a number of sources on the internet, or through an astrologer), or even studying which constellation the Moon is situated in at certain times, to increase the power of your spells and asking rituals. For example, you might like to 'ask' for a promotion at work during a New/Waxing Moon period, particularly if the Moon happens to fall under an auspicious sign for career advancement, such as Capricorn. Your natal Moon phase can also be used to similar effect, by researching when your Moon phase will coincide with a certain Lunar constellation position.

In most astrological interpretations the Sun is regarded as the most important, central feature of a natal chart. But to many the Moon is equally, if not more, important than the Sun sign. Many ancient cultures considered the Moon sign to be more significant. The Moon passes through the 12 signs about every 2.5 days, usually covering the whole zodiac in around 27.3 days. The Moon symbolises our inner world, the world of feeling, emotions, habitual responses, instincts, intuition, security and the subconscious. It describes our nurturing style and needs, our emotional response to life, our attitudes and likely reactions to others, our instinctive and habitual responses, the receptive feminine side of ourselves, our experience of our mother or mother figure, and our childhood experience. It represents the soul. In relationships it symbolises how we like to be nurtured and cared for, and the potential depth of our involvement on personal intimate levels.

For many centuries, people across the world have recognised that the Moon influences the affairs of all living things on planet Earth. The waxing Moon appears to have a drawing, increasing and enhancing effect, whereas the waning Moon has a decreasing, receding and withdrawing effect. All things that come into being are stamped with the qualities of the prevailing Moon stage. It seems that people born during certain Lunar phases tend to share specific attributes with other people born during this same phase. In turn, their attributes will be subtly different from those of individuals born during any of the other stages in the Moon cycle. Knowing exactly which phase of the Moon you were born under gives you all kinds of extraordinarily valuable insights into your character, emotions, behaviour and motivations in life. It can make you aware of your deepest underlying drives, the fundamental purpose that you are drawn towards in life and the contribution you can make to others and society during the course of your lifetime. This knowledge may enable you to intuit and make the most of your own personal cyclical pattern that you go through each month, and allow you to know when the most auspicious periods of time are for you and your affairs, nurture yourself and channel your energies in the most positive directions.

Because this Lunar pattern repeats itself every month, you will find that you can even pace yourself on a long-term basis. This will enable you to effectively target your efforts and goals on periods of time that you know will be potentially fortunate for you. You may in fact find that your birth phase corresponds with the days of the month when you have abundant energy, feel inspired and can generate new ideas with ease. During this period, you should work towards the fruition of your efforts, bring your dreams into light and reach for the stars!

The Lunar Phases Are:

★ New Moon
★ First/Waxing Crescent
★ First Quarter
★ Waxing Gibbous Moon
★ Full Moon
★ Waning Gibbous / Disseminating Moon
★ Last Quarter
★ Waning Crescent / Balsamic Moon
★ Back to the New Moon

SPELLS, MAGIC & WISHING WITH MOON PHASES

Though the Moon has eight astronomical phases, it is the three phases corresponding to maiden, mother and crone that are the most significant in spells, ritual, wish magic and psychic work. By tuning into the physical Moon we can understand and harness these distinct energy phases in our daily lives and magical worlds. The four primary Lunar phases are the New Moon, First Quarter, Full Moon and the Last Quarter. Depending on what sort of spell you wish to perform, your spell should take place during one of these cycles or time periods. Each phase of the Moon is good for some types of magic, but not so much for others.

NEW MOON, WAXING & FIRST QUARTER

In astronomical terms, the New Moon occurs when the Moon rises and sets at the same time as the Sun. Both bodies are found in the same position compared with the Earth. Therefore, a Solar eclipse can only ever occur at the New Moon, when the two luminaries are found, for a short time, in a perfect line relative to the Earth, with the Moon positioned between the Sun and the Earth. The New Moon's sunlit face is hidden from the Earth.

In astrological terms, the New Moon occurs at a time when the Sun and the Moon are found in the same degree of the zodiac and therefore occupy the same zodiac sign, forming a conjunction, or a 'fusing' of energies.

In astronomical terms, the First Quarter occurs seven days after the New Moon. Seen from the Earth, this phase makes the Moon like a crescent, forming the shape of a capital D.

In astrological terms, it occurs when the Sun and the Moon form a ninety-degree angle, or the square aspect, inside the zodiac, the Moon always preceding the Sun.

As the New Moon marks the beginning of a new cycle, it symbolises fresh starts. This is an exceptional time to work magic and make wishes for new beginnings, and for the conception and initiation of new projects. Use this Moon phase for improving health, the gradual increase of prosperity, attracting good luck, fertility magic, finding new love, friendship or romance, job hunting, making plans for the future and increasing your general spiritual or psychic awareness.

Overall, the Waxing Crescent and First Quarter Moon phases are appropriate for spells, rituals and workings that involve growth, healing and increase. This is a period of time lasting approximately two weeks, to draw things toward you and increase things, such as love, prosperity and new opportunities. During this period is the time to bless new projects, anything that requires energy to grow, such as gardens, business ventures, new homes, or educational pursuits. Personal growth and healing are accented, as is 'attraction magic' - drawing something to you such as love, abundance, health, success or a new path - and if done well, you can expect results by the next Full Moon. Magical workings for gain, increase or bringing things to you should be initiated when the Moon is waxing (or New, going from Dark to Full). A time for divination of all kinds, spells of spiritual intention, and for any creative project you wish to see birthed, with magical and fruitful results.

While making a wish within the first forty-eight hours after the New Moon is a powerful way of helping it come to fruition, the most potent time for making wishes is actually within the first eight hours of the exact time of its position. Write down your wish list within this first eight hours on a piece of appropriately coloured paper with a special writing tool, and be sure to capture the essence of your wish by wording it in a way that charges your emotions and simply feels 'right'. Make a maximum of ten wishes (less is perfectly fine too), as making too many wishes might disperse their energy too much to be effective. After writing down your list and releasing your wishes to the Universe in whichever form you feel happy with, keep your list and check on it in a few days', weeks' or months' time to assess whether anything has shifted in the direction of your listed dreams, desires or goals. I'll bet it has - or at the very least, something even better has arrived in its place!

Although the first forty-eight hours after the New Moon is the most potent time to make a special wish, you can begin Waxing Moon magic when you can see the crescent in the sky and continue until the day before the Full Moon. The closer to the Full Moon, the more intense the energies. In fact, a personally devised ritual using any special Lunar-associated materials over three days up to and including the Full Moon is excellent for something you require urgently or within a short timeframe.

In some cultures, people turn over silver coins or jewellery three times when the crescent Moon appears in the sky and make a wish. As the Moon grows, it is believed that prosperity and good fortune will grow too.

While the New Moon is not known as a time for 'banishing' or releasing things we no longer want in our lives, I feel that if we are to ask and wish for things, we need to make room to receive them. Making room means that the Universe can slot it right into our lives where we have cleared our paths for it. Clutter, unwanted things, unhappy relationships, possessions that no longer serve us, are all things we can banish. So, to help what you are asking for come into your life quicker, the New Moon is a particularly opportune time to throw a few things out so you can make way for the new and clear up some space for that which you are wishing for. What are you waiting for? Start creating a space for your wishes today!

FULL MOON

In astronomical terms, the Full Moon occurs 14 days after the New Moon, on the day when the Moon sets at the same time the Sun rises, or conversely. The two luminaries are effectively facing each other, with the Earth in between, the Sun shining its light onto the reflective Moon, giving it the fully lit up appearance of a giant, bright, perfectly round sphere. Indeed, its entire face is bathed in sunlight. A Lunar eclipse can only occur at the Full Moon, when the Sun, Moon and Earth are all in line, and the Earth hides the lit side of the Moon to us.

In astrological terms, a Full Moon occurs at the time when the Sun and Moon are 180 degrees apart inside the zodiac, and therefore positioned in opposite signs, forming an opposition aspect.

The highest energy occurs at the Full Moon, making this is a powerful time for all manner of magical workings. Use the Full Moon phase for any immediate need, a sudden boost of power or courage, psychic protection, a change of career or location, travel, healing acute health conditions, the consummation of love or a commitment, justice, ambition and promotion of all kinds. This phase lasts approximately 3 days - 24 hours before the exact Full Moon, the day of, and 24 hours after it, according to many sources - giving us 3 full days to perform our spells. However, we are not strictly limited to a three-day period; the power of this phase can actually be accessed for seven days - three days prior to, the night of, and the three days after the Full Moon. The Full Moon period is when the Moon is at her most powerful, being the most luminous and radiant part of the cycle. Known as the 'high tide' of psychic power, the Full Moon represents culmination, climax, fulfilment and abundance. The Full Moon governs all kinds of magic, including manifestation, banishing, and is particularly good for calling forth protection and heightening your intuitive abilities. The Full Moon contains magic that calls forth personal power, fertility, spiritual development, and psychic awareness. Cleansing of ritual tools, crystals, wish lists, Tarot decks, and the like can be done during this phase. Magic worked during the Full Moon often takes one complete cycle to come to fruition. Try also reaffirming your desires during the New Moon to give them an added nudge in the right direction.

LAST QUARTER OR WANING MOON

In astronomical terms, the Last Quarter, or Waning Moon, occurs twenty-one days after the New Moon. The time difference between the rising and setting of the two luminaries is reduced to what it was at the First Quarter. Viewed from the Earth, the Moon resembles a crescent whose lit up area is decreasing in size, forming the shape of a capital C.

In astrological terms, the Waning Moon occurs when the Sun and Moon are positioned at ninety degree angles of each other in the zodiac, forming the square aspect again. However, during this phase, the Sun is instead *ahead* of the Moon.

The Waning Moon represents the Lunar cycle from Full to Dark. Any spells and magic performed during this period is based purely around banishing and releasing. It could involve releasing things which no longer serve you (such as behaviours, material things, relationships and attitudes), banishing negative energies, and removing obstacles which are standing in the way of achieving your goals or dreams. The Waning Moon is the best time for cleansing, gently releasing, eliminating, expelling and completion. It is of great assistance when you are wanting to let go of something, or someone, gradually. The Dark of the Moon, the period when the Moon is no longer visible to the naked eye, until the New Moon, is the most useful time for divination of all kinds.

★ What is your natal Moon phase type?
Can you think of ways you can combine it with the power of your Sun sign to effect change and bring about wonderful happenings? ★

HARNESSING YOUR PERSONAL MOON MAGIC ★ MOON IN CAPRICORN

When the Moon is in your sign of Capricorn, it is a great time for working magic around: Structure, practical matters, resourcefulness, career advancement and promotions, patience, thrift, endurance, success, restraint, duties and obligations, sincerity, self-discipline and order. Suggested operations could be around rituals and spells to learn to work with authority figures, rules and business, or organisations. It is also an opportune time to tap into your inner authority, and try to strengthen it. Spells to help you build your savings account, call forth Divine justice (karma), or for a promotion in your current job or position in life. With the Moon in Capricorn, you can also seek to create order out of a chaotic or unwanted situation, cultivate greater self-discipline or wise caution, and to build the underlying structure or foundation for anything (such as a new idea).

THE MOON ★
WHAT IT REPRESENTS
IN THE HUMAN PSYCHE &
NATAL CHART

The Moon in the sky shines with the reflected light of the Sun. Although not a planet, the Moon is our nearest celestial neighbour and exerts a great influence upon us. The gravitational pull of the Moon affects our body fluids, which contribute to about 90 per cent of our biological make-up. It moves at approximately half a degree per hour and takes an average of 27.3 days to pass through all twelve zodiac signs, staying in each for around 2.5 days.

In astrology the Moon corresponds with the way in which we reflect and respond to what is going on around us. It has to do with our feelings, emotions and instincts and, in the same way the Moon influences the tides on planet Earth, it symbolises the ebb and flow of our emotional nature, our moods, fluctuations and changeability. The Moon is the archetype of the Mother, which is within us all, and represents the primary feminine principle in the natal chart. It is through the Moon that we express our parental instincts - caring, nurturing, protecting, sensitivity. The Moon has links with the past and the subconscious and it is from this almost primitive source that our natural instinctual forces flow.

The Moon is essentially a feminine principle and associates with the inner personality, receptivity, passivity and inward-oriented feelings. It can act as an inner guide to the deeper self, the unconscious self, figures half-shrouded in mystery, linking the hidden personal world of the subconscious to the clearer world of personal awareness.

The Moon is the innermost core of our being, private feelings, habitual reactions and subconscious habits. It is the caring, nurturing sustainer of life, the 'mother' of the zodiac. It tells us about how we seek security, our urge to nurture, our nurturing style, our responses and feelings and moods. The innermost core of our being, private feelings, subconscious habits. It is concerned with habits, mothering, habitual/instinctive responses and personality. It is our karma, our soul, our past.

The Moon represents our mother or mother figure, our feminine side, maternal instinct, our nurturing style and needs, our unconscious self, our emotional reactions, the subconscious, our feelings, instincts, intuition, receptivity, habits, what we need to feel secure, fluctuations, cycles, moods, and our childhood. Its position in the birth chart is very significant, because as well as revealing feminine qualities and the potential gentleness and tenderness of a being, the Moon also reveals important information about the experiences and expression of the five senses.

The Moon is essentially receptive and passive; it reflects the life experience rather than initiating it. Fluctuating and cyclical, the Moon is the planet (although technically a satellite) of the childhood experience, and instinctual reactions. It represents the mother (a child's experience and expectations of their mother), maternal instincts and the feminine principle, indicating how strongly these manifest in an individual, male or female.

As it represents what our childhood experience is likely to be, and childhood is essentially a time where our consciousness has not yet fully developed, our Moon sign traits seem to be more apparent in our younger years. We will usually show our Moon sign traits more so than our Sun sign traits during this developing period of infancy and early childhood, until we have the presence of mind to more consciously develop our ego and true core self (the Sun).

The symbol for the Moon ☽ is a representation of its crescent in its waxing phase from new to full, but it can also be seen as two half circles - these form a bowl shape, a receptacle, a feminine container that 'receives' and 'holds' anything put into it. The half circle, unlike the full circle of the Sun, is finite and incomplete, almost as if striving for wholeness.

The Moon represents our *soul*.

YOUR MOON SIGN

The Sun / Moon Polarity
Conscious & Unconscious, Night & Day,
Yin & Yang

"Man does, woman is."
Edward Edinger

Your Moon Sign, representing your soul, and your Sun sign, representing your spirit, work together to form the foundation of your basic personality, expression and nature. If you know what your Moon sign is, look it up below and read how it works with your Capricornian Sun to blend your mind, soul and spirit.

♈ **With the Moon in ARIES, Sun in Capricorn**, you are likely to be ★ Dutiful, persistent, a sore loser, wilful, ambitious, self-interested, purposeful, quick-thinking and acting, enterprising, shrewd, self-motivated, pioneering, adventurous yet grounded, impatient with others' shortcomings, moody and temperamental, a realist, eager to get ahead, action-oriented, successful, powerful, vital, robust, zealous, strong, entitled, competitive, able to combine fun with wisdom to good effect, pragmatic, resourceful, meticulous, commanding, an astute thinker, honest, able to blend realism with idealism, dictatorial, professional, impressive, a workaholic, bossy, authoritarian, detached, entrepreneurial, self-disciplined, recognition-seeking, precise, inspired, skilful, demanding, self-controlled, caustically witty, dedicated to winning at all costs, self-important, a great leader, a good delegator, easily enthused, self-sufficient, diligent, forthright, a perfectionist, impatient, irritable, steady, rational yet feisty, in possession of an indefatigable resilience, and able to ground your idealism.

Sun/Moon Harmony Rating ★ *7 out of 10*

♉ **With the Moon in TAURUS, Sun in Capricorn,** you are likely to be ★ Solid, possessive, stable, caring, dependable, cool, calm and collected, careful, deliberate, deeply sensual, greedy, consistent, dedicated, cynical, ambitious, stubborn, conscientious, dutiful, supportive, self-sacrificing, a staunch supporter of the status quo, dignified, graceful, cautious, domestic, routined, unimaginative, staid, materialistic, nature-loving, security-seeking, fruitful, self-restrained, down-to-Earth, diligent, financially savvy, organised, reserved, affectionate, in possession of a shrewd business sense, infinitely patient, slow and steady-paced, persevering, enduring, loyal, devoted, logical, stoic, faithful, peaceful, capable, resourceful, realistic, sensible, persistent, and dedicated to working hard for a substantial income to ensure security.

Sun/Moon Harmony Rating ★ *8 out of 10* **

♊ **With the Moon in GEMINI, Sun in Capricorn,** you are likely to be ★ Intelligent, clever, cunning, manipulative, a craftsperson, skilful, critical, analytical, astute, adaptable, independent, resourceful, bright, discerning, articulate, debonair, cerebral, emotionally conventional, detached, cool, conflicted between conservatism and having fun, a jack-of-all-trades and master-of-all, shrewd, polished, decisive, organised yet scattered, talented, quick, efficient, perceptive, communicative, discriminating, observant, applied, able to balance work and play, rational, nimble, clear-thinking, precise, practically intelligent, pragmatic and straightforward, objective, able to apply your mind to anything, nervous, in possession of mental ingenuity, refined in taste, persuasive, unemotional, upwardly mobile, logical, concise, alert, unsentimental, and able to reason.

Sun/Moon Harmony Rating ★ *8 out of 10*

♋ **With the Moon in CANCER, Sun in Capricorn,** you are likely to be ★ Tough but tender, gentle, devoted, caring, retiring, emotionally repressed, cynical, anxious, sacrificing, moody, dependable, sensitive, nourishing, timid yet tenacious, over-sensitivity, practical yet emotional, dutiful, sentimental, compassionate, private, conscientious, defensive, courteous, deeply sensual, enduringly loyal, tense, reliable, virtuous, prudish, doting, self-reflective, a complainer and whinger, pessimistic, prone to depression, self-critical and self-pitying, reticent, withdrawn, discerning, considerate, concerned for the welfare of others, helpful, protective, a good wise counsellor, supportive, and able to analyse and process your emotions.

Sun/Moon Harmony Rating ★ *7.5 out of 10*

♌ **With the Moon in LEO, Sun in Capricorn**, you are likely to be ★ Artistically refined, able to balance work and play, aesthetic, helpful, grounded but buoyant, understatedly charming, honourable, honest, proud yet humble, individualistic, wilful, discreet but radiant, expressive, vibrant, forceful, hospitable, a good host, self-centred, calm on the surface with a great strength within, self-controlled, gently artistic, dignified, bossy, in possession of a down-to-Earth zest, romantic but sceptical, quietly generous, gentle and warm-hearted, capable, trustworthy, sensually romantic, quality-seeking, affectionate, accomplished, recognition-seeking, snobbish, gently passionate, conflicted between vanity and modesty, praise-seeking, driven, a good leader and organiser, dedicated to excellent, controlling, dedicated, patient, pleasure-seeking, sensually indulgent, encouraging, supportive, skilful, an elitist, noble-minded, masterful, and high standards-oriented.

Sun/Moon Harmony Rating ★ *7.5 out of 10*

♍ **With the Moon in VIRGO, Sun in Capricorn**, you are likely to be ★ Critical, aloof, studious, focused, dignified, virtuous, cynical, discriminating, humble, modestly wise, lucid, responsible, sensual, cautious, controlled, methodical, precise, prudish, a perfectionist, stable, logical, respectful, judgemental, hard-working, cool, calm and collected, trustworthy, methodical, devoted, dedicated, practical, modest, reserved, helpful, analytical, thoughtful, productive, consistent, supportive, kind, scrupulous, efficient, caring, rigid, conventional, down-to-Earth, attentive, industrious, constructive, resourceful, objective, rational, cool-headed, dutiful, scathing, willing to help and do what needs to be done, pragmatic, skilful, reliable, persevering, stable, poised, and in possession of a good deal of common sense.

Sun/Moon Harmony Rating ★ 7.5 out of 10 **

♎ **With the Moon in LIBRA, Sun in Capricorn**, you are likely to be ★ Introverted, graceful, stylish, aesthetically aware, noble, orderly, emotionally elusive, high-minded, moderate, sophisticated, intelligent, peace-seeking, astute in business, tasteful, pleasant, romantic, modest, classy, liberal yet conservative, endearing, courteous, polite, elegant, patient, inclined to be opportunistic, ethereally sensual, attractive, artistic, quietly sociable, articulate, clear-headed, a friendly loner, refined, well-balanced, loving of simplicity, understatedly charming, a hider of feelings, gracious, shrewd, socially aware, chic, hospitable, pleasure-seeking, delightful, gently persuasive, artistically sensitive, charitable, helpful, rational, a practical idealist, and conflicted between lofty ambitions and relationships.

Sun/Moon Harmony Rating ★ 8.5 out of 10

♏ **With the Moon in SCORPIO, Sun in Capricorn,** you are likely to be ★ Intense, powerful, tireless, steadfast, unshakable, rigid, austere, persevering, all-or-nothing, narrow-minded, complex, cynical, strongly disciplined, manipulative, self-mastering, deeply aware of the self, tense, serious, strategic, perceptive, self-reliant, strongly principled, suspicious, concentrated, tightly controlled, serious, meticulous, substantial, ambitious, enduring, obsessive, deeply anxious, harsh, tight, pious, strong-willed, ruthless, sensually passionate, unable to tolerate fools, broody, aloof, fearless, scrutinising, ruthless, passionately dedicated, undiluted, single-minded, robust, highly resilient, discriminating, subjectively responsive, acutely intelligent, persistent, committed, repressed emotionally, self-sufficient, charged, astute, focused, unable to relax, heavy, resourceful, critical and judgemental, obsessive compulsive, unyielding, sustaining, controlling, shrewd, thorough, hard-working, penetrative, compulsive, secretive, intensely loyal, emotionally stoic, exacting, manipulative, and in possession of a difficult but strong temperament.

Sun/Moon Harmony Rating ★ *6.5 out of 10*

♐ **With the Moon in SAGITTARIUS, Sun in Capricorn**, you are likely to be ★ Helpful, dutiful, rational but idealistic, ambitious, witty, sarcastic, zealous, authoritative, earnest, morally strong, faithful, restless but controlled, cautiously adventurous, verbose, articulate, philosophical yet logical, broad-minded, able to see the big picture, ethical, responsible, moralistic, grounded yet seeking, cleverly perceptive, strong, charismatic, dry-humoured, adventurous yet conventional, urbane, a dedicated student and thinker, embracing of novel ideas, honest, reasonable, frank, studious, intelligent, mentally dextrous, prone to preach and boss, a good guide or mentor, distant from your feelings, emotionally nervous, mentally agile, gently optimistic, ardently sensual, gently exuberant, a lover of learning, aspiring, objective, ambitious, broad-minded yet rigid, and guided by reason and logic rather than emotion.

Sun/Moon Harmony Rating ★ 7.5 out of 10

♑ **With the Moon in CAPRICORN, Sun in Capricorn,** you are likely to be ★ Self-controlled, persevering, emotionally repressed, cool, aloof, dedicated, emotionally isolated, staunch, disciplined, conscientious, devoted, refined, shrewd, rational, trustworthy, dependable, defensive, cynical, down-to-Earth, steadfast, pragmatic, humble, a workaholic, dictatorial, resourceful, committed, driven to succeed, conventional, ambitious, reserved, pessimistic, able to overcome most obstacles, withdrawn, methodical, frugal, dignified, realistic, logical, industrious, self-restrained, helpful, organised, productive, efficient, reliable, organised, serious, critical, tight-fisted, timid, sensible, introverted, understanding of practical applications and wisdom, economical, practical, honourable, uptight, socially rigid, professional, fearful, sophisticated, autocratic, self-contained, materialistic, protective, and willing to work long and hard to achieve your goals.

Sun/Moon Harmony Rating ★ 7 out of 10

♒ **With the Moon in AQUARIUS, Sun in Capricorn,** you are likely to be ★ Objective, humane, impersonal, rational, thoughtful, cool-headed, observant, applied but scattered, solitary, concise, slightly eccentric, contrary, lucid, paradoxical, diligent, nervous, detached, cool, aloof, quirky yet practical, discontent, living an unusual lifestyle in some way, paradoxical, socially timid, dedicated to worthy ideals and causes, self-contained, attracted to academia, well-meaning, open to the unusual, emotionally repressed, helpful, sensible yet rebellious, a progressive thinker, dispassionately critical, standoffish, acutely aware of the human condition, kind, pragmatically helpful, contradictory, an intellectual, untouched by passions, philanthropic, changeable, dissatisfied, unique, a pragmatic humanitarian, inconsistent, respectful, unstable, sceptical, conflicted between solitude and being around groups, realistic yet idealistic, committed to principles and ideals, embracing of abstract concepts, and devoted to social causes.

Sun/Moon Harmony Rating ★ *7 out of 10*

♓ **With the Moon in PISCES, Sun in Capricorn**, you are likely to be ★ Compassionate, helpful, caring, able to mix realism with mysticism, ethereally sensual, insightful, idealistic yet grounded, artistic, wholesome, a natural counsellor, refined, gentle, kind, pessimistic, cynical, romantic, unstable, unsure, prone to depression, a martyr, sentimental, modest, downplaying of own abilities, supportive, a pragmatic poet, able to bring dreams into reality, needy, introverted, withdrawn, whimsical, despondent, easily discouraged, self-sacrificing, diffident, torn between being impractical and practical, evasive, melancholic, an escapist, sensitive, cleverly intuitive, perceptive, tough but tender, and torn between responsibilities and escapism.

Sun/Moon Harmony Rating ★ *7.5 out of 10*

** If your Moon is in Taurus or Virgo, your Sun and Moon will form what is known in astrology as a trine aspect. This aspect is the easiest, most flowing and harmonious astrological aspect, ensuring that your Sun and Moon, or spirit and soul, are well integrated. With both luminaries in Earth signs, this gives them the best possible degree of complementary energy - a blending of the elements suggests a balanced expression of personality. One drawback of the trine aspect lies in the fact that its easy flow can be *too* harmonious; if our path is too smooth and difficulties don't arise to challenge us from time to time, we can often become lazy and complacent, stunting our growth and spiritual evolution. As Earth signs, you share the art of practical application, devotion, rational thinking, logic, a love of beauty and peace, determination, pragmatism, sensibility, conservatism, realism, sensuality, fruitfulness and a gentle, caring approach to all your relationships and endeavours, but may be staid, rigid, unimaginative, materialistic, slow, lazy, narrow-minded and lacking in enthusiasm and zest.

YOUR BODY & HEALTH

> "A physician without a knowledge of astrology has no right to call himself a physician."
> **Hippocrates (born c. 460 BC)**

Hippocrates, the fifth century BC Greek physician and 'father of medicine' and supposed author of the Hippocratic Oath, maintained that no one should be allowed to practise medicine who had not first studied astrology. Another Greek physician, Claudius Galen, brought together a huge range of knowledge and ideas in the second century AD which dominated medical practice until the 17th century. Among his teachings was a diagnostic technique which assumed that illnesses and their treatments were affected by and governed by the phases of the Moon. For centuries, astrology was a compulsory component of medical training (and still is in some natural medicine degrees), albeit only one aspect of diagnosis and treatment.

Medical or health astrology concerns particular ways of determining and interpreting an individual's horoscope with particular reference to health issues - diagnosis of current dis-eases, identification of areas of bodily weaknesses, and the prescription of natural cures and remedies. In ancient times, and still even today, the movement of the stars and planets was believed to affect bodily functions, and to cause ailments, or cure them.

During the Middle Ages, many drawings of the 'zodiac man' were made, which showed which signs of the zodiac were related to each part of the body, providing information as to the best times of the year to undertake cures for ailments affecting the corresponding body parts.

Health astrology persists today in many forms and among astrologers themselves, from whom clients seek counsel on health-related issues, and while it certainly cannot be used diagnose a condition or dis-ease, one's Sun sign, along with other factors of the natal chart, can definitely indicate potential problem areas of weakness or possible troubles. This branch of astrology has been found to be surprisingly accurate in most cases. While mostly accurate, none of the following information should ever be used as a substitute for professional medical advice should you be personally concerned about any of the conditions or afflictions listed for your Sun sign.

CAPRICORNIAN HEALTH

"Generally speaking, if they avoid lingering illnesses caused by lingering depressions, the Capricorn tenacity for life is remarkable. But it's no fun to be the last leaf on the tree if you're suffering from arthritis and rheumatism. The Goat must seek the sunlight and laugh at the rain to stay healthy."
Linda Goodman

Capricorn is associated with the Knees, Joints, Ligaments, Bones, Skin, Hair, Nails, Teeth, Corpus Callosum, Synovial Fluid, Parathyroid Glands, Mastoid Bone, and Gall Bladder. Most Capricorns are less than robust when they are young, but their resistance to diseases seems to increase as they age.

Being sober, sensible and temperate, you are the most likely of the signs to live to a substantial age. One of the natural survivors of the zodiac, there is not much in the way of sickness that you can't shake off or come to terms with. It has been said that Capricorns are 'born old and grow young', therefore the older you are, the younger and more active you seem to be for your age.

Capricorns usually encounter three main health problems. The first occurs in childhood, when you are likely to be either sickly or weaker than most of your peers and to catch every minor complaint going around (but the resistance of the Capricorn child increases with age). The second problem is you are more liable to psychosomatic illnesses than most other signs. You are a great worrier and can literally worry yourself sick. Thirdly, you are subject to vague aches and pains, the most pernicious of which are rheumatism and arthritis. However, the health troubles that afflict you are not the kind that will shorten life; they are much more inclined to cause discomfort and irritations that, unfortunately, may persist for long periods of time.

Capricorn rules the muscles and the bones, particularly the knees. Everything that hardens and protects in the body is under its influence. It gives a tough, wiry constitution that is capable of undergoing extreme hardship. The symbol for Capricorn, the Goat, is a very hardy animal with qualities of endurance and the ability to survive in austere conditions. When struck by illness, you are usually slow but steady to recover, and persevere to overcome what ails you at all costs.

Anxiety, over-responsibility, over-work, gloominess and general pessimism tend to take their toll on Capricornian health however, so you need to learn to relax and occasionally lighten up and have some fun. Psychologically, you should guard against fear, worry, lack of vitality, withdrawal and depression, for your physical health complaints are often induced or aggravated by worry and introspection. Your worst health hazard is indeed your pessimism and angst, as these not only affect your appetite but also impair your entire constitution. And in any case, your unease and uncertainties are almost always irrational or exaggerated. In all compartments of your life you tend to look on the down side. You crave security and sometimes seek escape, but these are easily remedied by choosing a brighter attitude, and by surrounding yourself with sunnier company (many of your closest associates tend to be introverted and serious). Chronic fatigue can be a manifestation of your tendency to be melancholic. It is in your later years, when negativity and morbidity have become habitual, that the worst effects may be felt. With Capricorn people, excessive drinking is more likely to be a compensation for depression or the like than an addiction.

Being the great organiser and leader, you seem to thrive on clearing away obstacles and sorting out tangles in everyday affairs, and it is important to your health and spirit that you be busily involved in some sort of work or project, as you have a strong distaste for being idle or lazy. You become agitated when you have no responsibilities, but need to be careful that you do not overburden yourself by taking on more than your fair share of obligations. Often, because you are so adept at coping, others often load you up with duties - loved ones are probably the worst offenders, albeit unwittingly.

On a more positive note, your nervous system is highly developed and you are not easily unbalanced. You are robust and strong-willed, and in times of crisis, are the best equipped of anyone to take charge. But your problem will always lie in coming to terms with your internal pressures and sorrows.

The commonest physical ills of Capricorns are knee problems, joint inflammations such as arthritis and rheumatism, cartilage issues, skin disorders, constipation, toothache and earache. You should ensure you get enough calcium, as calcium deficiencies are common in Capricornians, and you are susceptible to bone and joint dis-eases such as osteoporosis, osteoarthritis, dental problems and knee joint issues. You may also be vulnerable to skin conditions such as eczema or acne.

Capricorn represents the energy of structure and form. Your nature is cool, dry and structured. As already mentioned, principal rulerships include the skin and bones, joints (especially the knees), cartilage and tendons, hair, nails, teeth and gall bladder.

As Capricorn is linked with the strong, consistent energy of Saturn, illnesses will be steadily overcome through determination, practicality and health wisdom. Saturn governs the Teeth, Spleen, Gall Bladder, Phlegm, Bones and Stones, Skin, Vagus Nerve, Joints, Ligaments, Sigmoid Colon, Mastoid Bone, Hearing and Sluggishness. It is also associated with the anterior lobe of the Pituitary Gland, which regulates the sex glands and affects bone and muscle structure.

Keeping yourself in excellent health overall, with a special awareness of Capricorn's vulnerable points, is key to achieving all you set out to do, and getting the most out of your life!

THE CELL SALTS ★ ASTROLOGICAL TONICS

Homeopathy and astrology have colluded to provide a wonderful list of astrological tonics, one particularly suited to each of the twelve signs. These are called 'homeopathic cell salts', 'tissue salts' or 'biochemic cell salts', and are available in most health food stores, are inexpensive and easy to take. They are considered to be gentle, effective and safe, even for children, people in fragile health states, and the elderly. Although the full picture, drawn from a full natal horoscope, gives a fuller, more accurate idea of an individual's unique constitution, even simply working with one's date of birth can be enough for the medical astrologer to suggest the use of a cell salt based upon the correlation with an individual's Sun sign. As well as the cell salts having a significant effect upon physical ailments, they can also profoundly influence the subtle energy bodies, including the mental, emotional, etheric and spiritual. Although the most common use of these salts is based upon each salt's correspondence with a Sun sign, use of the cell salt related to one's Moon sign can assist with addressing deeper underlying emotional issues, such as anxiety, depression, panic and fear. Use of the cell salt relating to your Moon sign will therefore help to restore your sense of safety, balance, security and emotional resilience. In the first seven years of life, when the Moon is the most influential sphere in our lives, Lunar cell salts are the most appropriate choice as a remedy or tonic.

For specific health problems, take both the salt of your Sun or Moon sign, *and* the salt that pertains to the specific condition. The same principle applies to the Ascendant sign, as the First House represents one's physical health, and especially if the Sun or Moon is a rising planet, which means rulership of the whole chart. For the purposes of this book, however, the cell salt that correlates with your Sun sign only is outlined.

TISSUE SALT FOR CAPRICORN ★ CALC PHOS.

Calcarea Phosphorica, or Calc Phos. (Calcium phosphate) is the cell salt for Capricorn. Calc Phos. is an important constituent of bones and is found in abundance in all tissues, fertile soil, blood plasma and corpuscles, saliva, bone, gastric juices, epidermal fibres, new blood cells, and the dentin of teeth. Regarded as a 'life-sustaining mineral', it has numerous important functions. It is essential for the proper growth and nutrition of the body, strengthens bones, helps to builds new blood cells, and improves gastric digestive function so all ingested vitamins and minerals are better assimilated. Calc Phos. is recommended for the alleviating of cramps, since it has a calming and relaxing effect on muscles and indeed the entire organism. Its sedative properties also make it a useful remedy for sleeplessness. In addition, Calc Phos. is a 'warming' salt and can be helpful when symptoms or complaints are exacerbated by cold and improve with warmth. It is also an excellent restorative remedy for convalescing people. Pregnant women, elderly people, teething babies and children respond well to this form of calcium as it is gentle and well-received by the body. The body requires larger amounts of Calc Phos. than any other tissue salt, especially during childhood, growth spurts, or after suffering a broken bone. Overall, Calc Phos. is of vital importance to the growth and maintenance of healthy cells, and is needed in the blood, ova and semen cells, liver, salivary glands and the thyroid gland. Since it often intensifies the action of other cell salts, it is a good companion remedy. Capricorn rules the skeletal system, and especially the teeth, joints and knees, so could benefit from this cell salt. As Capricorns are susceptible to worry and brittle bones, they may need this cell salt in their diet to settle the stomach, aid digestion, and build stronger bones.

EARTH SIGN CAPRICORN & THE MELANCHOLIC HUMOUR

Greek physician Hippocrates (460 - 370 BC) theorised that certain human behaviours were caused by body fluids, called 'humours'. Later, Galen of Pergamon (AD 131 - 200), a Greek physician, developed the first typology of temperaments to encompass many facets of the human psyche and physiology. These also related to the classical elements of Fire, Earth, Air and Water - as choleric, melancholic, sanguine and phlegmatic respectively. According to the Greeks who developed the temperament theory (the word stems from the Latin word *temperamentum*, meaning mixture), temperament is the 'mixture' of qualities that combine to form elements in physics and humours in medicine. The Greeks sought equilibrium in the four qualities of hot, cold, wet (moist), and dry, the elements of Earth, Air, Fire and Water, and the four humours of choler or yellow bile, melancholer or black bile, blood and phlegm. If balance was achieved, the person was said to be well- or even-tempered, and the importance of determining the temperament allowed for imbalances to be treated.

In ancient times, each of the four types of humours corresponded to a different personality type, which were associated with a domination of various biological functions. It was suggested that the temperaments came to clearest manifestation in childhood, between around the ages of six and fourteen of age, after which they become subordinate, but still influential, factors in our personality. It is important to note that your temperament is not your personality. However, your personality can incorporate parts of the temperament in its expression. Personality is shaped by both external and internal factors, whereas the temperament is innate, an inborn, inherent part of each individual.

The Earth element corresponds with the humour melancholic, which is characterised by long response time delay, and response sustained at length, if not seemingly permanently. Driven by the fear of rejection and the unknown, you tend to be rigid, moody, anxious, sober, pessimistic, unsociable, responsible and quiet.

The melancholic temperament is analogous with the Earth, which is the main element in autumn (or fall), the season with which Earth signs have many points in common. The nervous system and physical and mental powers reign supreme in melancholic types, although they may often behave in nervous, worried or unstable ways, too. The Mercurial (Virgo) melancholic is distinguishable from the Saturnian (Capricorn) melancholic through the former's obviously more eccentric and less withdrawn mannerisms.

A melancholic disposition represents anxiety, peace and inflexibility. Its taste is sweet and astringent, its nature alkaline, its indication black bile. The melancholic humour is associated with the physical and *solid* body ^, and with cold and dry conditions.

^ A couple of thousand years ago, the Mesopotamians, Chinese and Egyptians, and more recently the Arabs, practised a medicine called 'of three bodies'. According to the doctors of the ancient world (who often practised as astrologers as well), a human being had three bodies: the physical body, the ethereal (or vital) body and the astral body, imparting a holistic approach to health. In modern medicine, usually only the physical body is focused upon fully. According to tradition, this physical body comprises three principles or states corresponding to three primordial elements: *solid* (Earth), *liquid* (Water) and *gas* (Air). This is the material body, the physical outer cover of muscles, nerves and organs held together by the skeleton. The Fire element corresponds with the *astral* body, which sits outside the physical body in one's auric field.

MONEY ATTRIBUTES

Colour for Increased Earning Power ★ Forest Green

The following plants can be used by all zodiac signs to assist in attracting money ★ Ginger, Allspice, Clover, Orange, Marjoram, Cinnamon, Sassafras, Woodruff, Bergamot, Tonka Beans, Heliotrope, Alfalfa, Coltsfoot, Thyme, Mace, Irish Moss, Clove, Almond, Corn, Honeysuckle, Sesame, Nutmeg, Vetiver, Poppy, Jasmine, Dill and Elder Flower. To attract luck and success, try using any of the above, combined with any of the following: Alfalfa Seeds, Basil, Mustard Seeds, Vervain Leaves, Poppy Seeds, Rosemary, Lemon, Anise and Holly.

Striving for financial gain and abundance with a healthy inner moral compass is, in my view, one of the most noble goals we can set for ourselves. When we have more money, we are better placed to help ourselves and of course others; after all, as Abraham Maslow's Hierarchy of Needs model (1943) attests, once our primary and base survival needs have been satisfied, we can then advance higher towards loftier achievements, such as self-confidence, creativity and self-actualisation. Prosperity allows us to turn our attention to these more transcendental matters - to reach for lives not just of material comfort and luxuries, but of meaning, generosity, balance, harmony, fulfilment and joy. Our Sun sign can offer clues as to how we go about acquiring, earning, saving, maintaining, and allowing the overall flow of giving and receiving money. What's *your* money style?

Capricorns have an innate respect for and inner knowing of money and rarely if ever spend frivolously or impulsively. Purchases are typically of excellent quality and designed to last. Your cautious and shrewd nature means that you plan your financial future carefully, and savings, insurance and pension plans are drawn up meticulously. You rarely, if ever, take a risk with your money, however if you do, it is very calculated and almost always has a beneficial outcome. You are extremely careful and cautious in financial matters, and have an uncanny ability to create wealth through shrewdness, ambition, determination and wise, carefully planned investments.

Capricorn is the financial guru of the zodiac. It could be said that Capricorn is the sign of the business man or woman, and although that is a generalisation, it is true that you are often the hardest working and striving sign of the zodiac. Material success, prestige and status are important goals for you, and you will stop at nothing to achieve them. You strive for financial independence as you are loathe to rely on anyone for much at all; in fact, you might even save towards your own nursing home so your dear loved ones don't have to part with their own pennies. In essence, you are serious, conscientious, cautious and responsible with your finances, however much or little you have.

You seem to have an inborn, in-built sense of financial and business acumen and know instinctively how to race ahead of the pack. You use your own efforts to achieve wealth; with money itself you can be extremely detached, but you enjoy spending your earnings on fine quality possessions and investments that may increase in value over time.

You are an excellent saver and always have a stash, however small, put away in case of unexpected misfortunes (which, by the way, rarely seem to befall you as you tend to have a robust resistance to such things). Capricorns more than the other signs, must guard against being mean, possessive or stingy with their money however, as you are prone to being tight-fisted when it comes to sharing with others and to overall generosity. And make no mistake, although you are a hoarder who likes to conserve money, you are an efficient trader. After all, your key phrase is "I Use," and use you do - money, power, status, people, *anything* which will further you along the path towards prosperity. In fact, you use everything that comes your way in life; indeed, everything and anything that will enable you to climb your way, little by little, to the very top.

COLOURS

Chromatomancy, or divination by colour, is a form of energy therapy that has been used for thousands of years by many different cultures. It works on the principle that we make both instinctive and rational choices or preferences based on circumstances which are already present in ourselves; colour also has an effect on the energy in an environment, and we in turn respond consciously or subconsciously to our surroundings. If we look at the causes, and try to understand the reasons, as to why we are so receptive to one particular colour over another, we will see that there is a subtle link between certain hues and our emotional and instinctive individual reactions. The colour which we give to things results from a combination of three elements:

1. The light or the vibration of a body;

2. The context in which it is found and the interaction between its own light and that of its environment;

3. The sensitivity of the eye's retina which sees the body in question. Because of this, a colour can vary, depending on the individual's perceptions, namely, his sensitivity, his mood, and his view of reality. For a long time, people have understood that their vision of reality depends a lot on their moods, feelings and emotions.

Chromatotherapy, or colour healing, stems from this body of evidence, and its main application is the use of colours for healing purposes. Colours are generally associated with characteristics, feelings, stones, metals, plants and flowers, planets and even the zodiac signs. In varying cultures, they play a significant role in ceremonies and regalia.

We vibrate to the frequency of colour, shown through its continual movement and change in our aura ^. One of the most beautiful examples of colour is the rainbow. This architect of colour is caused by the refraction and internal reflection of light in raindrops. Colour can be perceived as either a pigment, or as illumination. The colour spectrum can be divided into eight main colours: red, orange, yellow, green, turquoise, blue, violet and magenta. Each colour has a wavelength and frequency that carry different therapeutic qualities which have indirect effects upon our health and bodily systems, and because of this, coupled with the fact that we as living energy centres emanate colour, colour can be a great medium in healing, calming, energising, increasing and attracting.

Aristotle, in the fourth century BCE, considered blue and yellow to be the true primary colours and related them to life's polarities: Sun and Moon, male and female, stimulation and sedation, in and out, expansion and contraction. He also associated colours with the four elements of Fire, Earth, Air and Water. Hippocrates, the father of medicine, used colour extensively in medicinal healing and recognised that the therapeutic effects of a white violet differed from those of a purple one. In the fifteenth century, Paracelsus placed particular importance on the role of colour in healing.

Each Sun sign and planetary body has a specific colour or colours which when used in combination with wishing rituals, can enhance their power immensely. Coloured candles can be used to good effect, as the fire energy of the flame/s increases the power of any wish, and flames are also a useful aid to meditating on, focusing upon or clarifying what you want. Coloured candles help to focus the energy for whatever purpose the colour is in sympathy with (e.g. green for money, pink for romance, orange for joy, etc.)

With all this in mind, wearing or using your Sun sign or ruling planet's magical colour/s on a regular basis will undoubtedly bring great benefits.

^ The aura is defined as an energy field, which interpenetrates with, and radiates beyond, the physical body. Clairvoyantly seen, the aura is full of light, colour and shade. The trained healer or seer sees or senses indications within the aura as to the spiritual, physical and emotional state of the individual. Much of the auric colour and energy emanates from the chakras.

YOUR LUCKY COLOURS

For Capricorn ★ Black, Grey, Brown, Dark Blue, Violet, Forest Green, Navy, all dark shades.

For Saturn ★ Green

As an Earth sign with a tendency to be sombre and reserved, Capricorns usually prefer classic, stylish, simple and conservative colours such as black, browns and dark greens.

Each of the eight colours of the rainbow spectrum also has a complementary colour to which it is matched. Red is complementary to turquoise, orange to blue, yellow to violet, and green to magenta. If these colour pairs enhance each other's most spellbinding qualities and energies, perhaps you could try wearing your Sun sign's lucky colour with its matching complementary colour in order to produce extra magical results! One of your lucky Capricornian colours is green, which complements magenta. Now you know your colours, you can dress for success!

FEATURE COLOURS ★ BLACK & (FOREST) GREEN

★ BLACK ★

Planetary Associations ★ Saturn, Pluto

Healing Qualities ★ Power, Domination, Protection, Elegance, Sophistication, Status, Control, Protection, Willpower, Banishing and Absorbing Negativity

Keywords ★ Mystery, Power, Authority, Luxury, Sexy, Confidence, Dedication, Self-Importance, Protective, Wealth, Outer Space, the Universe

Technically speaking, black is not a colour but rather the absence of colour that occurs when light is totally absorbed by a surface. This means that none of the light hitting a black is reflected back into your eyes, which is how you usually perceive colour, giving black a number of useful properties, such as: if you are feeling cold it's better to wear darker shades such as dark grey or black, as these will retain heat, making you feel warmer (in summer, however, white is the most effective colour for helping you keep your cool). Also, because black is the colour you arrive at when all colours are 'absorbed', it is ideal for soaking up negativity, thereby possessing protective qualities. A powerful and thought-provoking colour, black is the colour of Saturn and of the element of Spirit. Black is symbolic of the beginning and the end, the abyss, the culmination of things, the completion of a cycle, the void, termination, and the unknown. All colours are included in black, the Universal colour, which used to be considered evil, darkness and bad luck. According to Native American tradition each of the Four Winds has its own colour. Black is the colour of the West Wind and this usually augured ill fortune. Because when living matter breaks down it darkens and blackens, indicating that it no longer contains the vital life force, we associate this colour with decay, endings and mortality. Instinctively, we have an aversion to these concepts and naturally view them with suspicion. We also use phrases such as 'black magic', 'dark mood', the 'black death' (referring to the 14th century European plague pandemic during which millions perished), and 'blacklisted', which further contaminate our feelings around this mysterious and oft-maligned colour. Although it has a bad reputation, being associated with death, fear and mortality, it can be used for positive ends - that is, through absorbing negativity, binding, dealing with depression and grief, divination and for bringing things to a conclusion. Because it is associated with grief and endings, black is a useful colour to use for binding in spell and ritual work; and in crystal therapies, black stones can be used for overall divination, connecting one to the Earth (through grounding), to protect and even to treat depression or helplessness. It is the colour of power and domination but has important spiritual overtones, as can be seen in the yin-yang symbol. Black is also a colour of elegance and luxury that can suggest power and authority. It is a sophisticated colour, signifying status and achievement, as shown by those reaching the highest levels in martial arts being awarded a 'black belt'. Black can encourage introspection and is useful for situations where you want to feel in control. Black, being the colour of mysteries and secrets, can provide answers when we gaze, for example, at the 'black spaces' between the stars above, or indeed, into a black surface or sphere (black crystal balls can be used for 'scrying' or crystal-gazing in order to conjure images, illuminations or visions that can enlighten and guide our life's journey). Being connected to the Earth element, black can also help to ground you when you are feeling disconnected, 'floaty' and dislocated from the world. Due to its tendency to make things look smaller, in crystal work this could be applied to problems that you wish to diminish. Also seen as the colour of unrealised potential, of ideas yet to be manifested, it can be used in magical rituals to harness and take control of your inner powers so that you may attain your desires. Black overall can enhance self-confidence, feelings of self-control and authority, grounding and all-round connectedness.

★ GREEN ★

Planetary Associations ★ Saturn, Venus

Complementary Colour ★ Magenta

Healing Qualities ★ Balancing, Harmonising, Calming, Comforting, Relaxing, Soothing, Wellbeing, Freshness, Generosity

Keywords ★ Prosperity, Growth, Money, springtime, the Emerald City, Abundance, Fertility, Good Luck, Harmony

Green is a colour of balance and harmony; from a psychological perspective, it is a great balancer of the feelings and the emotions, creating an equilibrium between the head and the heart. The most restful colour on the eye, it is the middle colour of the rainbow - a bridge between the colours of physicality and spirituality. Green is the colour of Venus and of the element of Earth. It shares the Heart chakra, Anahata, with pink and when the hues of this energy centre are in balance you feel an abundance of love and happiness. Its healing powers come from its alignment with the natural forces and rhythms of the

Earth. It is the colour of nature, which can reconnect us to planet Earth, and we instinctively lean towards this colour when in need of peace or harmony. Green is also connected with spring, and the abundance of baby animals and seeds sprouting at this time, make it a youthful and playful colour. Being the colour of balance and sympathy, it has the power to bring the negative and positive energies of a person into balance. Likewise, it has the strength to integrate the right and left hemispheres of the brain, the right hemisphere being intuitive and the left being intellectual. It is also the colour of Spring, of growth, of rebirth and renewal. Green, being such a pervasive colour in the natural world, is regarded as a symbol of peace and ecology. It can be used in healing to promote fertility and beauty. In Feng Shui and other spiritual disciplines, it is said to attract money through its vibrational energy. As mentioned earlier, Green is the colour of the Heart chakra and bridges the gap between the physical and the spiritual worlds. Opening the Heart chakra allows one to love more, feel compassion and empathise with others. Meditating with a green crystal held over the Heart chakra can help to balance emotions. However, green can also evoke feelings of jealousy and envy when out of balance, hence the terms 'green with envy' and the 'green-eyed monster'. Darker shades of green can also symbolise wealth, avarice and greed. Despite some less desirable connections, this colour works to make your mood more like it: caring, contented, accepting, loving, nurturing and joyful. Green can also balance the three aspects of a person's being, namely the body, mind and spirit, creating a sense of wholeness and integration. Green is the midpoint colour of the rainbow spectrum, being neither at the hot nor the cold end. It occupies more space in the spectrum visible to the human eye than most colours. Positioned right in the middle of the rainbow spectrum, it gets along well with other colours and can be used alongside them to complement their effects and enhance and brighten duller hues such as grey or brown, rather than overpowering them. Coupled with blue, green is a great stress-reliever and natural tranquilliser. It is not always regarded as a gentle colour; for some, it can signify illness, such as when one's skin turns green if sick, and for others, it has connections with ghoulish monsters, aliens, zombies, vampires and dragons. Also strongly associated with the fairy world, it is linked with elves, sprites, dryads and leprechauns - who can all be very helpful to humankind, but can also be 'impish', mischievous, spiteful and malicious. But despite some negative associations, overall, there is no better colour if you are looking for new ideas or a fresh start, as green is the colour that symbolises and supports growth and natural change. Green is a wonderful all-round soother, balancer and harmoniser, and a beneficial tonic for the mind, body, spirit and heart.

Green and magenta, its complementary rainbow spectrum complementary colour, as well as black, are Capricorn's special LUCKY colours! The three can be worn or otherwise used together to dazzling and mesmerising effect.

CAPRICORN'S CHAKRA
CORRESPONDENCE ★ BASE

The word 'chakra' comes from the Sanskrit and means 'wheel', disc' or 'circle'. Chakras are vitally important to your physical health, emotional wellbeing and spiritual growth, and are regarded as a complete integrated system that works holistically. The chakras are funnel-shaped spinning energy vortexes of multicoloured light. These swirling vortexes of energy absorb and distribute life-force, the subtle energy known as *prana*. The seven master chakras - Root, Sacral, Solar Plexus, Heart, Throat, Third Eye and Crown - lie in the centre line of the body, with the first five embedded within the spinal column. Each chakra vibrates at a different vibrational frequency and on a different note, and responds to specific life issues or 'thought forms'.

The lower body chakras deal with physical issues. As we move up the body, the chakras correspond to increasingly spiritual concerns. As a consequence, each chakra's energy vibrates at a different rate, depending on whether they govern earthbound or ethereal issues. The lower chakras have slower and denser vibrations, while the higher chakras spin at faster speeds with higher vibrations.

Because the chakras have no physical manifestation and cannot be located using any scientific instrument, they have tended to be viewed with scepticism by many Western medical professionals, a distinction they share with energy points in acupuncture and the notion of meridians. Instead, they are believed to have been sensed intuitively by many people over many centuries, and indeed people in yoga positions and in deep meditation have reported experiencing the sensation of a surge of energy rising from the base of the spine and emerging through the top of the head. Some people have even said they have seen points of blue light when their *kundalini* energy has risen from the lowest chakra to the highest, as well as experiencing a profound sense of happiness and ecstasy.

In summary, the Universal Life Force enters the body through the Crown chakra at the top of the head. As it works its way through the body, it flows through the other centres. As it spreads to the Base chakra, it is said to arouse the kundalini energy, which yogis believe sleeps in a coiled serpentine form.

The chakra associated with Capricorn is the first, the Root or Base chakra, which governs and regulates issues of security, survival and fulfilment of our physical needs for food and shelter.

BASE CHAKRA

Location ★ Base of Spine
Colour ★ Red
Concerned with ★ Security & Survival
Gland ★ Gonads
Essential Oils ★ Benzoin, Vetiver, Patchouli
Animals ★ Bull, Elephant, Ox
Shape ★ Yellow Square
Element ★ Earth
Planets ★ Saturn, Earth
Zodiac Sign ★ Capricorn
Flower ★ Four-petalled Lotus

Energy State ★ Solid
Mantra ★ LAM

Positive Expression ★ Energetic, productive, grounded, stable, serves others, committed

Negative Expression (Blockage) ★ Angry, self-indulgent, aggressive, plodding, habitual, tied down, prone to anxiety, ungrounded, fearful about security and survival, flighty, difficulty letting go, lack of sense of belonging, weak constitution, overly practical, lacking dreams and imagination

The Base chakra, otherwise known as the Root chakra, is located at the base of the spine. Its Sanskrit name is *muladhara*, and its symbol is a four-petalled crimson lotus flower around a yellow square containing a downward-pointing white triangle. Harmony in this chakra is expressed as groundedness, stability and reliability. When this chakra is balanced you are caring, focused, self-confident, secure, strong and happy, but out of balance it can make you sexually predatory or frigid, manipulative or guilt-ridden. It corresponds to the adrenal glands and the coccygeal nerve plexus. Crystals that can be used to cleanse and balance this chakra are mostly red, black and brown stones, including: Garnet, Fire Agate, Bloodstone, Boji Stone, Red Calcite, Carnelian, Cuprite, Hematite, Brecciated Jasper, Brown Jasper, Red Jasper, Obsidian, Smoky Quartz, Ruby, Black Sapphire, Zircon and Black Tourmaline.

LUCKY CAREER TIPS & PATHS THAT WILL MAKE YOUR BANK BALANCE & SPIRITUAL SELF SOAR

The branch of astrology known as 'vocational astrology' encompasses the areas of one's calling, career path, or ideal profession. Careers, jobs, professions and occupations can all mean different things to different people, but to simplify the definition, I refer to a vocation as one's true calling, one's authentic path, and a dynamic way of life which pays an income in some form and leads to a deep fulfilment of personal and spiritual needs. An ideal vocation will provide self-fulfilment, ego satisfaction, and feed one's inner drive to achieve what they ultimately wish to achieve, whether that be to gain recognition, wealth or approval, to travel, to learn and fulfil an inner need for knowledge, an urge to serve others in some way, or an urge to improve personal, societal or Universal conditions.

In order to gain ultimate fulfilment and self-esteem, we all need a purpose in life. Many people gain this through their work, providing the job or career they choose suits their temperament, talents and aspirations. If our professional life is unsatisfactory or disharmonious in any way, frustration, unhappiness and even despair can result. Although your whole horoscope would need to be drawn up and interpreted in order to gain more substantial, deeper insights into your ideal career and purpose, you can begin by being guided by your Sun sign, which can give you many pointers to a suitable, and therefore successful, career path. You just never know, something in the following might jump out at you and make your soul dance immediately - and hopefully all the way to the bank!

With your Sun in Capricorn, you are a natural organiser and leader. Your practical skills of planning, building, ordering and managing resources will bring you much success in business, but your caution and conservatism can sometimes hold you back from your goals. Opportunities will open up when you acknowledge your own worth and power and take calculated risks. Your ideal vocation would be something that brings advancement and leadership opportunities.

Capricorn is essentially a down-to-Earth sign for whom the basic fundamentals of life are important. You like to build your career, family, home, finances, and overall lifestyle on a solid foundation, and feel uneasy when conditions are unstable, changeable or insecure. Unlikely to be attracted to any vocation based on imagination, creativity, fantasy, artistry or impossible dreams unless there are sound financial or practical reasons for doing so, you usually aim for something 'safe', realistic, practical and achievable.

Most Goats would do well in any type of field where good management, organisational skills, executive ability and careful planning are prerequisites. Being an Earth sign, making a living from the land may hold appeal for you, and careers based on such rural industries as Farming, Agriculture and Mining may be suitable.

Any type of occupation which has enduring qualities and which offers sufficient long-term prospects and opportunities for promotion will attract you. You seldom rush into anything because you like to think things out carefully, and this applies to your choice of career; many Goats spend many years studying for their specialist qualification - your patience and perseverance is second to none. Your tenacity and self-discipline will also be evident as you sure-footedly climb high up the ladders of career, material and financial success.

For the Saturnian and conventional Goat, the following fields may hold appeal:

Some fields of employment which are specifically related to Capricorn are: Plastering, Building, Restoration and Repair, Surveyor, Elderly Care, Excavation, Banking, Finance, Crystallography, Administration, Dentistry, Economics, Mineralogy, Government, Real Estate, Chiropractics, Politics, Osteopathy, Public or Civil Service, Bricklaying, Architecture, Civil Engineering, Pottery, Quarrying, Sculpture and Stone Masonry.

Capricorn is not a back-slapper, and she is not overtly socially gregarious or charming, instead preferring to work alone quietly and seriously behind the scenes. Often the most hard-working and ambitious of all the signs, you have the amazing ability to ignore any obstacles or impediments in your path which might prevent you from achieving your goals. You are dutiful, traditional and value integrity, making you an admired and respected member of any company. You love to lead and make an excellent authoritive figure, although at times you may be a little harsh on your subordinates.

Overall, the business world is a natural place for you, and whatever you choose to do you will undoubtedly apply yourself diligently, responsibly, seriously and conscientiously.

LUCKY PLACES WHERE YOUR ENERGY IS HEIGHTENED

As the Earth element and melancholic humour correspond with cold and dry conditions, arid but cool places suit your constitution, disposition and temperament. The following nations, countries and cities are also places whose vibrations are closely allied with the sign of Capricorn: Libya, Monaco, New Caledonia, Macedonia, Nicaragua, Nauru, India, Mauritius, Mexico, Bulgaria, Great Britain and the United Kingdom, Australia, Hong Kong, Afghanistan, Haiti, Lithuania, Sudan, Burma, Slovakia, Cameroon, Brunei, and the Shetlands (Orkney). Many parts of Europe, such as Greece, Belgium (Brussels), Bosnia, Albania, Poland, Sweden and England (Oxford) are also in tune with the Capricornian energy, as are mountainous and thorny regions. Taking a White House tour, visiting other famous parliamentary, traditional or governmental institutions, going to places of historical authoritative significance where powerful leaders have reigned or currently rule, climbing Mount Everest or taking a pilgrimage to any other mountainous region, trekking through a cool desert region, and indulging your senses and intellect in natural surroundings where the call of the Earth is strong in order to restore or refresh your mind, body and spirit, could very well be your ticket to Capricornian heaven!

GEMS & CRYSTALS

"People love stones, and apparently stones love people. Like the angels they may be, they seem endlessly willing to serve the wellbeing of humans and to help us achieve our desires …Unlike people of the ancient past, we now have access to virtually the entire mineral kingdom. We have the opportunity to work like modern alchemists, combining and arranging the stones and their currents, looking for combinations and patterns that can help us enhance our inner and outer lives."

Robert Simmons, *Stones of the New Consciousness*

Each crystal and mineral of the Earth embodies different qualities, patterns or potential expressions of the Divine language, the silent whispers of the Universe. If we can accept the fact that the human body is a sophisticated, multi-faceted antenna system comprised of a crystalline matrix that is constantly transmitting and receiving all manner of energies, it could then be assumed that energy and body workers who use quartz, shells and stones, which are also crystalline materials, have the power to promote resonant interactions with the liquid 'crystal' structures found in human tissues. It could even be said that we are all made of essentially the same substances and structures, and that crystals and gemstones vibrate at varying energetic levels which can connect with our own in order to 'buzz' and dance together to make a harmonious Uni-verse both within and without.

All crystals work through vibrational balancing and by channelling energy. The magic of crystals is in their colour, which is determined by the rate at which their atoms vibrate; these vibrations can be matched to the energy given by your own body's aura. And just as light can be focused and refracted through gemstones, so too can all kinds of psychic energy, from healing energies to Divine communications.

Gemstones can help us attune to higher vibrations and bring them into our own experience and being. This theory of crystal resonance suggests that the characteristic energy patterns emanated by any stone can be transferred into the 'liquid crystal medium' of our bodies through resonance. Our bodies, being composed of these tuneable liquids, can mimic and mirror any consistent vibrational pattern with which we come into contact; we can therefore resonate with the healthful qualities of various crystals and minerals.

Crystals and precious stones have been valued throughout world cultures over many centuries for their healing virtues and capacities to imbue courage, strength, invulnerability, clairvoyance, love and numerous other qualities. Wearing gemstones is one of the simplest and most effective self-healing practices you can undertake, and wearing or carrying those stones whose vibrations correspond with the qualities you wish to embody brings their energetic currents into engagement with your body.

Over time the phenomenon of energetic integration, may be felt tangibly and your own vibrational field may internalise the stone's currents and adjust to them and effectively 'store' them, making them, eventually, a part of your own vibrational make-up. And we seem to know from the resonances we feel within our bodies when in contact with these gemstones, that crystals emanate tangible, if oft immeasurable, currents.

Crystals act as transmitters and amplifiers of your will or intentions - as long as your will or intentions are in sympathy with the crystal's energy. The mineral kingdom refers to stones, minerals and crystals and the associations and vibrations they carry. When working with stones, we are working with several different layers of spiritual energies, and although they can be regarded as inanimate 'psychic batteries', they are actually moving, vibrating masses of energy which transmit potential and power into our lives. Some crystals and stones even have receptive powers, which means they can absorb energy and retain it within until cleansed or re-programmed.

Although it is untrue that the only stones you can usefully wear are the ones astrologically matched with your Sun sign or ruling planet, those which align with your Sun sign or ruling planet are your most fortuitous and therefore strongest 'attractors' and 'amplifiers'.

Twelve oracular gemstones were described in the Bible, as the author of *Exodus* (28-15 and 17-21) knew them. Yahweh spoke to Moses about the breastplate he would have to wear to train for priesthood, and described it to him in these words: "And thou shalt make the breastplate of judgement with cunning work; ... And thou shalt set in it settings of stones, even four rows of stones; the first row shall be a sardius, a topaz, and a carbuncle. And the second row shall be an emerald, a sapphire and a diamond. And the third row an opal, an agate and an amethyst. And the fourth row a beryl, and an onyx, and a jasper; they shall be set in hold in their inclosings. And the stones shall be with the children ... (all) twelve (of them)." Given that the compilers of the Bible lived during a time when astrological belief was prevalent in Babylon, it seems valid to assert that these previously named gemstones would have some astrological basis. Further, since these ancient people supposedly made correlations between each of the twelve precious stones, and one of the twelve zodiac signs, there are seven crystalline systems set down in crystallography (or the science of the laws which influence the formation, structure and geometric, physical and chemical properties of crystallised matter) as analogous with the seven traditional ruling planets of the zodiac.

However, nobody is under the rule of one planet alone. We are all in essence a complex mixture of every planet, many elements and varying aspects, depending on their positions, placements and prominence in our birth chart. Everything that goes on in the skies above us affects what is going on here on Earth, and also *within* us. Your lucky stones are to assist you to tune into your Sun sign's energy and planetary influences, but you are by no means limited to the ones listed for your sign alone. Above all, let your stones, whichever ones you choose, work for you and allow them to transport your very own unique and magical energy into the wider Universe.

> "Beautiful and strong is the material of stones, but more beautiful and much more powerful is the mystery that emanates from them."
> **Chinese Poet & Alchemist, Li Po, 8th Century A.D.**

CAPRICORNIAN & SATURNIAN LUCKY CRYSTALS, STONES & GEMS

Capricorn birth stones ★ Garnet, Turquoise, Smoky Quartz, Jet

December birth stones ★ Ruby, Turquoise, Bloodstone, Lapis Lazuli, Zircon, Tanzanite

January birth stones ★ Garnet, Zircon

Garnet, Turquoise, Smoky Quartz, Jet (your four primary birthstones), Zircon, Ruby (December and January birthstones), and Blue Sapphire (Saturn) are your luckiest stones, and at least one of these gems should be worn about your person to ensure good luck and increase your overall magnetism. Black Coral, White Onyx, Banded Agate, Snowflake Obsidian, Mahogany Obsidian, Black Pearl, Amethyst, Tiger's Eye, Black Onyx, Carnelian, Green and Black Tourmaline, Hematite, Tibetan Quartz, Titanium Quartz, Aragonite, Malachite, Stibnite, Chalcopyrite, Azurite, Amber, Fluorite, Galena, Labradorite, Magnetite, Clear Quartz and Peridot also align with Capricorn's energy.

CRYSTALS & THE PLANETS

All the Vedic texts agree in relating gems to planets. This verse from the *Jatax Parijat* links each gem to a planet:

'The ruby is the gem of the Lord of the Day (the Sun),
The shining pearl is the gem of the cold Moon,
Red coral is the gem of Mars,
The emerald is the gem of noble Mercury,
Yellow sapphire is the gem of Jupiter, instructor of gods,
Diamond is the gem of Venus, instructor of demons,
Blue sapphire is the gem of Saturn.'

Each planet influences its gem, and their curative power varies according to the position of its planet in the zodiac. Ayurvedic medicine has always paid attention to these details in their healing practices, often advising people to wear their corresponding zodiacal stone as a ring or a talisman.

CRYSTALS & THE ELEMENTS

Crystals are inextricably linked to the four elements, from their original creation to their potency and use in magical rituals and healing. Formed by the combination, in varying conditions, of different physical elements, such as metals, non-metals and gases, some stones require the enormous heat generated by volcanoes or deep thermal currents to bond their molecular makeup, while others may require pressure or water sources. The effects of the four elements of Fire, Earth, Air and Water is evident in these formation processes. The heat generated by Fire, pressure from the Earth, and the chemical reactions involved in absorbing elements from the Air and Water, all demonstrate the four elements in action to produce the correct conditions and ingredients necessary for the creation of crystals, lending them each their unique qualities.

CRYSTALS & THE EARTH ELEMENT

The most obvious elemental force for crystals is the Earth, in which they are found. Crystals are formed over millions of years, which naturally links them with qualities of perseverance, endurance and patience. These gemstones provide the stability of the Earth and the ability to remain, or become, grounded.

Some Earthy crystals are ★ Jet, Onyx, Aventurine, Magnetite, Emerald, Crysocolla, Smokey Quartz, Malachite and Jadeite.

THE CRYSTALLINE SYSTEM OF YOUR RULING PLANET SATURN

Associated with your traditional ruling planet Saturn, are Black Coral, Carnelian, Jet, Onyx and Black Pearl. This is the second crystalline system, known as quadratic, that is having an upright prism with a square base, and its characteristics seem to be connected with this planet. The stone which perhaps represents this system best, the Wulfenite (only relatively recently discovered), is nothing other than lead molybdate, which is analogous with Saturn.

CAPRICORN'S FEATURE CRYSTAL ★ GARNET

Garnet, whose name comes from the word 'grain', is a bright to dark red compound silicate. It is regarded as a symbol of sincerity, good faith, loyalty and honesty. This is a stone of vitality and dreams, and increases the flow of the body's natural energy systems. Relating to the mysteries of sex and regeneration, garnet is a stimulant and effective connector to our deepest memories. It is a useful stone to have during challenges and lawsuits, where courage or fortitude may be required. During such times of change or upheaval, it can provide a sense of grounding, calm and balance. It inspires service, cooperation, relaxation and 'going with the flow'. Garnet has an affinity for the Base and Sacral chakras, where it breaks down blockages and stimulates our untapped creative energy. It will also revitalise and balance energy in these chakras, bringing serenity or passion according to the need. Sometimes known as 'carbuncles' (when they are cut *en cabachon*, that is flat at the bottom or with a convex rounded top instead of facets), garnets occur in many different shades, the most well-known being deep red. Garnet also keeps us grounded, making us feel safe and secure. Garnet can help lift melancholy and will help you find your inner strength and full potential by releasing your fear of failure. It assists in boosting confidence, imparting courage, building strength of character, and enabling us to find our inner fortitude and resources. Garnet helps to dissolve unhelpful behavioural patterns and past hurts to allow you to become more self-empowered and move on. Further, if you are feeling impotent or stuck in plans that have not yet manifested, this stone assists in moving out of the stagnancy and into potent action. It is also useful in easing situations in which you feel trapped and there seems no way out, or where life has become chaotic or broken, offering hope in apparently hopeless circumstances. It can help with any sexual difficulties, both mentally and physically, and is a stone of love and commitment which brings warmth, devotion, constancy, faithfulness, understanding, sincerity, trust and honesty to a relationship. Innovative garnet encourages you to be more creative and stimulates the right brain, creating 'light-bulb' flashes of inspiration and thought. It is an energising and regenerative stone, especially for the two lowest bodily chakras, although it also works effectively on the Heart chakra. Garnet is a powerful attractor of abundance, and Grossular garnet or hexagonal green garnet are effective stones for creating a pentacle layout in magical workings. It is traditionally believed that wearing a square-cut garnet encourages success in business dealings. Garnet draws prosperity into your experience and offers support during challenges. It is interesting to note that skyscrapers built on New York's Manhattan Island have deep foundations driven into the island's bedrock, which contains a vast amount of garnet. It can activate other crystals, amplifying their effect.

CAPRICORNIAN POWER CRYSTALS

Around six thousand years ago, in ancient Mesopotamia, the Sumerians started studying precious stones and minerals, as well as the stars, with a view of improving their lives in many ways by probing the secrets and mysteries of the Universe. Their esoteric interests and knowledge were such that they began to grasp the general connections between the Earth and the heavens, or the Solar system as they knew it, and the functions of stones and minerals as a link between the two. Their method of making these connections was by colour (for example the Sun was allocated all yellow stones), as well as other spiritual links. The gemstones listed for the portion of your zodiac sign are given their status as your 'power crystals' due to the links that can be made between your primary planetary ruler/s and your mutable planetary ruler (listed last), and each stone's particular colour, chemical and mineral compositions, healing properties, and the number they are given (based on the Mohs scale of hardness: for example, diamond scores a perfect 10 out of 10), all of which combine to align with your planetary rulers. Working mindfully with your planet's special crystals is one way you can increase the flow of power and magic into your life.

POWER CRYSTALS FOR FIRST HALF CAPRICORNIANS ★ (21 December - 6 January)

Influenced by Saturn and Venus
Topaz, Chondrolite, Jet, Lazulite, Stichtite, Morion, Citrine, Amethyst

★ **TOPAZ** ★ A traditional stone of protection, topaz has long been believed to protect its wearer from harm. Usually orange-yellow or yellow-green in colour, topaz can also be found in blue, green, red, pink, yellow or colourless. It is believed that topaz originates from and bears the name of an island in the Red Sea off the coast of Egypt, which, according to legend, was plunged into thick fog day and night and solely inhabited by snakes. This island, known today as the Isle of St John, was infested with these snakes who were the guardians of the topaz. According to the legend, the flashes of these stones sparkling in the night gave a supernatural glow to the foggy island, and this famous luminosity which defied the dark forces of the night made the topaz gem a symbol of honesty, faith, purity, loyalty and righteousness. In ancient times amulets were made from topaz to protect the bearer from evil spirits or accidents, and it was believed that it changed colour to warn the bearer of imminent danger. The ancients also believed in its ability to arouse passions and intense feelings, to inspire enthusiasm and commitment, to regenerate the body, and to uncover acts of treachery and deceit, hence its connection and resonance with the zodiac sign of Scorpio also. African tribal people use it in their ceremonies to communicate with the spirit world and to attract and manifest both wealth and health. Overall, it is an excellent stone to use for attraction and desire-drawing purposes, attracting people to you on friendship, love and business levels, and magnetising your desires as long as they are for the greater good. Topaz has the power to magnetise prosperity, honour, glory and recognition of your worth. This stone's vibrant energy brings abundance, generosity, joy, success and good fortune, and is particularly supportive for affirmations and manifestation. An empathetic stone that directs energy to where it is needed most, it soothes, heals, recharges, stimulates, re-motivates, and aligns the meridians of the body. As well as promoting forgiveness and truth, it helps shed light upon one's path, tap into inner resources, and highlight goals. Eliminating doubt and uncertainty, topaz also encourages a sense of trust in the Universe, that enables you to simple *be* rather than *do*. This is an envisioning stone and helps you see the core of any issue. It has the capacity to see both the bigger picture and the minute detail, recognising how they interrelate. Excellent for cleansing the aura and for inducing relaxation, topaz (particularly golden, or imperial, topaz) acts like a battery and recharges spiritually and psychically, strengthening one's faith and optimism, reminding you of your Divine origins. With an affinity for the Sacral and Solar Plexus chakras, topaz encourages one to be benevolent in outlook and helps to promote a more selfless approach to life and be more considerate of the needs of others. It helps you discover your own inner wisdom and riches as well, making you feel confident and philanthropic and compelled to spread the good fortune and sunshine all around. As it can also reduce stress levels, it is a very useful stone for people involved in the caring professions or other stressful jobs. Encouraging relaxation and serenity, it is good for restoring calm and helping the mind to unwind. With its inherent protective properties, it is also effective in healing addictions and aiding detoxification - indeed, wearing a topaz crystal can give the immune system a boost and encourage it to cope with the difficulties of withdrawal. A piece of topaz can also be worn or carried when it feels like one's willpower is wavering, in any situation. An unusual characteristic of topaz is its apparent ability to puts its wearer in touch with life in other parts of the galaxy; it certainly can't hurt to try! As it enhances creativity, understanding and self-expression, topaz defines the essence of a true magic-worker; one who is courageous, a visionary, and filled with hope, inspiration and purpose.

★ **JET** ★ The most frequently used word in the English language to describe something extremely dark is 'jet', as in 'jet black'. This lustrous and velvety gemstone accords well with the zodiac sign of Capricorn, for its dark tint echoes the deeper shadows seen on their celestial ruler Saturn. Jet is a type of black fossilised wood that is actually a variety of hard and compacted coal. It needs tremendous pressure when forming. Jet is almost like a sister stone to amber, in that is not an actual stone (rather, a form of coal called lignite) and can also generate electrical charges when rubbed against wool or silk.

In fact, it can be worn with amber to protect you from harmful energies - the amber stores the positive energy, while jet absorbs the potentially harmful energy (jet absorbs negative energies like a sponge so must be cleansed regularly to be effective). Unlike amber, which is resin, jet is driftwood which was compressed under great pressure after being subjected to chemical action in stagnant water. It is also much more difficult to obtain than amber, as there is less of it in the world. It has been used as a talisman since Stone Age times, being used in olden times to protect from 'entities of darkness'. Dull black in colour, it has long had a reputation as a protective stone, being thought to possess the power to overcome spells and enchantments. The protective energies of this stone are also believed to keep travellers safe on their journeys, no matter what their mode of transportation. Jet is a receptive stone and it draws powerful energy, and has the ability to both repel negative energy and to transmute it into productive energy, depending on how you personally program it. Used since prehistoric times, it became most well-known during Victorian times when it was used for funeral jewellery. As well as being a shielding stone, jet can help you to open your Third Eye chakra and encourage psychic abilities to grow. As black is associated with the element of spirit or ether, the energy of this crystal will help to calm and balance your aura, enabling your psychic faculties to express themselves in a safe and calm environment. This would be especially beneficial before using the Tarot or other forms of divination. It is said that those who are attracted to this stone are 'old souls' who have a long experience of being incarnated on the Earth. Said to stabilise finances and protect businesses, it can be placed in a cash box or the Feng Shui wealth corner (far left rear) of one's house or business premises for these purposes. Psychologically, jet brings stability, emotional security and balance, promotes control over one's life and circumstances, alleviates depression and balances mood swings. It cleanses the Base chakra and stimulates the rise of the kundalini (life force/sexual energy) force when used in this region.

★ **CITRINE** ★ Citrine is known in crystal healing circles as the success, prosperity, abundance and happiness stone, and is an attractive, bright, golden-yellow gem that takes its name from the old French word 'citron', meaning 'lemon' or 'yellow'. The golden-yellow colour of citrine quartz is formed when high temperatures are applied to amethyst or smoky quartz. Citrine carries the power of your ruler the Sun, and has a particular affinity with the Solar Plexus chakra. Its beneficial energies also work well with the Sacral and Heart chakras. It is associated with good fortune, luck, abundance, manifestation, and increases personal power and energy. Citrine is an exceedingly beneficial stone, a powerful cleanser and regenerator, is warming, energising and highly creative. This is a willpower stone, being connected to the Sun, and is particularly helpful for helping to release old patterns of behaviours or thoughts that stand in the way of our achieving greatness. Being so highly Solar in nature, citrine energises every level of life, promotes clarity and puts us in touch with celestial Fire and the powers of our brightest luminary and the core essence of our self - the Sun; in this way, it can help to raise self-esteem and self-confidence. Because it is a stone of positivity, it dispels destructive tendencies, improves motivation, encourages self-expression, activates individuality and enhances creativity; in fact, it is excellent for dissolving blockages to creativity. Further, it is useful for overcoming depression, fears and phobias, and promotes the inner calm that enables wisdom to emerge. Citrine awakens the higher mind, stimulates inspiration and frees the mind of limitations, helping to turn ideas into reality. It amplifies and regenerates energy, and being the product of heat-treated amethyst or smoky quartz, it carries the forces of transmutation and inner alchemy. Its bright yellow colour is literally like a sunbeam shining into your life, helping you to gain insight or confidence when you need to manifest change. This stone helps you look forward optimistically to the future instead of hanging onto the past; it also promotes exploration and enjoyment of new experiences. It is an aura protector and has the ability to cleanse the chakras, especially the Solar Plexus and Sacral chakras. But it also activates the Crown chakra, opens the intuition and balances the subtle bodies, aligning them with the physical. It is a good stone to use if you wish to develop your psychic abilities, especially if you have problems trusting and acting on your instincts. Hold a piece of citrine in your hand when you are undertaking any psychic work, such as mediumship or scrying, and it will enhance your inspiration and reasoning capacities. Citrine is one of the stones of abundance. This dynamic stone teaches how to attract, manifest and keep wealth, prosperity and success. Citrine has the power to impart joy to all who behold it, and overall it promotes joy in life. It is a happy, generous stone that encourages wonder, enthusiasm and delight, filling any dark areas with cheer and light. Citrine's wonderful nature means that it can enliven you and connect you strongly with the light of your inner being. Working with this stone will help you instinctively 'put out there' what you most wish to attract. Transmuting energy and radiating positivity, and holding the energy of wealth, keep this stone in your cashbox or purse to attract prosperity. It is interesting to note that this stone never needs cleansing.

★ **AMETHYST** ★ An extremely well-known, common, easy-to-source and popular stone, this is the stone of spiritual power and psychic energy. Its colour varies from pale lilac to an intense purple, depending on its iron content. The Ancient Egyptians consecrated this stone to the god of wisdom, Thoth, while in Ancient Greece it was associated with Mercury. It has a high ethereal vibration and is an extremely powerful, healing and protective stone, particularly for those born in February and under the signs of Aquarius and Pisces. Amethyst is the birthstone for the month of February, and its name is derived from the Greek word *amethystos*, literally meaning "not intoxicated." Its violet colour is created by the presence of iron oxide impurities in its crystals. This charming stone awakens and activates our higher awareness and psychic abilities, and has been used since biblical times; it is mentioned in Exodus as one of the 12 sacred stones worn on the High Priest Aaron's breastplate. Amethyst has strong cleansing and healing powers, and its serenity assists with enhancing meditation and the reaching of higher states of consciousness. It fights against inferiority complexes, insecurities and fears, through calming states of stress. Connected with the Crown and Third Eye chakras, amethyst offers protection, wisdom, focus, power, access to divine understanding, ethereal awareness, and increases psychic abilities, healing and inner peace. It's best known use is for heightening and enhancing one's spiritual connections and insights; it can even open doors to other dimensions, planes and realities. Many spiritualists believe that it can also bring the divine into the mundane parts of your life, heighten your receptivity to all manner of things, and generally enhance *all* healing. The radiation of violet light issuing from amethyst has been placed on record as providing a calming influence upon the nerves, making it balancing and comforting to the wearer, and is said to be instrumental in slowing rapid and agitated bodily movements, and helpful in easing neuralgia, headaches, gout and stress-related insomnia. Amethyst can be worn on parts of the upper body to encourage conversations with your higher self, and is especially beneficial when worn over the throat or heart. Encouraging selflessness, intuition, spiritual wisdom and divine visualisation, amethyst can transmute earthly energies to the higher vibrations of etheric realms. As a stone of tranquillity and contentment, it can also dispel anger, irritability, mood swings, fear and negativity. Amethyst can act as a compassionate anchor and ensures that you are emanating your energy from a place of peace and understanding.

POWER CRYSTALS FOR SECOND HALF CAPRICORNIANS ★ (7 - 19 January)

Influenced by Saturn and Mercury
Tanzanite, Opal, Pineapple, Lapis Lazuli, Rock Crystal, Venus's hair

★ **TANZANITE** ★ Sometimes referred to by scientists as blue zoisite, tanzanite is an extraordinary purple-blue gem with violet lights flashing from its depths. A member of the zoisite family, tanzanite is a mineral with a hardness of 6.5 to 7, whose colours range from blue to blue-violet, although some crystals are golden to brownish yellow (when heated to around 900 degrees Fahrenheit, the yellow-toned types turn to blue or blue-violet). Tanzanite was first discovered as recently as 1967 in Tanzania, Africa, from where it derives its name, and was introduced by Tiffany and Co. in New York. Tanzanite has an affinity for the Throat, Third Eye and Crown chakras, and as such is a crystal which effectively links the mind and heart; tanzanite is used to integrate the energies of both, reminding one to stay centred in the heart's wisdom while evaluating the ideas of the mind, often opening a cascade of thoughts and insights while at the same time keeping one calmly anchored. Connected also with the Soul Star (above the head) chakra, it also helps one to speak from and adhere to the heart's truth, with all the resourcefulness and eloquence the mind can conjure. By activating our psychic abilities and raising our vibratory rate, tanzanite facilitates communication with the spiritual realms, enabling us to link with angelic beings, ascended masters, guides and other spiritual beings from other dimensions. In addition, tanzanite opens us up to 'receive' from these other worlds. This is a stone of transformation that dissolves old patterns of dis-ease and karma, helping us to move forward with renewed optimism and inspiration. It enhances healing at all levels, as well as protecting those who are doing the healing, and gives us a sense of direction as well as allowing us to manifest our powers for the highest good. In essence, this enchanting stone can be a teacher and healer to those who desire ascension into higher levels of awareness.

★ **OPAL** ★ This is a beautiful and delicate stone with a fine vibration, reminding us of the wondrous unfolding of the Divine Universe. As it contains all the colours of the other stones, it can be used to amplify all other stones' energies. Unlike most other gemstones, opal is not crystalline in form, but rather is defined as a mineraloid. It is an amorphous silica variety of quartz, is comparatively soft, and owes its beauty to the wonderful play of colour from its surface. The mineral is formed from the shells or skeletons of very tiny plant and animal organisms, and occurs in many different colours and varieties, such as fire opal, girasol quartz, moss opal, milk opal, precious opal and resin opal, among others. Bringing miraculous order to a vast array of patterns and colours, the opal unites heaven and Earth in a union of water and fire. The characteristically iridescent, rainbow hues of the gem are caused by irregular refraction of light from its surface, which is traversed by innumerable tiny cracks. In the process of its formation, the surface becomes covered by these cracks, and these crevices become filled in with a substance containing more or less water than the surrounding surface. A great irregularity and refraction and a play of colour varies according to the angle from which the gem is viewed: blue, perhaps when looked at in one direction, yellow or crimson if we view it from another. Known as the Queen of Gems, opal is one of the most beautiful stones and has been highly prized for thousands of years. Opals have always generated strong passions, according to the folklore of many cultures. In Ancient Egypt and Babylon, opals were considered a powerful healing gem, combining the qualities of fire and water, and were said to bring good luck. Opal was also sacred to medieval England, Greece and some Arabic societies. Opal is said to improve vitality by magnifying energy, enhance one's self-image, improve one's fortune or luck, have protective powers, stimulate cosmic consciousness and induce psychic visions. It is considered capable of opening up the Third Eye and Crown chakras, and above other minerals is used by many mystics to lead them into supernatural and otherworldly realms. Absorbent and reflective, on a spiritual level opal picks up thoughts and feelings, amplifies them, and returns them to Source. A protective and karmic stone, it teaches that what you put out comes back. An excellent aid for transformation, opal enhances self-worth and helps you understand your full potential. It stimulates originality and dynamic creativity, and encourages an interest in the arts. Opal is also associated with desire and eroticism, love and passion; it is a seductive stone that intensifies emotional states and dissolves inhibitions. It can also help you gain access to your true self, magnifying your personality traits and bringing them to the surface for healing. Overall, opal will work well with the emotional, mental, spiritual and etheric bodies. It can provide a much-needed burst of energy, boost self-confidence, enhance creativity and intuition, help release anger, and connect one to the Higher Self. Opal contains more water than any other mineral, up to 21 per cent, and is porous, so it should not be immersed in water or brought into contact with oils, as these may harm or destroy it.

★ **LAPIS LAZULI** ★ Lapis lazuli is a deep (royal) blue or bluish green mineral whose name, derived from the Latin/Arabic word *lazward*, meaning blue, refers to its striking colouration. The later Latin form *lazurius* and the French word *azure* are also linked with this stone's very special colour of blue. In fact, it can be taken quite literally to mean 'sky stone', from the Latin *lapis* meaning 'stone' and the Persian *lazward* meaning 'blue' or 'sky'. When polished it displays sparkling metallic flecks that are due to particles of iron pyrite within its matrix. Ancient manuscripts reveal that this gem was considered the sapphire of Ancient Greece, being described as a 'sapphire sprinkled with gold dust'. Centuries ago, these sparkles in the deep blue of the polished stone were compared to the twinkling of the stars in the heavenly firmament, and it was hence called the Heavenly Stone. Indeed, this is an ancient stone that can be traced back to Mesopotamian and Egyptian cultures. As lapis does not have a crystalline structure by definition it cannot be referred to as a crystal, but for the purposes of this text, I will refer to it as a crystal or a stone. Stimulating the Third Eye and balancing the Throat chakra, lapis enhances enlightenment, inspires confidence so one can express their emotions more easily, connects the physical to the astral plane, links one with the source of omnipotence, reveals inner truths, increases vitality, eases depression, and facilitates spiritual powers. As such, it stimulates enlightenment, psychic abilities, spiritual journeying, and mystical potency. Shielding the wearer during the process of spiritual development, it also allows the wearer to draw wisdom from natural sources. Bringing objectivity and clarity, it assists in discrimination, active listening, receptivity, comprehension, and other functions of the higher mind. It harmonises the physical, emotional, mental and spiritual levels of the being. This balancing brings with it a deep sense of inner self-knowing and connection. Overall, lapis lazuli reveals our inner 'voice', encourages self-awareness, and allows for uninhibited self-expression. It brings the enduring qualities of honesty, compassion and truth. A powerful thought amplifier, lapis encourages creativity through connection and attunement to 'the source'. Possessing enormous serenity, the stone releases stress, alleviates insomnia and brings deep peace. Lapis lazuli is a protective stone that enables contact with our ethereal guardians; indeed, it is one key to spiritual attainment. As it is a stone of great power, lapis should be worn with care if you are unfamiliar with its spirituality. This is because it can transform you into a channel for an abundance of energy to flow through, but is also the reason why it is so beloved by psychics and mediums. It should also not be worn for long periods at a time, not even all day, because such is its strength that it can elevate the higher senses until a receptive owner may want nothing else but its refining energy, leaving no thought for the body which houses the soul and spirit. Physically, lapis is a fine transmitter in the hands of a crystal therapist 'channelling' health to a patient. So many healing virtues are attributed to this stone that it is difficult to specify the most important, but it can be defined as an overall emotional sanctuary. Significantly, for those wishing to manifest something in their lives, it also helps us focus our energy and amplify it when we're sending it out into the Universe towards a specific goal. Ultimately, it helps you to confront truth, however and in whatever form you find it, and to accept what that truth's message teaches. As second-half Capricorn's power crystal, in colour, hardness and its constituent elements, lapis lazuli corresponds harmoniously with Saturn, while its metallic elements are ideal for Venus. A saying of the ancient Sumarian priests was: "He who carries with him into battle an amulet of Lapis carries with him the presence of his god." Which perhaps says it all.

★ **ROCK CRYSTAL** ★ Otherwise known as clear quartz, this is truly the master healer of the crystal world, the perfect all-rounder with wide-ranging healing applications. The word crystal comes from the Greek word *krystallos*, meaning ice. Clear quartz is thought to be the only crystal that is modifiable or 'programmable' to suit your needs *, as other crystals automatically contain their own specific resonance or natural signature. In ancient times quartz was thought of as a permanent form of ice, its clarity and purity having magical similarities to water and glass. A common, well-known and popular gem, rock crystal is an all-purpose 'jack-of-all-trades' stone because it contains the full spectrum of the visible white light - a broad spectrum healing energy which clears dis-ease from all levels. Clear quartz stabilises, focuses and amplifies the vital life-force, and its resonance will swiftly go to any area/s in need of healing or restructuring. It also activates, amplifies and channels the magic of any work you do or wishes you make, by receiving, storing, transforming, transmitting and magnifying all energy and thought forms. It is connected with all the chakras and increases the power of all other crystals. Kirlian photography ** has revealed that when a quartz crystal is held in the hand, the strength of the bio magnetic energy field is at least doubled. It therefore follows that placing one on any part of the body will increase the energy in that area. Its vibrations, which begin at about room temperature, giving this mineral an important role in all holistic practice, and whether held in the hand, placed on a person, or positioned in close proximity to any living thing, clear quartz enlarges the aura of everything near it, even increasing the healing powers of other minerals. Many healers find they obtain swifter results when the patient holds a piece of clear quartz. It was, and still is, the stone most favoured for crystal gazing or scrying, for its lustre quickly 'freezes' the optic nerve, with the result that outside impressions are suppressed and the eye is 'released' to gaze into its depths. This is a deep soul cleanser, which unblocks and regulates energy and emotions. It is balancing and harmonising, and can attune you to your spiritual purpose. Rock crystal is believed to strengthen the link between Earth and the heavens, enabling its user to see into other times and places, so it is a useful aid for psychic travelling and dream journeys. In various cultures, quartz crystal is reputed to be the most powerful crystal, the 'grandfather crystal', and the 'chief of the Stone People'. In essence, clear quartz is the most easily programmable and the most overall healing of crystals, and holds a unique importance in the universe of gems. It has zodiacal affinities with all the signs, and a special connection with second-half Capricornians.

* To program your clear quartz crystal, simply hold it on your Third Eye chakra (between and just above the physical eyes) and concentrate on the purpose for which you wish to use it. Be positive and receptive while you allow your crystal to fill with this energy. If you wish, you could also state the intention of the programming out loud, for example, 'I program this crystal for love / healing / meditation / abundance / protection or (insert your own word here)'.

** Kirlian photography is a method of photography that takes images of the bio magnetic sheath or aura surrounding the body.

★ **VENUS'S HAIR** ★ properly named rutilated quartz and also known as 'angel hair', Venus's hair is actually clear rock crystal with fine, hair-like 'needles' of golden and reddish hue. Its appearance is that of long thick 'threads' in clear crystal. These strands comprise the reddish-brown mineral known as rutile, which carries an ethereal vibration that enhances attunement to the Divine and higher self. Venus's hair is an effective integrator of energy at any level. It heightens the energetic impulse of quartz and is a very efficient vibrational healer. It is said to have the perfect balance of cosmic light and to be an illuminator for the soul, promoting spiritual growth and cleansing and energising the aura. Protective against psychic attack, it is useful in supporting one's energy field during emotional release or confrontation with the darker aspects of the psyche. It also connects one to soul lessons, soul plans, and the present life purpose. Excellent for alleviating exhaustion and energy depletion, it can also ease dark moods and depression, and soothe anxiety, stress, fears, phobias and self-loathing. Venus's hair can be used to encourage your belief in yourself if you are feeling negative or self-critical; it can de-clutter your mind and change your mental outlook to a more cheerful, hopeful one. Rutilated quartz is a powerful healer which enhances the life force, encourages inspiration and will uplift the healing energies of all other stones. On a mystical level, its aids scrying, channelling and astral travel, and is also helpful for therapists as it filters negative energies from clients, while at the same time supporting their energy field. Overall, Venus's hair facilitates contact with the highest spiritual guidance and breaks down those barriers which are hindering one's personal progress and evolution. Wherever you are on the Path, carrying or wearing rutilated quartz, or Venus's hair as it is more mystically known, will aid your vitality and optimism along the journey.

YOUR LUCKY NUMBERS

Your lucky numbers are ★ 7 for Capricorn ^ & 8 for Saturn (also, see 'Lucky Magic Square of Saturn')

LUCKY MAGIC SQUARE OF SATURN

In Western occult tradition, each planet has traditionally been associated with a series of numbers and particular arrangements of those numbers. One such method of numerological organisation is the magic square. Magic squares date back to ancient times, appearing in China about 3,000 years ago. The first Chinese square is seen in the scroll of the river Lo - the Lo-Shu, a scroll believed to have been created by Fuh-Hi, the mythical founder of Chinese civilisation. Certain squares came to be linked with the planets; these associations came from the Babylonians. Each *kamea*, or magic square, is linked with a particular planet, and each of the squares has a *seal*, which is the geometric pattern created by following the numbers in order of their value. This pattern touches upon all the numbers of the square and the seal is used to represent the entire square. An intelligence and a spirit are also associated with each kamea, derived from the key numbers contained within it, using a Hebrew form of numerology. This intelligence is viewed as an inspiring, guiding and informing entity.

The 'Magic Square of Saturn' is divided into 9 cells, or squares, three across and three down. The sum of the numbers in the vertical, horizontal and diagonal lines is a constant of 15. The total of these numbers is 45. Therefore, the numbers 3, 9, 15 and 45 are also assigned to Saturn.

YOUR NUMEROLOGY NUMBER & LUCKY SUN SIGN NUMBERS

"Everything that exists has a vibration. The vibration of sound, music, colour, matter, even our words, thoughts, and names show form. All vibration is measurable. To measure we need numbers. Numbers are the basis of all. Numbers are the key to all mysteries."
Shirley Blackwell Lawrence, *Behind Numerology*

Numerology is essentially the metaphysical * 'science' of numbers. The use of numbers in magic is its cornerstone of power. The ancient Greek philosopher and mathematician Pythagoras, born around 590 BC, embarked on a thirty-year spiritual quest studying with important religious and esoteric teachers and healers to find the mystery of 'The Hidden Light', and came to see mankind as living in three worlds: the natural, the human and the Divine. He asserted that all things can be expressed in numerical terms, because they are ultimately reducible to numbers. Pythagoras stated that "Numbers are the first things of all of Nature" and followed the theory that "Nothing can exist without numbers."

Many believe that numbers have an arcane, mystical relationship with words, and with inanimate and animate objects; the interpretations that arose from these relationships date back to a time when the dawning intelligence of primitive man first visualised the meaning of numbers and associated it with spiritual significance. Numerology is the science of the exploration of this relationship in order to discover hidden meanings, forecast the future or interpret the character of a person. In its more modern applications, a series of figures which correspond to an individual's name and date of birth are calculated, and practitioners believe one's prospects, fortune and character can be deciphered from the results ^.

So what is numerology and how does one use it? Everything in the Universe has a vibrational frequency, an energy, a force, all vibrating at various rates, and we as humans are no exception, the difference between one person and another is their rate of vibration. This force or energy is constantly in motion and changing, and we can even 'tune into' and feel our vibrations if we are still for long enough.

Along with letters, sounds, colours, crystals, and many other things, it is believed that numbers also have vibrations, and when we are able to familiarise ourselves with our own numerical frequencies, we can use this familiarity to add power and magic to our lives. The numbers of our birth date, the letters of our names, and the numbers of our Sun sign and ruling planets, all have a unique vibrational frequency, and herein lies the key to understanding our self and our journey through life. Numerology refers to the knowledge contained within the numbers of our birth date and our name, and this is our own personal magic which can greatly assist us through life.

* Metaphysics is the study of those sciences that extend beyond the physical or tangible

HOW TO FIND YOUR NUMEROLOGY NUMBER

^ Your Sun sign's number was added up according to the principle of corresponding a number with a letter, for example 1=A, 2=B, 3=C and so on in sequence and up to 9=I, then beginning again at number 1 for the next letter J and following this same sequence. Following this system, the sum of the letters in Capricorn vibrates to the number 7.

Your personal numerology number is determined by adding up all the numbers in your birth date until they reach a two-digit figure. The two resulting numbers are then added together again to form a single digit, which is your personal numerology number. For example, someone born on 3 February 1983, would add the digits 3 + 2 + 1 + 9 + 8 + 3 = 26 = (reduced to two digits) 8. So that person's personal numerology birth number is 8.

Each primary number or birth number from 1 to 9 has a specific meaning and is governed by a planetary force. The principle of numerology reduces all numbers down to the following: 1 to 9, and 10, 11, 13 and 22 *. The last four numbers only apply to people specially concerned with the occult and spiritualism - and can be studied at greater length through other sources if so desired - and can in any case be reduced further to a single digit if preferred. Your birth number contains a unique power, and therein lie your strengths, shortcomings and opportunities. It is beyond the scope of this book to outline your individual numerology number possibilities, so for the purposes of astrological applications, I have only included your Sun sign and ruling planet's special numbers.

* The numbers 10 and 13, and the master numbers 11 and 22, can be further reduced to one digit if so desired; however, they can be interpreted as they are without further reduction. The choice is personal.

BASIC MEANINGS & KEYWORDS

1 ★ Sun. Masculine influence, beginnings, independence, inventiveness, originality, leadership, exploration, innovation, ambition
2 ★ Moon. Feminine influence, cooperation, partnership, tact, diplomacy, harmony, unity, emotions, imagination, adaptability
3 ★ Jupiter. Communication, expression, youthfulness, self-confidence, creativity, inspiration, optimism, curiosity
4 ★ Uranus. Order, form, security, stability, patience, restriction, work, values, practicality
5 ★ Mercury. Freedom, inconsistency, change, variety, travel, activity, learned
6 ★ Venus. Love, home, family, sense of duty, responsibility, marriage, justice, nurturing, balance, gentleness, peace, friendship
7 ★ Neptune. Analysis, wisdom, mystical, spiritual, solitude, precision, research, integrity, mystery, psychic perceptions

8 ★ Saturn. Money, power, success, organisation, hard work, business, health, purpose, control, authority, mastery

9 ★ Mars. Completion, endings, Universal, service, humanity, philanthropy, loyalty

10 ★ Fortunate, creative, vibrant, stable, optimistic, original, successful, determined, individualistic

11 ★ Master number. Prophecies, inspiration, moral courage, missionary, long-suffering, foolhardiness, enlightenment, invention

13 ★ Misunderstood, fearful, changeable, interested in the occult, fatalistic, flexible, sacred, beguiling

22 ★ Master number. Powerful, successful, idealistic, attracted to the occult, creative, wise, successful, masterful, spiritually understanding

★ THE NUMBER 8 - FOR SATURN ★

Names ★ Octave, Octagon, Ogdoad

Arithmomantic connections with the letters of the alphabet ★ H, Q and Z

Number 8 is a strong, successful and material vibration. The Octahedron, the number 8, or the Ogdoad was greatly esteemed in Ancient Egypt, where it was customary to have 8 people in each boat taking part in sacred processions on the River Nile. Eight is the most balanced of numbers - a fact that, whether by accident or design, is perfectly reflected in the symmetrical Arabic symbol or numeral '8' that we use to represent it. Eight is the number of material success, prosperity and abundance. Financial troubles are said to ease by moving to a dwelling with a number that adds up to eight. Similarly, the number 8 can be used in all money magic. Eight remains a whole number when divided by one half and one quarter, and is therefore the most indestructible of the even numbers. It is twice 4, and so incorporates the rebellious contradictions of that number. The symbol '8' also demonstrates indestructibility in that no matter at which point we start to draw it, we always end up where we started. Like the zero symbol or the circle, it has no end and no beginning, and therefore stands as a symbol of eternity; in fact, when placed on its side, the figure '8' is a symbol for everlasting life. In the Major Arcana of the Tarot, the eighth card 'Justice' shows a woman sitting on a throne which resembles the capital letter H - Heith in Hebrew stands for H, the eighth letter of the Hebrew alphabet. In China, the lotus flower with eight petals symbolises the eight paths to follow in order to find the way of the Buddha.

Ruled by Saturn, 8 can symbolise a ruthlessness, but is also a symbol of the material world, survival, destiny, eternity, analysis, efficiency, infinity, and a coolly controlled character. Number 8 types love being bossy and in control, making them very competent at anything related to the material planes. You can be cruel, bullish, forceful, tense, narrow, insensitive, greedy and intolerant. Number 8 is a strange, difficult number, which can mean sorrow, yet it is associated with worldly success. This is the number of self-mastery, importance, success and abundance. It's a very powerful number for business and commerce, but it does like to flaunt itself and therefore there is a tendency towards showing off. However, it is perfect for highly ambitious people who love a glamorous lifestyle, and in particular for sporting enthusiasts. It is also the number of Divine law, so some sort of karmic situation may manifest which will teach you an important lesson or lessons. Eight characters are authoritative, accomplished, organised, business-minded, leaders, powerful, materialistic, balanced, realistic, successful, capable, worldly and excellent judges of character. Number 8 people have great willpower and individuality, but you may appear cold. In fact, you have deep and intense feelings, and are often misunderstood by others.

Overall, number 8 governs the material world and is ruled by the planet which aligns with this realm: Saturn. Its special day is Saturday. The number 8 promotes prosperity and encourages us to understand the exchange of energy and to concentrate on what we give and, perhaps more importantly, how we receive.

Alchemy ★ Eight stands for the octave. It is also the number of architecture and structure, where two sets of four can be combined elegantly together. The steps of the octave, which we associate mostly with notes in music and also possessing a vibrationally-connected connotation, are said to represent a cosmic order, in which you find a similar note at the top to that at the bottom, but at a different pitch or level. The octave is generally seen as a 'vertical' structure. Eight can be found in the octagon, or can be seen as two interlaced squares, or an eight-fold star.

LUCKY 'MAGIC HOURS' OR 'TIME UNITS'

One rule of magic, luck and power, as already outlined elsewhere in this book, can be found within the well-known phrase, "As above, so below." From the most ancient times, the planets were said to rule Earthly destinies and powers. Days of the week were named after the seven planets which were the only ones then known: Sun Day, Moon Day, Mars Day (French: Mardi), Mercury Day (French: Mercredi), Jove Day (French: Jeudi), Venus Day (French: Vendredi) and Saturn Day.

The planetary hours are based on an ancient astrological system, the Chaldean order of the planets. The Chaldean order indicates the relative orbital velocity of the planets, and from a heliocentric (helios = The Sun) perspective, this sequence also indicates the relative distance of the planets from the Sun (the Sun switching places with the Earth in this sequence), and the distance of the Moon from the Earth.

Before an action is taken in daily life, or a transaction undertaken, for instance, it is possible to choose the appropriate day and hour that will provide the greatest chances of success. By studying the planetary hours system, you will discover which actions are propitious to which of the seven planets or 'star-gods' and at what time it would be advisable to undertake them.

The planetary hours system uses this Chaldean order to divide time, and each planetary hour of the planetary day is ruled by a different planet. The order is repeated, starting with the slowest: Saturn - then, Jupiter, Mars, Sun, Venus, Mercury, Moon, then back to Saturn, Jupiter, Mars, etc, ad infinitum. The planet that rules the first hour of the day is also the ruler of that whole day and gives the day its name. So the first hour of Saturday is ruled by Saturn, the first hour of Sunday by the Sun, and so on. It is important, for the purposes of using specific planetary energies for our magic and wishes, to note that planetary hours are not considered the same length as our normal time-keeping slots of sixty minutes. Each day is split into time periods, day time and night time, beginning at around sunrise and sunset respectively. These two time periods are each divided into twelve equal-length hours, which are the planetary hours. So the planetary hours of the day and the planetary hours of the night will be of different lengths, except during the equinoxes when light and darkness are balanced.

In sequence, the Sun, Moon and the five visible planets each exerts its own special influence over a twenty-four-hour period. I like to call your planet's special day and hour the 'Magic Hour'.

Magic rituals to draw luck and love to you should be conducted at astrologically correct times and with the appropriate instruments, tools, cards, herbs, flowers, oils and plants which are linked with the ruling planet. For example, a love ritual, spell or potion demands a concoction of any or all of the above ruled by Venus. Do not be underestimate rulerships, for they wield an unseen power that can help make our dreams, big and small, come true.

Further, as specific hours of each day are ruled by certain planets, if you are really serious about attracting some power, luck or magic into your life, it is imperative that you wish, pray or ask at the most opportune times for your Sun sign. There are two methods you can use for fine-tuning your magical workings. The first method is to perform your spell, ritual or wishing on the day your Sun sign's ruling planet during the planetary hour that signifies the essence of what you are asking for (e.g. A Capricorn who is looking for love might perform a love-seeking ritual on a Saturday, during a Venus-ruled planetary hour). Alternatively, if you wish to summon the power of your Sun sign's own ruling planet, then that same Capricorn might perform their love-seeking ritual on a Friday (ruled by Venus) during Saturn's planetary hour.

The nature of that which you are asking for, such as love, travel opportunities, money, career guidance, protection or friendship for example, should always be considered when choosing the day or hour during which your magic will be heightened.

The answer to the question why are there seven days in a week, is a very important one to know in unravelling the secret of your Magic Hours. Ancient people recognised the supreme importance of the seven heavenly spheres, which comprised those which could be seen by the naked eye: the Sun, Moon, Mercury, Venus, Mars, Jupiter and Saturn. They then named each of the seven days of the week after one of those spheres and assigned that planetary 'ruler' to one day of the week. As viewed from Earth, these seven spheres appear to move at varying speeds, and the ancients used this factor to arrange them in order of varying speed. If you intend to use your Magic Hours to attract wonderful things, you must memorise that sequence because it is what forms the basis of the whole system.

Whenever you intend to use your Magic Hours or, perhaps more accurately, Magic *Time Units*, it is important to find out the exact time of sunrise for the area in which you live, as sunrise marks the time when your planet's magic is at its most powerful on its specific day. So, at sunrise on Sunday, the Sun rules the hour following the sunrise, the Moon rules the first hour following sunrise on a Monday, and through the week the pattern is repeated, with each day's ruling planet beginning the cycle in that first hour after dawn. It is logical then, that the rest of the planets, in sequence, follow on with one planet per hour for that day thereafter for the rest of the 24-hour cycle, creating a Magic Hour or Time Unit for each planet throughout the day and night, depending on which planet rules that particular day and is therefore the first in line.

If you wish to explore the idea in more depth, it is worth noting first and foremost that each day contains twenty-four hours, but, depending on the season, day and night will be of varying lengths. In summer, daylight is longer than darkness, whereas the reverse applies in winter. During autumn and spring, day and night are usually about equal. Therefore, although a complete day always contains twenty-four hours, there are not always twelve hours between sunrise and sunset and another twelve hours between sundown and the following sunrise. So, depending on the season (and location), a time unit may be shorter than one hour, longer than one hour, or equal to one hour. So whenever you intend to use your Magic Time Units, it is important to find out the exact time of sunrise and sunset for the area in which you live. The next step is to divide the amount of day time (if day when you wish to work your 'magic', otherwise the same following theory applies to night time) into twelve equal sections by calculating the number of hours and minutes between sunrise and sunset and divide by twelve. An example is if the Sun rises at 6.27 a.m. and sets at 5.49 p.m., the amount of time contained in this day is eleven hours and twenty-two minutes. Convert this total into minutes (682) and then divide that figure by twelve (57). Therefore, each of the twelve daylight time units will be 57 minutes on that day.

Although this wonderful method of using astrology is very ancient, it may be completely new to you. You are in for a pleasant surprise though, because if you are willing to delve into a little research and put the system to the test, rich rewards are in store for you!

YOUR LUCKY DAY ★ SATURDAY

Planet ★ Saturn
Basic Energy ★ Restriction, Crossroads, Authority
Basic Magic ★ Banishing, Rewards, Wisdom
Element ★ Earth
Colours ★ Black or Midnight Blue
Energy Keywords ★ Caution, Responsibility, Rigidity, Sternness, Justice, Seriousness, Defence, Authority, Time, Fear, Humility, Law, Patience, Pessimism, Age, Respect, Sincerity, Restraint, Severity, Wisdom, Thrift

Saturday is the day of Saturn, your planetary ruler. In commonly used calendars, Saturday is the seventh day of the week, though in others it is the sixth. The Romans named Saturday *Saturni dies*, meaning 'Saturn's Day' no later than the 2nd century for the planet Saturn, which was believed to control the first hour of that day. Some cultures and religions observe Saturday as Shabbat or Sabbath, which stretches from sundown Friday to sundown Saturday and is the day of rest. Other religions distinguish between Saturday (Sabbath) and the Lord's Day (Sunday). Black Saturday, a day named after the beginning of tragic bushfires in Victoria Australia, Holy Saturday, the day before Easter, and Lazarus Saturday, the day before Palm Sunday which is part of the 'Holy Week', are some well-known examples with which Saturn's day is associated.

Saturday ends the week in most calendars, and is ruled by dark-browed Saturn, father of the gods and ruler of time. His help can be sought for anything to do with old age, and with establishing or breaking down boundaries, limitations and structures. His magic works slowly but although subtle it can be extremely powerful, if you have the patience to allow him to work with you on whatever you are wishing for.

In the folk rhyme 'Monday's Child', 'Saturday's child works hard for a living'. It is a day of Leadership, Ambition, Authority, Hard Work, Perseverance, Dedication, Responsibility and Duty, and an opportune day for making wishes or working magic involving long-term goals, careers, institutions, establishments, security, investments, karma, 'reversals', building structure, protection, solitude, privacy, determination, endings, blocking, renewing and transforming.

SATURN'S MAGIC TIME UNITS (BASED ON THE PLANETARY HOURS) FOR EACH DAY OF THE WEEK

SATURDAY ★ First and Eighth time units after sunrise
SUNDAY ★ Fifth and Twelfth time units after sunrise
MONDAY ★ Second and Ninth time units after sunrise
TUESDAY ★ Sixth time unit after sunrise
WEDNESDAY ★ Third and Tenth time units after sunrise
THURSDAY ★ Seventh time unit after sunrise
FRIDAY ★ Fourth and Eleventh time units after sunrise

**

Choose the Hour/s of Saturn to start a long-term project, build, construct, lay down the basis or foundation for an ambitious venture, ask for wise advice, enter into a long-term commitment, start a fundamental curative treatment, devote yourself to serious study, or to examine a complicated dossier.

** Please note that for the purposes of simplification, the information regarding 'Saturn's Magic Time Units' is a very diluted and simplified version of using magical times to your advantage. These hours cover only daylight hours, or the first twelve hours after sunrise, and do not take into account magical times after sunset or throughout the night. 'Hours' is also a deceptive term, as most 'time periods' used in this system are less than an hour, but for the purposes of simplifying the technique, I refer to them as Magic Hours (to keep with the tradition of the term 'planetary hours') rather than magic 'time units', which is what they really are. Should you wish to do further research on your ruling planet's most powerful time units, or require further information about the planet/s from which you are seeking 'energy' from in order to assist your wish-making, other sources may provide you with more comprehensive and detailed information.

A LITTLE NEW MOON / MAGICAL TIME UNIT WISH RITUAL

Step 1 ~ Choose the Magical Hour and/or day that matches your intentions. The first dawn hour of Sunday, ruled by the Sun, is a great time for all-purpose magic, success, joy, abundance, prosperity, bliss, personal power & all-round expansion.

Step 2 ~ Write out a little wish list with the appropriate coloured pen on the colour paper which corresponds to your desire.

Step 3 ~ Choose a small stone of your choosing that is connected to your wish (or a number of stones that are perhaps linked with your planetary ruler's number, for example 8 for Saturn).

Step 4 ~ Find a nice patch of soil in your garden or any special place to you, dig into it, affirm your wish in your mind, place the crystal/s and piece of paper in the hole, then place a plant on top of the crystal/s and wish list.

Step 5 ~ Fill the soil back in over the roots of the plant and feed it with a little water out of a magical vessel (a small genie bottle would be ideal).

Step 6 ~ Thank the Earth, the Universe and the Sun (or whatever planet you are summoning the power from) for bringing forth your desires.

Step 7 ~ Repeat all day long: "Thank You, Thank You, Thank You!"

Step 8 ~ Watch your plant - and your wish - grow bigger and bigger as time goes on!

YOUR LUCKY CHARM/TALISMANS

The following are three 'materials' or talismanic symbols from which to make your lucky charms, and the planetary energy under which to do it, corresponding with your Sun sign:

CAPRICORN ★ Garnet, Cat, Lead, Saturn

"When any star ascends fortunately, take a stone and herb that are under that star, make a ring of the metal that is congruous therewith, and in that fix the stone with the herb under it."
Henry Cornelius Agrippa, *On Occult Philosophy*

Charms, talismans and amulets are among the oldest forms of magic. A charm or talisman is a symbol, often used to communicate a thought, prayer or wish to, or to make a connection with the Divine. It is usually in the form of an object, which has been imbued with mysterious and magical powers. A charm may be as simple as a stone, a flower or a feather, or it might be a parchment bearing writing; the meaning and significance that you attribute to the symbol is what is important. It can be created by yourself (to best effect) or by someone else, and works as a tool to activate our subconscious mind.

You can use general charms such as a cross, or a universally lucky symbol such as a horseshoe, but you will exude and therefore attract more potency and protection if you make and wear the appropriate charms with the matching gemstone, set in the right metal and created under the corresponding planetary influence. While most people wear silver or gold, cheaper tin or copper may be more appropriate and indeed beneficial for your Sun sign. An amulet (for protection) or a talisman or charm (for luck), must also be made, ordered, designed or purchased on the appropriate day of the week for its power to be most effective. Your day, as previously described, is Saturday.

You can even go further and create or buy your amulet or charm at one of the hours and/or days when your planet is exerting its most powerful influence. It may sound complicated and requiring of forethought and effort, but if you are going to summon magic and are superstitious enough to truly *believe* that you can do this (and remember pure belief in something is the starting point of all manifestation), you should be scrupulous enough to do it properly. For your planet's day and time, please consult the information under the previous headings 'Your Lucky Day' and 'Saturn's Magic Time Units'.

GODS, GODDESSES, ANIMAL TOTEMS & OTHER 'GUIDES'

Gods, goddesses and guides can be summoned to help you live your life to its optimal best. Some are connected with your Sun sign, while others may be of your own personal choosing, ones you may feel particularly drawn towards. Those which align with your ruling planet and your Sun sign, give a good indication of those who will shine a guiding light along your desired path, but you can choose your own too, based upon exploration, observations, research, meditation or simple intuition - I believe choosing your own, based on your inner *knowing* or guidance system, is a very powerful magical tool. However, to get you started, following are some animal spirit guide ideas for your contemplation. Good luck!

YOUR LUCKY ANIMALS & BIRDS

Dog, Elephant, Goat, Owl, Toad, Bear, Mole,
Crocodile, Cloven-hoofed Animals, Bat, Serpent,
Vulture, (Snow) Goose

"Somewhere beyond the walls of our awareness …
the wilderness side, the hunter side, the seeking side
of ourselves is waiting to return."
Laurens van der Post, *The Heart of the Hunter*

"(People) everywhere are being made acutely aware of
the fact that something essentially to life and
wellbeing is flickering very low in the human species
and threatening to go out entirely. This 'something'
has to do with such values as love, unselfishness,
sincerity, loyalty to one's best friend, honesty,
enthusiasm, humility, goodness, happiness … fun.
Practically every animal has these assets in
abundance and is eager to share them, given the
opportunity and the encouragement."
Jay Allen Boone, *Kinship with All Life*

Some astrological systems, such as Shamanistic *
or Native American Astrology, tell us that the Sun
sign we were born under has a corresponding animal
totem, which informs us about our characteristics and
act as a kind of spiritual guide or mentor throughout
our life's journey. These totems are described as Solar
totems, because many of them share similarities with
the Solar system and the sign the Sun was passing
through at the time of our birth, and therefore relate
to animals and animal behaviours which also

correspond to environmental conditions and seasonal changes. These animals encompass many aspects of the Solar system, from seasonal relationships, to creature instincts, to reciprocal links with the planetary vibrations, and 'clans' within nature that you are inherently closely connected with through your date of birth.

Carl Jung, a master of dream analysis and interpretation, proposed that animals symbolise our natural instincts, operating through our dreams. He theorised that certain dream symbols, among them animals, represent core emotions and concepts, archetypes that will hold true for all of us the world over, regardless of so-called 'divisions' such as sex, customs, age or culture. In *Man and His Symbols*, Jung states that primitive societies believed that each person had a bush soul and a human soul. The bush soul incarnates as a tree or animal - a totem - and when the bush soul is harmed or injured, the human soul is considered injured as well.

Some of the most important and powerful spirit guides are those belonging to the animal kingdom. Both in ancient times and in some traditional modern tribal systems, people consult with animals for their wisdom and personal power. Even though most societies today have drifted away from this connection, it has never really left us, and different creatures continue to communicate with us on both the physical and spiritual planes in an attempt to speak to our souls and spirits.

As part of the teaching world, animals can bring us wisdom and survival skills, while others show us how to adapt, transcend or morph. Others still can remind us the importance of play and humour, and guide us around how to overcome life's challenges. Many are known for their loyalty and ability to love unconditionally and without judgement, while some have a grounded and healthy detachment, remaining true to themselves rather than pleasing others, an important lesson in itself. Whatever the qualities of the unique animal guides for your Sun sign, all have some enlightening soul-awakening traits that can teach us much about our own true inner selves. Ultimately, your animal spirit guides, and in particular your Solar totem animal, endow you with qualities that will enhance your life and help to activate your creativity, wisdom and intuition, helping to heal the broken or return the lost pieces of your soul and reconnect you to the natural world.

Your Solar totem animal (listed last on your lucky birds and animals list) is not the same as an animal spirit guide, which is based on metaphysical principles and is also based on your soul's mission in this embodiment - however, you can definitely make your birth Solar totem animal your spiritual guide if you wish, as you may find that its qualities, traits, symbolism and messages strongly reflect and define your own nature - or what you aspire to become, manifest or draw towards you. Your birth totem power animal comes from a place of trust and innocence, and represents the essence of your creative inner child. If you spend some time meditating on your Solar totem animal, asking what lessons it can teach, and reflect deeply on its character, life and habits, you may find it connects with you on a deep spiritual level and you can make the necessary changes to your life to draw in more magic and power.

Overall, if your life is stagnant or in need of healing or an energy boost, you can request your animal spirit or spirits to come and help you change your vibration, awaken your truth and arouse your inner forces. If you are aware of your animal spirit's presence in your life every day, you can use its particular energies to support, guide and teach you. And above all, pay attention to any signs and expressions of its lessons, and remember to thank your chosen animal guide for helping you.

* Shamanism is a traditional spiritual practice of the Native American culture. A shaman, one who practices this age-old art, is an intermediary between the human world and the world of the spirits. He inherits his magical powers at birth, but spends many years as an apprentice, so that he is usually much older in age before he is able to practice and call upon his skills. People ask for a shaman's help when there is a crisis on either a personal or wider spread scale, such as famine, drought, war or illness. The shaman makes contact with the spirits by going into a trance. First, he may perform a series of rituals, which usually include drumming, singing and chanting, and when these have brought on the right conditions, he leaves his body behind to travel to the other world. There he meets with the spirits of his ancestors, who inform him what must be done to relieve the suffering of his people. If the shaman is asked to cure someone of a dis-ease, then the spirits may accompany him to find the correct medicinal herbs or treatments for his patient.

YOUR FEATURE ANIMAL ★ GOOSE

The Goose's Message ★ The destination at the top is more important than the climb
Brings the totem gift of ★ Excellence, perseverance, setting goals and achieving them
Shares the power energies of ★ Ambition, drive, competitiveness
Brings forth and teaches the magic of ★ Unique humour, sensuality and warmth

The Goose is often seen as a symbol of protection and is therefore associated with some of the warrior gods such as Mars. The Goose is also seen as a symbol of marital happiness, aspiration and freedom. These commanding birds have long been revered: The Goose was a sacred bird in the Roman temples of Juno, it was associated with the North Wind in Greek mythology, and is a Native American totem for the Winter Solstice. The Greeks associated it with Hermes the messenger and to the ancient Egyptians the Goose had direct links to the gods, believing the Goose could fly to the gods, and so they became the symbol of the soul of the pharaoh. Native Americans believed that the Goose is an omen of the winter weather to come. When the Goose flies high, it is a sign of good weather; when it flies low, then there is bad weather ahead, and if the geese fly south in early August, then this is an indication of a severe winter to come. In Eastern cultures, the Goose is an important bird associated with the Sun and masculine elements.

The Snow Goose brings clarity to our Earthly dreams and helps us to trust our intuition about which way to go and to know instinctively when it is right to change direction. While some branches of wisdom advise that we should never go back, the Snow Goose teaches that you certainly can and sometimes should.

The Goose symbolises cooperation, the sacred circle, communication and dedication. As a potent symbol of the Sacred Circle, the Goose reminds us of the sanctity of the cycles of our lives, and the time when Canadian Geese migrate highlights the passages of the Great Circle of the Year.

Extremely compassionate and communal, a Goose will never leave an ill or wounded bird behind; they are caring, loving and selfless.

The Goose can also discern when to lead and when to follow, and they alternate in their roles for these positions, teaching us the value of leadership as not being a burden or a privilege, but a shared opportunity and responsibility. As a member of the flock, this bird is an especially useful ally in helping us to communicate our needs and to speak up when necessary - whether to assert oneself or to protect others.

The Goose, also being symbols of fertility and fidelity, mean that people born under this totem often have deep-rooted faith and belief that there is one special person out there just for them.

Persevering, dogged and with an unlimited capacity for ambition, if you want something done and done properly, give it to a Goose. The Goose is determined to succeed at all costs, but first needs to conquer the inner critic. Once she has overcome the internal struggles of striving so high, she will accomplish great things. Driven and at times dominating, they are excellent in business and competitive sports. The Goose may suffer from obsessive, compulsive or extreme behaviours which may become her demise; however, in a supportive nurturing environment, the Goose is passionate, gregarious, humorous, sensual, and usually excels at everything she puts her mind to.

SPIRITUAL KEEPER ★ BUFFALO

Your spiritual keeper guides your spiritual growth and brings illumination. Your spiritual keeper is determined by the season in which you were born. Regarded as the 'keepers' or 'caretakers' of the Universe, the four Directions or alignments were also referred to by the Native Americans as the Four Winds because their presence was *felt* rather than seen. The Direction to which your birth time belongs influences the nature of your inner senses. The North Direction's totem is the Buffalo. The Buffalo is a symbol of the mind and its sustenance - knowledge. The Buffalo (or Bison) is a revered symbol and a mighty albeit confronting animal, each beast weighing up to a tonne. It teaches us the gifts of provision, gratitude, abundance, prosperity, blessing, stability, consistency and strength. Its medicine includes manifestation, protection, Earth creativity, courage, knowledge, generosity, sharing, and giving for the greater good. The Buffalo brings you the endurance and power to walk the Great Road of pure intent that leads to happiness, health and fulfilment, bringing the sustenance that offers renewal and rebirth after a long, arduous winter. The power of the North's influence is primarily with the mind and wisdom, and the specific influence of this direction on Buffalo people is on intuitive sense, enabling you to Divine hidden truths, and endowing you with a deep sensitivity both to others' feelings and to mystical matters. Having this animal as your spiritual keeper bestows you with the gifts of a clear and keen mind, a quiet wisdom, and the power of renewing your energies from your own inner resources. The Buffalo is a reminder of the greater whole and its symbolism illustrates, in magical ways, the interconnectedness of everything in the world - and the wider Universe. Your animal keeper the Buffalo is, above all, a potent symbol of oneness and abundance.

CLAN ★ TURTLE

Your clan animal comes from a place of inner knowing and intuition, helping you to discover the essence and magic of your true self. The Turtle is the totem of the Earth clan and in mythology, during a time when there was only water and nowhere for the people and animals to go, the Turtle made a great sacrifice by letting everyone come and live on her back. In the Far East a talisman carved in the form of a Turtle is believed to have power over all kinds of magic; the Chinese and Japanese also wear charms in the shape of Turtles to ensure a long life. In ancient times, the shape of a Turtle's shell suggested the dome of the sky and the creature became a symbol of heavenly virtue. The medicine of the Turtle is Mother Earth. The Turtle can be your guide to connect with our Earth Mother for healing and wisdom, and reminds us, in return, to tread gently and with respect. In fact, you have a responsibility to our Mother to protect her, and also to remind others to appreciate her bountiful beauty that provides so much for life itself. People of this clan tend to be brave, stubborn, strong and loyal. Methodical and practical, you possess a great determination but also like to take things one step at a time - with steady, slow-paced grace. Although some Turtle clan people tend to be as hard as a rock, you have a need to personify roots, growth and stability, much like the Earth itself does. You are revitalised most strongly by visiting natural places frequently and instinctively feel connected to rocks; in fact, you instinctively feel drawn to be around rock formations and need to have rocks in some form or another around you in your personal environment. Indeed, the rocks will speak to you, if you listen, but you must be careful not to become too much like them - that is, immovable, inflexible and too firmly rooted in the one place out of a need for comfort, safety or security. In essence, Turtle clan souls focus on the tasks at hand with the determination, persistence, diligence and perseverance of one who is aligned with a true Mission. To connect with your clan animal, visualise yourself walking at a slow and steady pace, with no worry for shelter as you carry your home on your back. You also have no concern for how fast you are travelling along the Path, for you know that you will arrive exactly where and when you are meant to. Nor do you fear attack from predators as you feel assured that the armour on your back will guard against attack. These lessons, once learned and incorporated into your life, are the blessings of being born of the Turtle.

YOUR CORRESPONDING CHINESE ASTROLOGY ANIMAL

The Chinese Zodiac, known as Sheng Xiao (literally meaning 'birth likeness'), is based on a twelve-year cycle, each year in that cycle related to a particular animal. These animals are: Rat, Ox, Tiger, Rabbit, Dragon, Snake, Horse, Sheep, Monkey, Rooster, Dog and Pig. The selection and order of the animals that so influence people's lives, particularly in East Asian cultures, originated in the Han Dynasty (202 BC - 220 AD) and was based upon each animal's traits, characteristics, tendencies and living habits. Further, ancient people observed that there were twelve Full Moons in a year, and that, among other similarly related celestial observations, suggests its origins are also based on astronomical concepts.

The legend of the Chinese zodiac's story usually begins with the Jade Emperor, or Buddha (depending on who is telling the tale), summoning all the animals of the Universe for a race or a banquet. The twelve animals of the zodiac all appeared at the palace, and the order in which they arrived determined the order of the Chinese zodiac.

Each oriental animal corresponds with a Western astrology sign. For Capricorn, it is the Ox.

> "Mine is the stabilising force
> That perpetuates the cycle of life.
> I stand immobile against the
> Test of adversity,
> Resolute and unimpeachable.
> I seek to serve integrity,
> To bear the burdens of righteousness.
> I abide by the laws of nature -
> Patiently pushing the wheel of Fate.
> Thus, I shall weave my destiny.
> *I am the Ox."*
> **Theodora Lau**

Chinese name for the Ox ★ NIU
Ranking Order ★ Second
Hours ruled by the Ox ★ 1 a.m. to 3 a.m.
Direction ★ North-Northeast
Season and principle month ★ Winter - January
Corresponds to the Western sign ★ Capricorn

★ **OX** ★ *Fixed Element Water*

★ Keywords ★
Calm, relaxed, patient, self-assured, sincere, brave, intelligent, sociable, resolute, stable, purposeful, stubborn, diligent

The Ox is the second sign of the Chinese horoscope. For centuries this dutiful creature has pulled the plough, making it one of humanity's most helpful and useful animals, and indeed people have respected oxen since ancient times. The Ancient Greeks considered oxen sacred and in Ancient

Greece, white oxen were sacrificed to their god Zeus and black oxen were sacrificed to Hades, god of the underworld. Solid and dependable, favouring routine and method, the Ox is very stubborn and through sheer perseverance is able to succeed where others might give up or fail. Traditionally a yin animal, oxen are bright, inspiring, self-sacrificing and original. Of all the Chinese animals, the Ox is the best at parenting, as it is the most nurturing of the Chinese zodiac animals. The ox is a symbol of strength, calm, patience and kindness. You are very eloquent and happy to be in the public eye, and while you don't talk a lot, you are able to hold your audience riveted when you do. Romance for you is not an overt affair and you are essentially down-to-Earth and cautious, with a mostly hidden but deep ardour and ability to contain your emotions. If your loved ones are patient, you reward them with great loyalty and many indulgences.

YOUR METALS

Capricornian power metals are Lead, Pewter and Plutonium.

Although the magic power of crystals is widely recognised and applied, the influence radiating from metals is often overlooked. Metal, too, emits a powerful energy and in fact, in Chinese philosophy, metal is considered so essential and powerful that it is classified as one of the elements, alongside Air, Fire, Earth and Water.

As already mentioned earlier in the book, throughout the writings of early philosophers and theorists, there are countless references to the unmistakable mystic connection between the seven known planets of the time, and Earthly affairs, ailments and objects. Seven metals were connected with the seven planets, to which seven colours and the seven 'transformations' were added. So the ancient alchemist came to share the astrological doctrine that each planet ruled a mineral: the Sun ruled gold, the Moon silver, Mars iron, Venus copper, Saturn lead, Jupiter tin, and Mercury quicksilver. Consequently, in alchemical symbolism the same sign came to represent the nominated metal and its corresponding planet.

LEAD

Lead is a chemical element in the carbon group with the symbol Pb (from Latin *plumbum*), and is a malleable, soft, corrosion-resistant, ductile and heavy metal which tarnishes to a dull greyish colour when exposed to air. When melted into a liquid, it has a shiny chrome lustre, and has been commonly used for thousands of years because it is widespread, easy to extract and easy to work with. Worldwide production and consumption of lead is increasing, with Australia, China and the United States accounting for more than half of primary production. However, with current usage rates, the supply of lead is estimated to run out in around forty years.

Contrary to popular belief, pencil leads in wooden pencils have never been made from lead, but rather a type of graphite called plumbago. Lead has many applications, including in the construction industry, batteries, pigments, the ballast keel of sailboats, cable sheathing, radiation protection, scuba diving weight belts, automobile parts and car batteries, electronic soldering, stained glass windows, organ pipes, gun bullets, ceramic glazes and plumbing.

Lead, however useful for many things, has its downside. If inhaled or swallowed, lead is a highly poisonous metal, affecting almost every organ, tissue and system in the body. The main target for lead toxicity is the nervous system, but it can also cause weakness in limbs and extremities, as well as rises in blood pressure. In pregnant women, high levels of exposure can cause miscarriage. Chronic, high-level exposure can also cause adverse brain and blood conditions, and has been linked to learning and other developmental disorders.

Lead is easy to work with, but it is toxic and therefore should not come into contact with bare skin. One way of using lead is to use parchment as a base and draw a circle around the symbols with a lead pin. Pewter can be and is often used as an alternative, because perhaps your power metal lead is best left to its more practical outer-world applications, well away from the body.

PLUTONIUM

Plutonium is a transuranic radioactive chemical element with the symbol Pu and is named after your ruling planet Pluto, following from the two previous elements uranium and neptunium (also named after planets). Like most metals, plutonium has a bright silvery appearance at first, but when exposed to air it tarnishes and oxidises very quickly to a dull grey. When exposed to moist air, plutonium forms oxides and hydrides that expand up to 70 per cent in volume, which in turn can flake off as a powder that can spontaneously ignite. These properties, combined with it being radioactive and accumulative in human tissue such as bones, make the handling of plutonium dangerous.

Mostly a by-product of nuclear reactions, plutonium was produced in useful quantities for the first time as a major part of the Manhattan Project during World War II, which developed the first atomic bombs. The Fat Man bombs used in the bombing of Nagasaki in 1945, had plutonium cores.

As well as being used in the first few atomic bombs, plutonium is still used in nuclear weapons, and is also a key material in the development of nuclear power, and as a source energy on space missions.

There are two aspects to the harmful effects of plutonium: its radioactivity and its heavy metal toxic effects. Metallic plutonium can become pyrophoric under the right conditions, meaning that it poses an extreme fire and explosive hazard. More dangerous when inhaled than ingested, it has been linked to cancer, radiation sickness, genetic damage and death, perhaps not the most desirable element to be dealing with. But powerful nonetheless, which is fitting for the deeply compelling and affecting Capricornian nature.

PLANTS, HERBS, SPICES, TREES, SHRUBS, FLOWERS, SCENTS & INCENSE

Plants have long been associated with magic, medicinal properties, superstition, nutrition and even astrology. In ancient times, some were endowed with magical properties based upon beliefs of the time, but also upon anecdotal evidence that some herbal concoctions, flowers or essences helped alleviate and even cure uncomfortable, painful or dis-eased physical or mental states. Whether these were based upon 'old wives' tales' or beliefs in supernatural forces matters little, for in modern times we can prove and indeed *have* proven through scientific research and controlled experiments, that plants have their place in our health and medicine cabinets. Some 'magical' plants have aphrodisiac or narcotic properties, while others have formidable toxic effects, but all are considered in some way to affect the human system on physical, spiritual and psychological levels. Plants such as cocoa, tobacco and coffee, which have accompanied humans over the course of millennia, are still, more than ever, an integral part of our daily lives. They still incite the same pleasures, the same fascinations, and the same dangers, and some still carry the same taboos. It is interesting to note that more than 80 per cent of chemical medicines in existence today, and found in pharmacists' dispensaries, are made from plants.

In modern astrology herbs are often associated with the zodiac signs and have evolved from an old system where a specific planet rules each herb. The planet that governs a herb is chosen according to its appearance, scent and where it grows; herbs are additionally categorised as hot or cold, and dry or moist. In this way you can see how the nature of the herb corresponds to the nature of the planet. If you are familiar with your ruling planets' basic associations, you will find it easy to match it to herbs. Although you can simply buy whatever herbs you wish to use for your magic, the optimum effect will be obtained if you can gather them at a favourable astrological time. Once you are armed with astrological knowledge, you can choose a time when the planet that rules your chosen herb is in a position of strength. Keep in mind that each planet rules a substantial amount of plants, so if one isn't easily obtained, it should be simply to find another one to use for the same purpose.

There sometimes seems to be a wide variance in the list of herbs associated with a specific astrological influence. This is because the different parts of the plant have different rulerships and uses. For example, whichever planet rules it, a plant that bears fruit is naturally related to Jupiter, its flowers relate to Venus, seed or bark to Mercury, leaves to the Moon, wood to Mars, and roots to Saturn. So, as well as the planet that traditionally rules the plant, it can be regarded as having a secondary ruler according to the part of the plant being used. Although you don't need to work with a highly complex system of deciding which herb will suit your purposes, you can make your magical workings more powerful by paying attention to some of these nuances.

Essentially, different scents, herbs, flowers and plants have their own specific vibrations. Their essences should be worn on your skin (you can make up your own combinations using essential oils or flower waters), burned in an oil burner, inhaled from a cloth, diffused in a bath or bowl of steam, or burned as incense sticks. Many plants, herbs and spices, however used, contain gentle yet effective energies which will affect not only your wishing ceremonies, but also your moods, associations and emotions, which can assist in carrying your wonderful Self in the direction of your dreams. Lifted up on incense smoke, for example, your wish is carried out to the wider Universe. Try making your own, out of any or all of your power plants, woods, flowers, shrubs, trees or herbs!

Thirty-three magical, mythical plants are: Cocoa, rosemary, tobacco, thyme, wheat, coffee, sugar cane, cinnamon, hemp, tea, pumpkin, foxglove, incense, amanita (a mushroom), tarragon, pepper, rice, belladonna, reed, ginseng, clove, ginger, sage, maize, mistletoe, lily, mandrake, St John's Wort, poppy, peyote, cinchona, verbena and the vine *. How many of your Capricornian 'lucky plants' (listed under the next sub-category, 'Your Lucky Plants, Herbs, Spices', etc.) can be found on this Magical 33 List?

YOUR LUCKY PLANTS, HERBS, SPICES, TREES, SHRUBS, FLOWERS, SCENTS, OILS & INCENSE

Holly, Carnation, Yew, Pine, Shepherd's Purse, Elm, Fumitory, Solomon's Seal, Comfrey, Sarsaparilla, Cypress, Knot Grass, Gardenia, Orange Blossom, Nightshade, White Oak, Aspen, Thyme, Ivy, Hellebore, Amaranthus, Pansy, Henbane, Thuja, Magnolia, Belladonna, Willow, Heartsease, Sorrel (French), Slippery Elm, Poplar, Hemp, Baby's Breath, Pine, Camellia, Rue, Thrift, Wintergreen, Fuchsia, Red and Black Poppy, Horsetail, Cumin, Capers, Sage, Knapweed, Nasturtium, Mallow *

For Saturn ★ Aconite, Hemlock, Deadly Nightshade, Horsetail, Yew. Woody perennials also relate to Saturn. These include Chamomile, Linden Flowers, Thistle & Black Poppy Seeds *

* Some plant products can be poisonous, toxic, hallucinogenic or even fatal if consumed. Always research first.

YOUR SPECIAL POWER FLOWERS

CAPRICORN IN GENERAL ★ Carnation

OTHER BIRTH FLOWERS ★ Ivy, Pansy, Rue, Snowdrop, Amaranthus & Nightshade

DECEMBER BORN ★ Holly ★ Although it is one of the most enduring symbols of Christmas, holly was the gift of good luck among the Romans celebrating their midwinter festivals. The northern tribes of that great nation draped holly over doorways as shelter for friendly woodland spirits who would bring good fortune into their homes. It is believed that sprigs of holly in the house at Christmas time will bring favourable luck. Holly, emblematic of physical and spiritual renewal, also bestows the gifts of foresight, strength and resilience on those who are born in December.

JANUARY BORN ★ Carnation ★ To those born in January, the much-loved carnation promises a life of variety and empowers them with the quality of courage. Carnations remove negative energy, especially in close relationships, and in the Netherlands, red carnations are associated with love, energy and optimism. The carnation is an important flower in the Christian tradition, as it is believed carnations sprung up everywhere the Virgin Mary's tears fell as she walked to her son's crucifixion. In Mexico they are known as 'the flowers of the dead', as they are strewn around the bodies of the deceased as they are prepared for burial. Carnation can offer one protection and, depending on the colour, encouragement, love or admiration.

YOUR FOODS

Pulsing beneath the solid composure of the Goat is a taste for the deeply sensual. Security, panache, style and good taste live at the sensuous heart of Capricornian appetites. Stable, consistent, cool and dedicated, the Capricorn is sometimes hard to please when it comes to food. You relish most cuisines, as all types of foods appeal to you, however you are not adventurous and are shy when trying new things; you would prefer to stick with the tried, tested and true. A predictable routine is best suited to you, as you don't like eating at strange hours or on the run (although having dinner late in the office is fine as you can combine your two favourite things that way: eating and working). You are essentially a sensible eater and eat mostly that which you deem to be nutritional, healthful or useful in some way. Overall, the more tender loving care, time and patience are put into making the dish, the more appealing you will find it! Slow-cooked and home-style were made for the Capricornian palate, just as long as you can pack it up to take into work for second helpings, as you hate to waste food in any way. Being so frugal and economical, you will never reject leftovers. You can, however be inconsistent at times: although you will gladly eat a humble cheese sandwich if offered, you are used to perfection and precision, and will demand that whatever you are served is presented on a starched white tablecloth, with well-polished cutlery (yes, even for a sandwich!), sparkling crystal and pristine plates. Hastily made, deep-fried, poorly presented, messy, exotic and adventurous are definitely not on the menu for the Goat.

CAPRICORN POWER FOODS

> "Let food be your medicine;
> let medicine be your food."
> **Hippocrates**

Sour, bitter, sharp, savoury tastes appeal to the Capricornian palate. Winter Foods, Salted Nuts, Onions, Spinach, Silverbeet, Christmas Flavours such as Roast Turkey, Spit Roasts, Rich Brown Gravies, Creamed Potatoes, Puddings, Quinces, Vegetables set in Gelatine or Marrow Jelly, Subterranean Vegetables (Potatoes, Celeriac, Salsify, Chicory, Swedes, Radishes, Kohlrabi, Sea-kale Beetroot, Artichokes, Eggplants), Barley, Eggs, Cheese, Prunes, Almonds, Rye, Bread, Fish, Goat's Milk, Malt, Starchy Foods, Earthy-flavoured Root Vegetables and Fruits. Your power beverages are Pure Guarana Powder (for its Earthy taste and stamina-inducing qualities), Gin and Tonic, and Aged and Fortified Wines. *

---

* Caution: Always use essential oils, alcohol and/or herbs with caution and research each one prior to use, as not all are safe for use by certain people, or under certain conditions such as pregnancy, intoxication or illness. Some herbs and oils may be hallucinogenic, toxic in high doses, or produce other undesirable effects, and may be considered potentially harmful or hazardous if used or consumed before operating machinery, driving, or combined with alcohol or other drugs. Always consult a qualified practitioner or undertake thorough research from

reliable sources before use or consumption of any of the listed essential oils, herbs or foods.

YOUR LUCKY WOOD ★ EBONY
(Great to make a magic wand out of!)

Native Americans referred to trees as 'Standing People' because they stand firm, obtaining strength from their connection with the Earth. They therefore teach us the importance of being grounded, while at the same time listening to, and reaching towards, our higher aspirations. In Norse mythology, Yggdrasil, the tree of life, is a cosmic map that represents all life. The tree has its roots in the Underworld, is linked to the Earth through its trunk and its branches reach into the air of the Otherworld of spirit. The dryad, or tree's spirit, needs to be respected and asked when 'taking' from a tree for the purposes of magic. The essence of tree magic lies in understanding the qualities of each type. These can be drawn on for such things as healing and spell-casting. For example, the rowan tree grows high up the sides of mountains, often in hard-to-reach places, so if you need to develop tenacity or access to difficult spiritual spaces, you can call on this tree; the oak tree is durable and strong, so if you are needing fortification or firmness, you can gain power from this tree. When respected as living, breathing beings, trees can provide insights into the workings of Nature, cycles, and our own inner essence. Each birth time is associated with a particular kind of tree, the basic qualities of which complement the nature of those born during that time. Appreciate the beauty of your affinity tree and study its nature carefully, for it has a connection with your own nature and lessons to impart.

EBONY ★ Ebony is well-known as one of the most powerful of woods. Ebony is both a masculine and feminine wood, combining those two energies, and also the five elements of Fire, Earth, Air, Water and Spirit, with an emphasis on Water. The power of ebony transcends boundaries; in fact, it can be used in any types of magical workings, and in conjunction with any of the elements. Well known as the most powerful of the magical woods, it has the power to change, attract positive luck, balance energies, and break down social barriers. Ebony wood is protective and so can be used in making amulets. Ebony wands are said to give the magic-worker pure, unadulterated power. Ebony is believed to be the most dynamic wood from which to make a wand, and is especially useful in the seeking of spiritual knowledge and the exploration of one's emotional and intuitive faculties.

YOUR SACRED CELTIC CALENDAR TREE ★ BIRCH

BIRCH ★ (24 December - 20 January)

The Celts and other ancient peoples had many beliefs and traditions based around the magical lore of trees. The system of Celtic tree astrology was developed out of a natural connection with the Druids' knowledge of Earth cycles and their reverence for the sacred knowledge they believed was held by trees. The Druids had a profound connection with trees and regarded them as vessels of infinite wisdom. Their calendar, being based on a Lunar year of thirteen months, contains a tree for each of these

Lunar months, corresponding with (but not exactly) each of the twelve western astrology zodiac signs, which are based on the Solar calendar.

BIRCH ★ The word birch comes from the Sanskrit root *bharg^*, which means 'shining', for the areas in which it grows contain snow which melts and sends cascades of water down its trunk, the birch bark taking on an appearance of liquid glitter. When it rains, the bark becomes so wet and dark, it is named the black birch. Birch carries properties of protection, exorcism, healing and purification.

The medicine of the cherry birch lies in its inner bark, which contains a rich, fragrant oil known commercially as wintergreen. The name wintergreen hints at the birch's effectiveness as a transitional plant between winter and spring. Spiritually, the black birch assists us in locating within our own bodies the signs of spring which have been buried under winter's cold, barren landscape and its oil assists us in shedding our protective winter layer to make way for our fresh 'green' selves to sprout.

The cherry birch thrives when it grows near water, giving us a signature of its gift as a tonic to the Watery elements and needs of the human body. In Russian tradition, birch trees were deeply revered through song and story. But while eastern European folklore focuses on the protective powers of birches, the Nordic countries consider birch the symbol of the Earth Mother, embodying the female, cyclical powers of growth and healing. Traditionally, witches' brooms are made of birch twigs, twine and wood, so if you feel drawn to witchcraft and the feminine aspects of magic and spirit, then birch wood might be a wise choice for you.

The immense durability of birch bark has been put to many uses; from Native American canoes and ropes to writing parchment. Using birch bark as a medium for the written word strengthens your connection to the tree's claim of being a 'tree of knowledge' and a gateway to new ideas and worlds. The tough substance of this bark indeed survives long after the original tree has died. Although strong, it is easy to work with.

In western Europe, the beautiful and graceful birch is referred to as the 'Lady of the Woods', belonging to the element of Water and under the dominion of the planet Venus. It is believed that if one wishes to communicate with the goddess, one should sit silently in a grove of birches and listen for her whispers, which travel on the gentle wisps of wind.

Throughout its life cycle, the birch continues to be both a useful and versatile resource. As a pioneer tree, it gives way to other larger trees, sacrificing itself to make way for new life. It is therefore associated with the circle of life, endings and beginnings, and new growth.

The birch tree is the Celtic tree of beginnings, an association springing from the fact that it is the first tree to grow back after a forest fire. The birch also sheds its bark, which suggests further links with renewal, as the old and worn-out is released to make way for the new. Creating and carrying a staff or wand made out of white birch wood is an ancient, wise way of allying one's self with qualities of communication, truth, perception and clearer vision. Wands can be fashioned and used to point the way to clear intent and fresh beginnings in life, or a kind of rebirthing of the soul.

The silver birch tree has special associations with the Moon as, interestingly, its bark reflects the moonlight, making the tree appear to glow in the light of a Full Moon.

ESPECIALLY FOR AUSTRALIANS
(OF ALL ZODIAC SIGNS)

If you live in Australia, here are two Australian-based magical woods, for those who prefer to source their woods closer to home and nature. Australia has a less documented history than many European civilisations, but still has no less mythology and legends swirling in its mists of time.

EUCALYPTUS ★ Eucalyptus is very plentiful and has a wonderfully intoxicating, distinctive, clean aroma which is reminiscent of the continent's vast areas of bushland, and has played an important ceremonial and medicinal role in the culture of Australian Aborigines, who have inhabited the nation for 40,000 to 50,000 years. Eucalyptus is a wood of feminine energy whose elemental association is Earth and main origin is Australia. One of the strongest healing woods known, eucalyptus wood has been used for centuries for medicinal as well as ritualistic purposes. Heady and Earthy, the energy of this wood is clean and pure. Eucalyptus is recommended for the promotion of good, robust health, and is also related to luck, especially if regarding knowledge. An excellent tool in divination, particularly when worn as a charm to invoke luck, it brings the wearer or user good fortune when used in rituals seeking positive results.

LEOPARDWOOD (or LACEWOOD) ★
Leopardwood or the Leopard Tree, so named because of its spotted wood, carries the energies of both the masculine and the feminine, Mars (Aries, Scorpio) and Venus (Taurus, Libra), and its main affinity is with the Water element (Cancer, Scorpio, Pisces). Leopardwood is a very useful tool for divination and is associated with positive luck, earning it the label 'gambler's wood'. Overall, its energy is very positive, making it an ideal wood for use in almost any ritual or spell, especially those concerning luck, magic and divination.

THE POWER OF LOVE

Each Sun sign exudes their own love and romance style. This style is an energy unique to that sign, and has the power to magnetise to that person their true, soulful match. Unhappy or unsuccessful relationships are often the result of incompatible Sun signs, personal values, goals, hopes, viewpoints or expectations. I believe everyone has a perfect soul partner (or three!) who is especially for them, and just knowing that special person or persons are out there can illuminate your life's romantic path. In this lifetime, we may not find that person or persons, but can still experience the joys and wonders of many other significant relationships which enrich and add tremendous meaning to our lives. Some partnerships are only fleeting, but the feelings they give us can last a lifetime, while others are more enduring, and the rewards they give us and lessons they teach us can last a lifetime too. Small gestures of love on a frequent basis, consistent nurturing and communication, and making the effort to understand each other, are just four ways to keep the fires of passion and romance burning long after the initially roaring fire has diminished into glowing embers.

Your whole natal chart would need to be examined to form an overall picture of your romantic nature, and although the Sun is a fantastic starting point, it is not the sole consideration. Regarding these other planets, in Carl Jung's studies on psychological astrology, and in traditional synastry (the comparing of two people's natal charts to determine overall compatibility), the harmonious link between the Sun in one person's chart and the Moon in the other's (usually the man's Sun and the woman's Moon) is considered the best indication for a happy and enduring relationship. More specifically, the sextile aspect, an angle of 60 degrees, appeared most frequently between the Sun of one and the Moon of the other in fulfilling relationships. Other positive planetary contacts, such as one person's Moon to another's Venus, or the Mars to the Moon (again, traditional indications of attraction and harmony) also occurred frequently.

The feminine personal planets in a male's chart (Moon and Venus), and the masculine personal planets in a female's chart (Sun and Mars) tell a lot about the inner self and how this is projected onto relationships. However helpful chart analysis is in telling a story about your relationship style and approach, it all depends not on your chart, but on what you do with the resources at your disposal, which your chart can indeed tell you a lot about. Relationships and marriages involving harmonious planetary and zodiacal energies between the two people tend to last longer because they are simply more 'flowing' and easier.

The signs in which the four personal and 'relationship' planets - the Sun, the Moon, Venus and Mars - are placed, coupled with the aspects they make with the other planets in the chart, give important clues into understanding the often unconscious drives within you that shape your relating style, tastes, mannerisms and patterns.

Expanding upon the other planetary considerations is beyond the scope of this book, but it is useful to know, particularly if you are interested in examining the dynamics of a current relationship a bit deeper, or are wishing to attract a new one into your life. But for now, your Sun sign is a wonderful place to start! Your Solar sign is regarded as being at the core of the complex - and very fun - study of relationships! So for now, we will begin this study of love with your essence, your core self, the brightest light shining from within - your Sun sign!

SOME LUCKY-IN-LOVE TIPS
GENERAL HINTS

★ To attract and retain love, the Heart chakra (an energy centre within the body) needs to be balanced and clear from blockages. The Heart chakra is located in the region of the physical heart. Its Sanskrit name is *anahata*, and its symbol is a twelve-petal green lotus flower whose centre contains a green circle and two intersecting triangles making up a six-pointed star representing balance (and also could be said to symbolise six as the number of Venus). Its element is Air and its colour is green. Balance in this chakra is expressed as unconditional love for ourselves and others. Crystals that can be used to cleanse and balance this chakra are mostly green and pink stones.

★ Pink candles (two, representing a couple, or six, representing Venus, is preferable) can be used in love spells.

★ Any 'love-attracting' wishing rituals should be done on a Friday (ruled by Venus) night around the time of the New Moon (signifying the principle of increase and growth).

★ Basil, otherwise known as witch's herb or St Joseph's wort, is said to be the most potent lover herb of all. Basil vibrates to the energy of Mars, which is all about lust and sexual energy, and it is used prolifically in all sorts of love potions and rituals throughout the world.

★ Ginger has a reputation as a potent sexual tonic and aphrodisiac *. Arousing and warm, it can increase sensual vitality, particularly in men. Being warming and spicy, its vibration aligns with Mars. Saffron is also regarded as a potent, albeit expensive, aphrodisiac!

★ Wear red and pink (associated with Mars and Venus respectively), as these colours in all their shades are said to incite passion, lust and romance. Green is also connected with the heart by virtue of its association with the Heart chakra and the planet Venus, and its links with fertility, nature, abundance of all kinds, and new growth.

★ Call upon some higher spiritual help. When working your 'love magic', some planetary influences, goddesses and gods that you can call upon are: Aphrodite, Venus and Eros/Cupid, and other lesser known deities such as Juno Lucina, Demeter, Freya, Ishtar, Circe and Hathor.

★ The planet Venus has developed a rich culture of gods and goddesses associated with her varying levels of love and passion. These include the virgin - Brighid; the fertile woman - Aphrodite, (the Greek goddess); and of course Venus (the Roman equivalent); the mother and provider - Demeter; and desirous or physical love - Eros/Cupid (Venus's son).

★ The pine tree is sacred to Adonis (Venus's lover) and is said to balance the male and female energies. Pine is cleansing and protective and, as an evergreen, symbolises life. Its cones represent fertility.

★ Cardamom is said to have aphrodisiac qualities

★ The three almost universally recognised symbols of love are the goddesses Venus and Aphrodite, and the Cupid. Venus is the patroness of flowers and vegetation, and represents the regenerative cycle of creation, as well as beauty, herbs and physical love. She can be called upon for general love wishes and rituals. The dove, roses, rings, copper, apples, rosemary and the ankh are some of her sacred symbols. Aphrodite is a Greek goddess who has the ability to brings lovers together. Her names mean 'of the sea' as she is believed to have been born of the foam of the ocean. She can be called upon in ceremonies and spells for affection, love, marriage and partnership. Some of her associated symbols are the Flower of Aphrodite, swans, dolphins, frankincense and myrrh. Cupid, the cherubic winged boy with a bow and arrow, is the Roman name, and Eros is the Greek name for the same deity. The son of Venus/Aphrodite, he is an aspect that represents lustful love and desire.

★ Heartsease, another name for the wild pansy, Latin viola tricolour, was one of the most popular additives to the love potions of the ancient Romans and Greeks.

★ In centuries past, when people were more in tune with nature and its cycles, ceremonies, rituals and festivals were held on certain dates or times of year. The following are some examples, and you can reawaken their powers through craft and ceremony: February 2 is Bridhid's Day, or Bride's Day, and represents the white goddess; February 14 is Valentine's Day, traditionally the greatest and most well-known love 'celebration' of the year; March 1 is one of the festival days of Juno Lucina, the light bearer and goddess of women and marriage; the month of April is especially linked to the love goddess Aphrodite; the Summer solstice which falls on or around June 21 is an important time for reconnecting with the spirit of love, fertility and marriage; August 1 is the first of three harvest festivals in the Celtic calendar: The Harvest Festival honours Demeter, the goddess of love, as bountiful mother and faithful wife; the Festival of Lights, Diwali, in October, is sacred to Lakshmi, the Hindu goddess of happiness, love, and good fortune; the Winter solstice which falls on or around December 21, marks the turning point from long dark nights to lengthening days, and is the time of the wheel of love when virgin goddesses gave birth to their children - it is also fittingly symbolised by evergreens such as pine, ivy and holly; in Mexico, December 31, the last night of the year, is traditionally 'wishing night' and is an opportune time to make a wish for a lover in the coming year, using evergreen branches to enhance your request.

* The term 'aphrodisiac' is derived from Aphrodite, the Greek goddess of love, beauty, lust and sensuality

★ GEMSTONES ★

When it comes to calling love into your life using crystals, the general rule is that any of the pink or green stones are closely aligned with matters of the heart and can therefore help you to entice the affections you seek. Although your Sun sign has its very own special gemstones, outlined elsewhere in the book, the following stones can be used by all the signs (except for the first point, which are your own sign's feature stones), as their energies and qualities contain the power to attract and create love in all its forms, from self-love to deeper soulful connections with another, or to increase states of being which open the heart, thus enhancing your abilities to magnetise love.

★ Garnet, Turquoise, Smoky Quartz and Jet ★
Using your Capricornian luckiest crystals is a fabulous start to working on heightening your romantic zest, and making your sensual energy more potent. Blue Sapphire is also useful in raising your attracting powers.

★ Rose Quartz is the ultimate love stone. It invites love into your life by helping to open your heart to receive love, and gently reminding you that you are worthy of love. Connected with the Heart chakra, it is the stone of unconditional love, enhancing all forms of it and opening up the heart. It is excellent for increasing self-worth and acceptance. The colour of rose quartz is pink, the colour of Venus, the amorous planet of desire and nurturance. Balancing and calming, it helps to heal emotional pain. Wear this stone, keep some beside your bed, or sleep with some under your pillow to remind you that love it coming your way - and that you whole*heart*edly deserve it!

★ Green Aventurine is considered the 'opportunity and luck stone'. Connected with the Heart chakra, it helps us to recognise opportunities and is said to place us exactly where we need to be for good things to transpire, as energetically it opens our mind and heart to increased perception to recognise lucky elements. It also promotes new growth, optimism, and is an overall attractor of good fortune, adventure and abundance.

★ Jade, on a spiritual level, has an affinity with the Heart chakra. It harmonises relationships, and encourages compassion and the establishment of strong bonds.

★ Emerald is reputedly a stone of constancy in love, and is said to have been brought to Earth from the planet Venus. Because it is green, it also holds deep associations with the Heart chakra.

★ Rhodochrosite can be used to attract one's soul mate. This stone, as with all the pink stones, can be used as an effective love magnet. It encourages you to appreciate yourself by teaching you that you are worthy of love, wholeness and happiness - and so opening you up to receive.

★ Malachite, Citrine, Rhodonite, Moonstone, Morganite, Beryl, Ruby, Mangano Calcite, Garnet, Red and Pink Tourmaline, Tugtupite, Rutilated Quartz, Lodestone, Peridot and Lapis Lazuli are also known for their love properties, and can be used or worn to invite romance into your life, or to bring and retain enduring love.

★ Clear Quartz can be used with any of these listed crystals to amplify their metaphysical properties.

★ Shells: Although shells are not technically a crystal, but rather a natural elemental material, they are associated with love and are sacred to Aphrodite, the Greek love goddess, and are often used in magic talismans to attract romance.

★ ESSENTIAL OILS ★

The following essential oils are known for their aphrodisiac or love-attracting properties also, and can be worn as perfumes on the skin, used in an oil burner or vaporiser, dispersed in a bath, used in spell-casting and wishing rituals, sprinkled on your pillow to imbue your dreams with inspired romantic notions, or in any other creative ways you can think of! **

★ Essential oils, flowers and herbs which contain natural pheromones or like substances, or increase pheromone levels in the body, are: Lavender, Frankincense, Jasmine, Nutmeg, Ylang Ylang, Sandalwood, Patchouli and Asian Agarwood (Oud).

★ The prime love oil, which holds Universal appeal, is rose. Reputedly excellent for both the mind and body, roses are the basis of more than 95 per cent of women's fragrances, and the petals have a long tradition of uplifting the spirits and soothing the soul. *Rosa damascena* is believed to be good for attracting love, while *R. centifolia*, the French rose oil base, is regarded as an aphrodisiac. Rose is traditionally accepted as the all-encompassing Universal fragrance of love, blessed with a reputation for opening up the hearts of all those who come under its spell.

★ Cedarwood oil has been used since ancient times in incense and perfumes. Its deep, woody scent helps to stimulate the Base chakra, increasing sexual passion and desire. Its sedative qualities aid relaxation and encourage openness. In herbal magic, it is also associated with spells for wealth and abundance.

★ Neroli, Geranium, Almond (as a base), Basil, Thyme, Vetiver, Gardenia, Vanilla, Rose Otto, Apple, Cardamom, Lotus, Orange, Ginger, Bergamot, Rosewood and Clary Sage are also exquisitely seductive and sensual, and can be used in any way you like to bring to you that which your heart desires. These oils, when mixed with your own pheromones and magical intentions, will naturally enhance your point of attraction!

** Always research first and use with caution.

CAPRICORN ★ LOVE STYLE

Loyalty, protection, help and considered advice are facets of your understated way of demonstrating affection to your partner. Careful in your selection of a mate, you prefer long-term commitments and devotion over flings and flirty dalliances. Conquering a Capricorn is not exactly the easiest task, seeing you are generally reserved, if not sceptical, and perhaps a little shy when it comes to being wooed. But if you are the wooer, you will use every charm in the book to perfection to win the heart of your desired - and to great effect, because your perseverance and stamina is second to none, and you will not stop until you achieve your ultimate aim. If you are rejected, you are resilient and possess a profound inner strength which allows you to stoically pick yourself up and keep climbing. Despite your notorious self-control and caution in romance, you can be very sentimental and warm when your heart is opened up by love. A gentle, sensual lover, you usually have a high regard for family and find it important to honour your duties, obligations and commitments to your special loved one. It is a rare Capricorn who believes in love at first sight, as all decisions of the heart need to be well thought out and you don't enter amorous adventures as light-heartedly as most other signs do. You keep your cards close to your chest and your heart well away from your sleeve, until you can trust enough to let your inner warmth (yes, it is in there!) shine through. You are also surprisingly tender, given your tough exterior, and make a delightful and dedicated partner whose feelings run much deeper than others would know. When you give away your heart, it is usually forever. You take marriage vows and married life very seriously and your enduring tenacity allows you to live up to the solemn line of "Till death do us part." Capricorn places more value on respect, duty, loyalty and the power of the family bond than she does on wild passion, grand love, and frivolous adventures. Secretly, every Goat seeks out, whether consciously or not, a partner who is successful or ambitious in some way, one who is like-minded, and who can ultimately provide you with the security and stability you so crave in love and life. If you can take down your suit of armour, relinquish control, loosen up, accept sympathy, reveal your vulnerabilities, receive affection readily, share your dry wit and unleash your unerring devotion, your relationships will become richer and more fulfilling. And seeing you are usually so old and wise in spirit, if you can find someone who can help you free your inner child to romp and play more openly and freely, you may just have met your perfect match!

LUCKY IN LOVE? CAPRICORN ★ COMPATIBILITY

* Please note the following is based on your Sun sign alone. For a whole and integrated approach to relationship compatibility, your whole natal chart would need to be taken into consideration. Synastry (*syn*: acting or considered together, united; *astry*: pertaining to the stars) is a branch of astrology which delves into more complex areas, and is based upon the natal charts of the two people concerned, to determine overall compatibility, potential conflicts and suitability based upon celestial influences. For the purposes of length, the below information is simplified and only refers to Sun sign connections.

Capricorn ★ Aries ♑ ♈

This is a challenging match and likely to test your patience. When the Ram tells it 'like it is' or tries to force the pace, the gentle but strong Goat may want out. But if you two decide to cooperate, you can achieve a lot together. If Aries tries to get into competition with the Goat, the Goat may throw Earth on the Ram's ideas and dampen his fiery passion. Earth and Fire can be a difficult combination at the best of times, but you are both Cardinal signs, so you do share the qualities of leadership, initiative and drive. But Capricorn, an Earth sign, is traditional, sensible, practical, conventional and structured, while Aries is spontaneous, bold, buoyant and extroverted, making your natures inherently different. Aries's ruling planet Mars is impatient and fiery whereas Capricorn's ruler Saturn is sombre, cautious and deliberate. The Goat likes to plan ahead, while the Ram prefers to push through the fence and act now. Capricorn and Aries both have highly ambitious natures, but the way they express these is completely different - Capricorn is single-minded, ruthless, and will stop at nothing to reach the top, while Aries is a big softie at heart, completely at odds with Capricorn's sometimes cool, authoritative character. Arien behaviour often undermines Capricorn's desire for stability, security and consistency. The Ram seeks out thrills, adventures, novelty and action, while the Goat is rigid, conservative, straight and respectful. However, you share an enviable competitive streak and fighting spirit of a high order, and if you can channel your energies into developing a rapport and natural respect for each other, a mutually fulfilling relationship could very well develop. Overall though, Aries's impetuous and irresponsible streak will unnerve and unsettle the quiet, steady Goat, who just wants to live a peaceful - albeit constantly striving and achieving - life. If you can both exercise tolerance for each other's differences, there is a chance your horns and your strong characters can intertwine and join forces - and you may just make it over the finish line *together*.

Overall compatibility rating ★ 6.5 out of 10
Lucky Romance Tip ★ To attract an Aries, wear the colours red or orange, and use the crystal diamond

Capricorn ★ Taurus ♑ ♉

Two Earth signs combine to create stability, security and shared aspirations. The Goat feels right at home with the Bull, yet together you may get bogged down in routine, stuck in a rut and the shine may quickly disappear from your romance. But overall, the lusty Bull and the horny Goat make a pleasing combination. With Capricorn's strength and Taurus's good taste, you could build an empire together - or never leave home! Taurus admires Capricorn's ambition, goal-mindedness and will for advancement, and the Capricorn appreciates the Bull's nurturing, sensuous, solid nature. You two seem to have a natural affinity and agreement that promises lasting happiness. The Bull may even help the Goat to loosen up a little and relax her self-control. Security-conscious Taurus will resonate with Capricorn's practical, basic attitudes, realistic approach, perseverance and conservatism. Being Earth signs, you are both likely to be sensible, reasonable, patient and responsible, so most issues can be worked through in a rational, logical manner. Big, burning flames of passion may be absent here, and there is a danger here that life could become a little too serious at times, but injecting some light-hearted fun and frivolous activities into your time together, should ease this very easy-to-solve problem. Indeed, you have great potential to grow old together.

Overall compatibility rating ★ 9 out of 10

Lucky Romance Tip ★ To attract a Taurus, wear the colours pink or green, and use the crystal rose quartz

Capricorn ★ Gemini ♑ ♊

Gemini bemuses Capricorn with his flighty and childlike wonder and innocence. But the Goat's initial attraction to the Twins may turn to apprehension and withdrawal when she uncovers Gemini's cheeky and nonchalant carelessness, which doesn't sit well with Capricorn's practical, realistic approach to life.

Gemini will appreciate the dry Capricornian sense of humour. However, the Goat tends to take life too seriously, and the Twins may be too flighty for them in turn, although Capricorn can provide Gemini with a much-needed stabilising influence. In return, the Gemini could help Capricorn see the fun side to life. Overall though, Gemini has very little in common with the Goat. Although he can respect her solid achievements, he may find her wall of staunch reserve and reticence rather off-putting. While Gemini, an Air sign, is changeable, restless, lively, scatterbrained, edgy, stimulating and wayward, Capricorn, an Earth sign, is traditional, sensible, controlled, pragmatic, conventional and structured. Capricorn is tight, sometimes mean and ruthless, and tenacious in her striving for lofty goals and ambitions, while Gemini is carefree but ever-friendly, and independent, determined to reach his many ideals using charm, eloquence, cunning and flying by the seat of his cheeky pants to get where and what he wants. Indeed, mischievous Geminian behaviour often undermines Capricorn's desire for stability, security and consistency. While the Goat is rigid, cautious, methodical and respectful, the Gemini flits from person to person and adapts to any new situation. However, you do share minds of a high order, and if you can channel your energies into your intellectual rapport and natural respect for each other, a mutually fulfilling relationship could very well unfold. And although your characters are very different, you can enrich each other with your unique gifts. Indeed, the young at heart spirit of the Twins can complement the wisdom and experience of the Goat, providing you are both willing to communicate to find common ground. Your life together may prove challenging at times, because Gemini so often changes direction, whereas steady Capricorn will pursue a goal to its conclusion. Gemini is easily distracted, while Capricorn has a single-minded vision and stays on the path. In this way, Capricorn rarely understands the highly strung, quicksilver ways of the crafty Twins. However, on the whole, there is something lacking emotionally which can make romance between you difficult and strained.

Overall compatibility rating ★ 6 out of 10
Lucky Romance Tip ★ To attract a Gemini, wear the colours light blue or yellow, and use the crystal citrine

Capricorn ★ Cancer ♑ ♋

You and your natural astrological opposite have a lot in common - and also a lot to teach and learn from each other. Cancer's sentimental, dependent nature will either melt Capricorn's heart and bring out the Crab's protective instincts, or make Cancer turn cold and suspicious. This is a generally harmonious combination of opposite temperaments, which could result in real success. If you apportion your roles wisely, you will certainly have the basis for a happy home environment. However, because you are zodiacal opposites, this partnership could be both complementary *and* competitive. If the Goat gives top priority to ambition and success, the sensitive Crab may feel left out, hurt or neglected. Cancer needs assurance, sentiment, warmth and constant care, which Capricorn often withholds for whatever reasons. However, the Crab will appreciate the security, stability and consistency that the Goat can ultimately provide in spades, and both are deeply sensual and introverted, meaning you will share many nights curled up on the couch and be quite content with this arrangement. Overall, Capricorn is a conditional lover when the circumstances call for it, which may unsettle the unconditional, devoted Cancerian, who gives her all to her loved ones. As well, the sometimes cold Capricorn is too icy for the warmth-seeking Cancer, and Capricorn may not understand the Crab's moods and sulkiness. The Goat's spirit is more independent than the Crab's clingy nature will tolerate, and Capricorn's discipline, guardedness, and emotional self-restraint will not serve to coax Cancer out of her reserve. If you can work through your polarities and reach a middle ground, this relationship has fair potential and good odds of enduring.

Overall compatibility rating ★ 7 out of 10
Lucky Romance Tip ★ To attract a Cancerian, wear the colours silver or white, and use the crystal moonstone

Capricorn ★ Leo ♑ ♌

The Lion's need for praise and centre stage irritates and confuses the modest Goat, and since you two are at odds by nature and differ in almost every respect, this romance has the potential to be a huge learning experience. Capricorn's Earth can put out Leo's Fire, particularly in this case. Although you are both strong, determined personalities, you are very different; the Lion needs fun and action, while the Goat needs calm, steady progress. As well, Leo enjoys the journey while Capricorn revels in the destination. Capricorn will seem distant and aloof to the open and friendly Leo and her lack of spontaneity may be frustrating to the demonstrative and playful Lion. The Goat's cool, indifferent nature may hurt Leo's precious pride and is at odds with the Lion's warm, outgoing expression. Your rulers the Sun and Saturn, also differ considerably - the brilliant, grandiose Sun seeks to shine and experience, while the austere, conservative Saturn strives for practical and serious applications. Frugal, sensible Capricorn will not tolerate Leo's extravagant, lavish, generous lifestyle, and joyful and affectionate Leo will find Capricorn's veiled sensuality too difficult to reach. Leo likes to live life to the full, in the here and now, whereas Capricorn, being more cautious, needs to plan for the future. Capricorn will show calm reserve if Leo sulks, and the Lion will seek more amorous company if he feels that Capricorn doesn't care. However, Leo has the power to melt the Goat's ice and if Capricorn can let her guard down, she is caring, giving and devoted, providing a stable, nurturing and steadying influence to the relationship. Further, she is disciplined enough to recognise when and where the partnership may need work, and will dedicate all her energies and resources into making it work if she feels it is worthwhile. If the Goat can lighten up a little and the Lion can learn to live with Capricorn's seriousness, these two have a reasonably good chance of bridging the gap between them. In any case, they will be unfailingly loyal to one another if the relationship is worth their effort.

Overall compatibility rating ★ 6 out of 10
Lucky Romance Tip ★ To attract a Leo, wear the colours gold or orange, and use the crystal ruby

Capricorn ★ Virgo ♑ ♍

You both share the Earthy need for ambition and to have social respectability and financial security. You can easily empathise, love and respect each other, but beware of playing on each other's over-active conscience. Virgo appreciates the Goat's steadfast approach and devoted nature and can easily relate to Capricorn's needs, being happy to help with Capricorn's lofty ambitions, provided the Virgin doesn't get caught up in the petty details - for the Goat will often have high aims which will not be hindered by anyone. You both belong to the Earth element, so you have your feet firmly on the ground, and you enjoy and appreciate the practical, realistic necessities of life, love and work. Both of you are conscientious, devoted, dedicated and reliable, with a strong sense of duty and responsibility, but these qualities can create a blessing *and* a curse, for you are both prone to falling victim to situations of 'all work and no play'. This, coupled with your serious, cool, aloof natures, can make for a very solemn union. Both of you tend to be workaholics during at least one period in your life, which can strain the relationship and give rise to resentment and cutting remarks. Your ruling planets, wise, self-disciplined Saturn and intellectual Mercury, are well matched for business and practical purposes, but there could be a lack of feelings, warmth, play and romantic zest. Both appreciate each other's systematic, orderly and methodical approaches to life, but when applied to love, these same characteristics may not work so well. You are both industrious and agree on all the essential things, but should ever beware of neglecting life's pleasures. Overall, however, your Earthy, sensual natures are likely to work well together and one thing is guaranteed - you are dedicated to and can depend on each other, sometimes forever.

Overall compatibility rating ★ 6 out of 10
Lucky Romance Tip ★ To attract a Virgo, wear the colours white or yellow, and use the crystal sapphire

Capricorn ★ Libra ♑ ♎

This is quite a challenging match, but once you learn to enjoy your differences, you may find each other surprisingly delightful company. The Scales' wit, elegance, grace, charm and eloquence will win the sensuous Goat over, but Capricorn's Earthy practicalities aren't always compatible with Libra's intellectual idealism. Libra's Venusian nature, with its liberal softness and love of pleasure, meets a rather cold, hard rock in Capricorn. The Goat's stern control of emotions and behaviour can turn the loving, gregarious Libran off. This is not the most workable of combinations, as hard-working Capricorn may view Libra's breezy socialising as trivial and lazy. There is generally not enough common ground here for real rapport to grow, and as Air does not mix easily with Earth, it may be hard to bridge any gaps between you. If Libra can learn to live with the Goat's natural reserve, he will be rewarded with someone who is loyal, protects, and makes effective decisions about their love and life. Indeed, the Scales can't handle the practical details of life and will either avoid them at all costs, or hand them over to someone who can - which in this case is the Goat. Libra craves affection and sharing, and Capricorn doesn't wear her heart on her sleeve, nor does she demonstrate love or warmth easily, so Libra could be left feeling neglected and unloved. Carefree Libra enjoys self-indulgence, ease and luxury, whereas frugal Capricorn takes life very seriously, thrives on responsibility and duty, and can cope with austerity a lot better than soppy, soft Libra can. If this partnership is to work, the Goat would do well to remember that the sharing of love, affection and beautiful experiences is as necessary to Libra as breathing air. Capricorn will frown upon Libra's frivolous handling of money and flirtatious behaviour, even if it is directed at *her*. Further, the Goat likes to take things slowly, steadily and cautiously, while the much more impressionable and easygoing Libra will fall for a romantic trick every time. If Libra takes the time to see behind the aloof façade of the cool Capricorn, it could be well worth his while, because he will find there a sensuous, devoted, caring partner in the Goat. But Libra is often too busy whirling and whizzing around his social circle to delve deeper than what can be seen at face value.

Overall compatibility rating ★ 6 out of 10
Lucky Romance Tip ★ To attract a Libran, wear the colours pink and blue, and use the crystal opal

Capricorn ★ Scorpio ♑ ♏

Both naturally reserved, self-controlled, suspicious and secretive, you will also tend towards being loyal to and protective of each other. However, Scorpio may demand too much of the Goat emotionally and keep her from climbing the mountain as high as she'd like to. But generally, you two make for a compatible pair as you share similar goals - based on respect, power and security among other things. The Goat may seem insensitive to the Scorpion at times, but will certainly respect her privacy and need to be introspective. You are both incisive, clear-sighted and consistent, and you both rely on your wits, instincts and resources to get by in life, no matter whose toes you step on - even each other's. Both intense and driven, but in considerably different ways, you could set fire to the bedroom or create a formidable, unbreakable bond. In any case, you are both unerringly faithful, dedicated, determined, wilful and do not stop until you have reached any goal you set for yourself. Scorpio will admire the Capricorn's abundant drive and Capricorn will appreciate the Scorpio's cool, steady, unwavering influence. When conflicts arise however, you can become bitter enemies, as neither is forgiving or compromising and you are both ruthless and brutal in battle. Neither of you will back down, as this would be a weakness, so any serious rifts will not be easily or quickly resolved. Earth and Water are generally harmonious though, so if you can find mutual characteristics, of which there are many, and capitalise on these, your relationship stands a good chance of being a strong, passionate bond which will weather any storm. Yours has great potential to develop into a strong, resilient and powerful match indeed. Just watch your sarcasm and bite.

Overall compatibility rating ★ 7.5 out of 10
Lucky Romance Tip ★ To attract a Scorpio, wear the colours red or burgundy, and use the crystal malachite

Capricorn ★ Sagittarius ♑ ♐

With the Archer's clownish and wandering ways, he can either bring out the Goat's gallantry or stern disapproval. If the Sagittarian restless spirit begins to take flight, Capricorn will turn cold. The Goat's practicality and hard-nosed realism can suffocate the Archer's Fire. Sagittarius's bubbly mirth and innate goodwill may begin to lessen under the influence of the tough, rigid Capricorn. Pragmatic Capricorn will look closely and critically at Sagittarius's never-ending ideals, plans and bigger picture schemes, which will frustrate the liberal Archer and make him feel sober and stifled. Yet, more than any of the other signs, Capricorn can help to ground the lofty Sagittarian ideals and bring them to tangible fruition, which the Archer will greatly appreciate. But the differences between you may weigh your union down over time, as the marked contrast between Fire and Earth is so very evident here. While Capricorn is dutiful, responsible, cautious, serious, prudent, cynical and conservative, the Sagittarius is naturally hopeful, optimistic, buoyant, careless and impulsive. The Sagittarius's tendency to be extravagant and not care about consequences may be unnerving to the much more calculated, methodical Capricorn. Furthermore, your ruling plants bring another restrictive influence to this partnership, as Saturn relates to contraction, boundaries, limitation and restriction, while Jupiter epitomises expansion, abundance, boundlessness and increase. Although opposites *can* attract, the vast differences inherent in your characters may make your relationship seem like hard slog at times. But you both aim high, so your ambitious streaks could combine to reach great heights and achieve wonderfully special things.

Overall compatibility rating ★ 5.5 out of 10
Lucky Romance Tip ★ To attract a Sagittarius, wear the colour deep purple or royal blue, and use the crystal zircon

Capricorn ★ Capricorn ♑ ♑

If you two stand still for long enough you may take root, such is your Earthy stability and groundedness. Mutual respect, powerful sexuality and similar concerns will also usually bind you together. This double dose of Earth simply multiplies your conservative, realistic, controlled, disciplined and practical approach to life and love. But you may risk taking life so seriously that you miss out on the many light-hearted adventures on life's menu. If you are both striving for the same goals and climbing the same mountain, your combined conscientious efforts will ensure great success. But if you start ascending different hills, resentment and bitterness could taint your relationship and cool your sensual passion. You need also beware of being competitive and playing power games with each other, as this will breed disputes that over time can erode your relationship. One thing is certain with this duo: you are both loyal, dedicated and committed, so if you do encounter romance problems, you will both work through them and persevere to make your union work out; rarely will a Capricorn walk away without trying every single avenue of resolution with their partner. Your biggest risk is becoming stuck in a relationship rut, which makes it all the more important to embrace other people and bring them into your circle, if for nothing else but to inject a bit of fun and spontaneity, which the two of you may be seriously lacking in. Although your relationship takes a lot of development in the beginning and a lengthy warm-up period before you finally become as 'one', once you have decided to be together exclusively, this can indeed be a meeting of minds, ambitions, sensuous delights and mutually satisfying, albeit veiled, desire. You stand a good chance of surviving to a ripe old age in union if you can remind yourselves to have fun often, for play is the glue that will bind you together.

Overall compatibility rating ★ 7.5 out of 10
Lucky Romance Tip ★ To attract another Capricorn, wear the colours brown or black, and use the crystal garnet.

Capricorn ★ Aquarius ♑ ♒

Capricorn supports the status quo and Aquarius likes to shake it up. The Goat should either loosen up and respect the Water Bearer's often kooky ideals, or choose another mountain to climb. While Aquarius, an Air sign, is erratic, unusual, disobedient, inventive, unorthodox and more than a little wayward, Capricorn, an Earth sign, is traditional, sensible, practical, conventional and structured. Air and Earth do not mix very harmoniously, and your modes, Fixed and Cardinal, will also prove an obstacle to you two seeing eye to eye. Capricorn is tight, sometimes mean, and tenacious, striving for goals and lofty ambitions, while Aquarius is unpredictable but ever-friendly, and independent, determined to reach their ideals in a completely different way. Aquarian behaviour often undermines Capricorn's desire for stability, security and consistency. The rebellious Water Bearer likes to rock the boat, challenge the establishment, question authority, seek out thrills and break down outworn traditions, while the Goat is rigid, conservative and respectful of tradition and authority. You do share minds of a high order however, and if you can channel your energies into your intellectual rapport and natural respect for each other, a mutually fulfilling relationship could very well develop. Overall, Aquarius's capriciousness and unruly streak will unnerve and shock the quiet, steady Goat, who just wants to live a peaceful - albeit constantly achieving - life. Only time - of which Capricorn has an abundance - will tell with this pairing.

Overall compatibility rating ★ 6 out of 10
Lucky Romance Tip ★ To attract an Aquarian, wear the colours electric blue or turquoise, and use the crystal aquamarine

Capricorn ★ Pisces ♑ ♓

Pisces brings out the Goat's protective urge, making Capricorn feel lighter and somehow enriched. The Fish's patience, gentleness, acceptance, persuasive charm and soft manners are food for the Capricorn's soul. But she might try to swim away if Capricorn tries to control her. Earth has an affinity with Water and although there is a great difference between your two signs, you do complement each other in many ways. Pisces finds it easy to merge with and adapt to people and situations which are safe, strong and secure, and Capricorn is the epitome of safety, strength and security. However, while Pisces is elusive, indirect, sensitive, emotional, fluid, sentimental, unworldly and romantic, Capricorn does not wear her heart on her sleeve and is serious, practical, solid, competitive, worldly, sensible, practical, conventional, structured, organised and worldly. While sensual, Capricorn is not known for being overtly romantic or readily charming, which doesn't seem to bother Pisces too much, as long as the steady Goat can provide a shelter and protect the Fish from the harsh elements of life. Pisces may be a little over-sensitive to Capricorn's lack of outward emotional expression, and Capricorn may find Pisces's deeply feeling nature a little difficult to handle. In Capricorn's ordered and organised world, there seems no place for a slippery and timid Fish, and Piscean behaviour often undermines Capricorn's desire for stability and consistency. The traditional Goat, however rigid, is conservative, traditional and respectful, and will treat the mermaid or merman with an inner tenderness, devotion and kindness like no other sign. A mutually fulfilling relationship could very well develop if Capricorn can learn to live with Pisces's tendency to dilly-dally and waver, and if Pisces is not intimidated or hurt by Capricorn's biting, ambitious, striving, win-at-all-costs nature.

While you both have different motivations and needs, you also share a need for peace, occasional solitude, profound connection with another, the deep sharing of thoughts, and gentle, sensuous affections.

Overall compatibility rating ★ 6.5 out of 10
Lucky Romance Tip ★ To attract a Pisces, wear the colours mauve or sea green, and use the crystal amethyst

YOUR TAROT CARDS ★ FOR LUCK, MAGIC, ENERGY, ABUNDANCE, QUESTING & MEANING
THE DEVIL & THE WORLD

Tarot and astrology are inextricably linked. All the cards of the Major Arcana, which comprises 22 of the Tarot's 78 cards, are 'ruled by' or connected with either one of the twelve zodiac signs, the planets and luminaries, or one of the four elements.

The 22 Major Arcana cards contain the richest symbolism of all the cards in the Tarot deck, each carrying a myriad of messages for the reader to decipher. The symbolism contained within these images represents the archetypal aspects of your character. It also describes the path your soul takes through each stage of life, revealing clues through which you can explore different parts of yourself. Each of the cards also represents an aspect of Universal human experience and has a name that either directly conveys the meaning of the card, such as Strength or Justice, or depicts individuals that represent these human archetypes, such as the Hermit or the Empress. The illustrations on each card contain one or more figures and tuning into a card's imagery enables you to grasp its meaning intuitively. Consider the demeanour of the characters, whether it is day or night, the background, any symbols, the buildings, the colours, the vegetation, the weather and the season. Every card has its own story to impart, and through entering that story you can gain deeper insights into the full picture of your journey so far, as well as illuminating your path ahead.

I have outlined two cards here for your sign: The Devil and The World, which have links to your zodiac sign itself Capricorn, your ruling planet Saturn, and your element of Earth. These two cards will have special meaning for your sign, and can carry powerful messages and lessons for you to reflect upon.

★ THE DEVIL ★
Ruled by Capricorn

Keywords ★ Temptation, Excesses, Entrapment, Bondage

★ KEY THEMES ★

Temptations ★ Bondage ★ Compulsions ★ False Sense of Entrapment ★ Dependency ★ Bad Influence ★ Overly Focused on Material Things ★ Negative or Fear-Based Thoughts ★ Guilt ★ Refusal to Face the Truth or Take Responsibility for a Situation ★ Addictions ★ Off-Balance ★ Excess ★ Irrepressible Urges ★ Instincts ★ Power Expressed in the Physical and Material World ★ A Passionate, Creative Person, Either Productive or Destructive, Ready to Use Any Possible Means to Reach Desired Ends ★ Firm Willpower ★ Strong Psyche ★ Financial and Material Aims and Achievements ★ Selfish Desire

Number ★ 15
Astrological Associations ★ Capricorn & Cancer

THE MESSAGE ★ The Devil is a complex card full of paradoxical meanings. In Jungian terms, we could regard the Devil as the collective 'shadow' that our culture has projected onto us, a symbol of societal bondage and power. This card serves to remind us of our shadow side and the evil we can do to ourselves if we fail to break free from our chains and bondages. Traditionally, and particularly to the collective medieval psyche, the Devil was a living force of evil and thus greatly feared. However, in modern Tarot decks, the meaning of this card is more in line with Cabbalistic thought, which sees the Devil as the 'tester' or the quality controller - indeed a negative force, but one which provides the challenges and hardships against which you have to strive in your life. For without this active, discordant force, there would be nothing to strive against, and therefore little chance to progress. The main idea in this card is that of bondage and this can take many forms, most of which tie you down or give you the feeling of being trapped. It can indicate enslavement to something or someone, and could be an idea, a relationship, a way of life, an unhappy job, a bad habit or a self-destructive pattern. But this card's message is that this perceived entrapment isn't real; it isn't based in reality, but rather the ego and the shadowy self that lurks deep within. Your trap is of your own making and, even though you may imagine you can't escape its constriction, there is a way out if only you can see it. You will remain enslaved to the challenging situation until you acknowledge that you are in fact your *own* imprisoner and *you* hold the key to unlock your chains.

THE STORY ★ The Devil is the archetypal face of evil. He compels us to look deeper into ourselves to examine our motives and untamed desires. Blinded to his spiritual nature, the Devil looks down on his captors, his slitted eyes suggestive of a complete obsession with and surrender to the material world. The Devil expresses the worst side of human nature: following decadent impulses blindly and judging things only by their surface value. This is the dark side of the soul, ignorant of what is 'real' and valuable. Though he may be merely mischievous at times, he will try to take advantage of any situation and cannot be trusted. Capricorn, the cardinal Earth sign attributed to the Devil, represents these manifestations in the continual attempt to scale peaks, sometimes at any cost. If Capricorn's competitive and ambitious streak turns to selfish gratification, power and wealth, it can become destructive. However, we have to acknowledge that within each of us resides an invisible, wild, gratification-seeking spirit, wanting expression, yearning for freedom. The outcome of the repression of this wildness can lead to robotic, dull, mechanistic, monotonous ways of living, which eventually manifest themselves as violence and aggression, often unpredictable, for when this free spirit breaks free from its reins, we often use expressions such as: "The Devil made me do it." Demanding instant satisfaction, love is lacking in the Devil for he sees it as a sign of weakness and distraction. However, he *will* set free those who choose to see beyond their own damaging material and selfish desires.

THE AWAKENING ★ The Devil in traditional form, puts fear into our hearts - but for our own good. He shows us the error of our ways and highlights the failings and trappings of ignorance and excess. An encounter with the Devil brings back your deepest fears. To overcome these, you need to change the emphasis from physical concerns, to those of the spirit. Your bondage is the result of your limited beliefs about the world and your resorting to deceit to get what you want. The first step in breaking out of bondage is to protest, by saying "No!" for example, which requires courage and conviction, a strong belief in self, and an unstoppable impulse toward freeing the wild spirit within. Saying "No!" to private thought forms and thinking habits that cripple us emotionally is empowering. Every person who has given up an addiction or said no to a pressing temptation, understands what effort and victory truly mean. You have within the power to change and use your beliefs, through visualisation, new habits, actions, free will and affirmations that are in harmony with natural and cosmic laws. In essence the Devil may exist in some form in each one of us, but it can always be exorcised.

THE LESSON ★ The Devil suggests the possibility of great power if energy can be released rather than imprisoned. The image of the Devil as the Greek God Pan, who was worshipped as a fertile, life-giving god of abundance, has attained a bad reputation over the centuries and, as a result, we have learned to feel ashamed of our instinctive urges. The Devil card points out that it is necessary to accept all aspects of our nature - dark, shadowy *and* light - so that our repressed fears can be released to give way to positive, liberated energies. If we don't allow this, inhibitions and phobias can develop in the unconscious, preventing healthy growth and expression. The 'devil' in us must therefore be faced so we can come to terms with him and put his forces to better use. Whether you are the one wielding the power or the one feeling the effects of submission, your soul is in need of liberation. The Devil carries the message and lesson that if such blocks can be overcome, the prospects for growth and progress are much brighter.

SYMBOLISM *★ The Devil card may evoke an initial response of fear, but its actual message is that you can overcome your inner 'demons'. The Devil symbolises the fearful, shadowy aspects of the psyche, and reflects what can occur when you are governed by the unconscious, ruled by the primeval mind, rather than by logic, intuition and wisdom. He symbolises that you are being controlled by your inner forces and fears, signifying obsessions, sexuality without love, and a sensation of being powerless.

The chains around the 'captives' at his feet are loose enough for them to break free, indicating that they should have the courage to do just that, and that in any case, they have the choice to break loose from the ties that restrict them.

The Devil is commonly depicted in the Tarot as half-man, half-goat, with bat wings and horns, which connects him with the Greek God Pan, who was the god of untamed nature and sexuality. Lustful and sensual, he was not malicious or evil, however, he represents our natural urges which, if left to their own devices, tend to be more troublesome than if they are managed and owned. This is symbolised by his naked prisoners, whose chains hang loosely and could be broken free from if they chose to do so.

The image of the Devil is a familiar if sinister one. This is the card of the dangers of materialism. The Devil rules the tyranny of the physical body and the senses and is the bearer of the inevitable, such as disasters and misery.

At this stage of the Tarot journey, you are confronted with the fact that the equilibrium you have been experiencing is found to be more fragile than you first realised, and you are forced to face your fears. Temptations appear that are difficult to resist or overcome and your strengthening self-awareness battles to prevent you becoming ensnared by issues of obsession, sexuality, materialism or power.

The two characters chained to each other at the Devil's feet in this card are, it would seem, prisoners of the Devil. But in reality, the Devil is a figment of their imagination, their thoughts, their desires and their wishes, hence lends the sense that their entrapment and imprisonment is merely an illusion. These two figures represent humanity; he has apparent power over them, but in his wisdom he has made their shackles loose enough for them to escape. It is they who are foolish if they do not take advantage of this, and release themselves from their situation. He makes us aware that only oneself can rid oneself of the psychological bonds inhibiting oneself.

Although the Devil is the tempter, who preys on your fears in order to gain power over you and chain you to an illusion, in essence, he really insists that you are not as trapped in your problems or situation as you might think.

This card reveals an excess, an imperious desire, a blind impulse, a pressing or irrepressible need to act, to reach one's aims or to satisfy them. This need is often blocked and if it is released it needs careful guidance to realise the positive aspects of the desire and thus encourage growth.

Its divinatory meanings are subordination, ravage, possessive instinct, bondage, malevolence, downfall, inability to realise one's goals, violence, shock, intense creativity, fatality, self-punishment, temptation to evil, self-destruction, unrealised success, power, weird experiences, bad outside influence or advice, black magic and unexpected failures. It is connected with lust and greed, with a refusal to recognise anything else but pleasure for its own sake. It signifies unyielding power, discontent, depression, overwhelming forces and an immovable object which cannot be overcome yet may be worked around.

In meeting with your darker self, this will signify the beginning of freedom, release from bondage, the throwing off of shackles, a light at the end of the tunnel, the undertaking of more charitable deeds and thoughts, the recognition of your needs by another person, the overcoming of severe handicaps, the beginning of spiritual understanding, and the overcoming and conquering of bad habits, thoughts or addictions that have kept you limited for so long.

Capricorns are recommended to carry one of these cards with them to illumine their paths, and to magnetise that for which they are asking. Go forth and claim the magic which is yours!

★ THE WORLD/UNIVERSE ★
Ruled by Saturn & the Element of Earth

Keywords ★ Completion, Attainment, Fulfilment

★ KEY THEMES ★
★ Arrival! ★ Completion ★ Fulfilment of Hopes and Dreams ★ Crowning Achievement ★ Total Success ★ Dreams Come True ★ Expansion ★ Aspirations ★ Idealism ★ Acclaim ★ A Prize or Goal Reached ★ Graduation ★ Accomplishment ★ Attainment ★ Contentment ★ Gratitude ★ The Path Toward Enlightenment ★ Perfection ★ Freedom ★ A Move to the Next Level ★ Cosmic Awareness ★ Expanded Consciousness ★ Joy ★ Great Outlook ★

Meditation ★ "I have completed one journey and will now rebirth myself to begin a brand new one. I welcome every chance to grow and learn."

Number ★ 21
Astrological Signs ★ Capricorn, Taurus, Virgo & Aquarius

THE MESSAGE ★ You have arrived at the beginning of the Path to Enlightenment, or could be considerably advanced along it by now. The World card suggests a job well done - you have happily completed something of great significance. Enjoy these feelings of wholeness and completion as your amazing accomplishments have been well-earned. You're now ready to move onto something new. You have grown spiritually and have evolved to a whole new level in your understanding of the Universe and your place in it. As well as this, you have attained complete clarity, cosmic awareness, significant enlightenment, an expanded consciousness and above all, the true freedom that accompanies all this.

THE STORY ★ A statue of a woman has come to life and is dancing, looking back at a leaf she holds in her outstretched hand. Just as the Earth, Divine Mother of us all, evolved from the stars and materialised into reality, so have our physical selves been created out of the same essence so that we may dance the dance of life just as She dances through the cosmos. This dream-like journey is one of going deep within and finding our essential harmony with All There Is. When we arrive at the knowledge of who we really are we gain The World.

THE AWAKENING ★ The World is a symbol of accomplishment, of an end which is also a beginning. The journey is completed! Upon reaching the World your goal is attained and you are suffused with joy and fulfilment. Life is fully and rapturously embraced, and you are free to experience all that it offers. You realise that the end of a journey merely leads to the first step on a new one. By uniting and balancing your long-sought after inner harmony with the skills you have learned in this lifetime so far, you have achieved true success and The World can be yours. Although hard work has been required to attain this, material rewards and inner peace are promised. But overall, you must view your life in the context of the whole of life and All There Is, before you can gain the wisdom you seek. The World imparts the message that each one of us carries a world inside of us, which is neither unattainable, illusory or utopian. It is simply what we are. All the elements are gathered here so that our conscience may awaken and our future will unfold as it is meant to before us.

SYMBOLISM *★ The World card symbolises completion and renewal. It incorporates the wisdom gathered throughout the journey of the previous 21 cards. The World embodies the essence of success, arrival, fulfilment and happiness. It shows a willingness to embrace life fully and to welcome in the new.

The central figure in the World card, hermaphroditic in appearance, symbolises the integration of the masculine and feminine principles to form a complete, unified entity. The wreath is a symbol of triumph, success, rebirth and renewal, while the surrounding creatures embody different aspects of human nature.

One of the most ancient symbols of alchemy is that of Ouroboros, the dragon or serpent which lies in a circle with its tail in its mouth. This sleeping creature must be awoken for its potential to be realised, and its energies released, for us to begin - and achieve - the process of self-transformation. The circle around the dragon, a symbol without end and without beginning, symbolises the fact that one's beginning can also be found in its end, and vice versa. And so the symbol for Ouroboros never loses its meaning, for its meaning is eternity and in a sense the journey is never really completed; each ending is followed by a new beginning. Even if we eventually arrive back at the place where we first began our journey, nothing will be the same; all is transformed.

The World (or Universe), the final card of the Major Arcana, is the supreme symbol of unity and wholeness. It commonly depicts a dancing figure holding the Magician's wand and encircled by a laurel wreath. The wand is symbolic of the magic of self-transformation, while the laurel is the plant of success, victory and high achievement. The circle represents the Ouroboros (a serpent or dragon eating its own tail), a symbol of eternity. In each corner are the four Fixed signs of the zodiac: Taurus the Bull, Leo the Lion, Scorpio the Eagle and Aquarius the Man, which correspond to the four seasons of spring, summer, autumn and winter respectively, the four evangelical qualities of Man: humanity, spirituality, courage and strength, and also the four elements, which the alchemists combined to create a perfect fifth - the 'quintessence', or fifth element. This fifth element is symbolised by the central figure in the card, a genderless hermaphrodite, an image of the reconciliation of opposites, and also of balance. The card's number is twenty-one, the number of completion (three times seven, the two most magically significant numbers). The wreath may also represent zero, the symbol of infinity, with which you started the journey; therefore, the end of one journey is marking the beginning of another.

Astrologically, the World seems to be the most strongly related to the Midheaven, which is the highest point in the sky at the moment of birth. The World's divinatory meanings are completion, perfection, the rewards of labour, inner satisfaction, the end result of all your efforts, success, synthesis, fulfilment, capability, eternal life, admiration from others, ultimate change, and triumph in all your undertakings. As a symbol of completion, attainment, success and self-knowledge, she suggests that you remind yourself of what you have already achieved, and know that others are aware of you, appreciate and truly admire your past efforts. She tells you that you are now entering an extremely rewarding phase of your life when you will enjoy the benefits of all your hard work.

The World marks the end of a period of time, or the completion of a task, which has its new beginnings as a seed within. It denotes a time of celebration and the wonderful feelings that accompany any occasion during which something is finished, or made whole. It represents a deeply satisfying sense of achievement and fulfilment, suggestive of a peak experience - and expanded horizons ahead. On another level, however, any accomplishment or completion may be followed afterwards by a feeling of emptiness or deflation, as the goal has been realised and the dream made a reality. At this point, the crowned dancing figure who celebrates reaching the finishing mark, suddenly morphs again to embody a foetal-like being, waiting to re-evolve and rebirth itself as the Fool in the never-ending circular journey; in this way, The World symbolises the ending of one cycle and the commencement of another, and indeed The World represents a course that has now come full circle, and suggests you can rest on your laurels for a time before moving onto this next phase, as you have rightly earned it. You now understand your place within that system, and are ready to begin a new phase from the beginning, but this time with an elevated, higher sense of acquired wisdom, spiritual truth and inner knowing.

* Please note that the images described are not found in all Tarot decks. The images in different decks can differ considerably.

THE TAROT'S SUIT OF PENTACLES ★ REPRESENTING THE EARTH ELEMENT

The Pentacle, or five-pointed star, that symbolises Earth in nature magic is often displayed as a central feature on the Suit of Pentacles cards. The Pentacles (known in some old decks as Coins or Discs) represent the Earth element - the energy that keeps us grounded, and the physical or material side of life. They represent the outer manifestation of our spiritual nature, and signify fertility and fecundity in all its forms - sensuality, sensual pleasures, sex and procreation, and the grounding and anchoring of creative energy. The Pentacles tell you about your relationship with the material world, resources, status, tangible assets, and also with your work. Being of the Earth realm, the Pentacles are also associated with prosperity, hard work, financial progress and practical concerns. They can represent the mastery of life's material aspects, or the ambition and striving directed towards achieving them. In essence, the Pentacles are connected with matters that are financial, economic, monetary, or concerning stability. They highlight your attitudes to wealth, work, possessions and success. Dealing with the practicalities of life, they reflect our thinking and actions around earthlier issues, and can inform us of areas where we seek greater stability in our lives. You experience the story of the Pentacles through your relationship with the tangible, physical aspects of yourself - through your attitudes towards your body, sensuality, success, work and worldly goods. A healthy approach towards all of these provides you with a sense of confidence that deepens your perspective on life. Focusing on this suit can help us become more grounded and can reconnect you to life and creativity through linking your Earthy nature to your spiritual essence. The Pentacles provide a solid framework that can be used as a springboard to attainment. Without the foundation of the Pentacles, the effectiveness of the other suits and their elemental correspondences (emotional Water, intellectual Air and enterprising Fire) would be hindered. In a deck of playing cards, the Pentacles correspond to the suit of Diamonds.

THE LUCKY 13 ★ CAPRICORNIAN TIPS FOR INCREASED MAGIC, LUCK & MAGNETISM

1 ★ Incorporate Capricornian symbols into your daily life to remind yourself of your soul's mission

2 ★ Use the crystal Garnet in any form in your daily life - wear it, meditate with it, hold it and carry it with you everywhere! Garnet is a stone of love and commitment which brings warmth, devotion, constancy, faithfulness, understanding, sincerity, trust and honesty to a relationship. It encourages you to be more creative and stimulates 'light-bulb' flashes of inspiration and thought. An energising and regenerative stone, garnet helps to dissolve unhelpful behavioural patterns and past hurts to allow you to become more self-empowered and move on. Further, if you are feeling impotent or stuck in plans that have not yet manifested, this stone assists in moving out of the stagnancy and into potent action. Garnet is a powerful attractor of abundance, drawing prosperity into your experience, and can activate other crystals, amplifying their effect. For Capricorns, garnet enhances emotions or states of being that can assist in attracting wonderful things to you.

3 ★ Wear or surround yourself with the colours black, brown and forest green.

4 ★ Learn the way of the Crab by learning greater compassion, deeper feelings, the value of domestic bliss, and how to show your care and affection for others more readily. Cancer has much to teach the Capricornian soul. Swim in the ocean with wild abandon ... Wear a daisy chain in your hair ... Get in touch with your emotions ... Explore your deeper feelings, yearnings and motives ... Nurture others more ... Work less ... Spend more time with your family ... Enjoy your or others' children ... Forget about practical concerns for a time ... Use your imagination to climb to higher and higher places ... Learn to cook ... Get in touch with your maternal side ... Enjoy the sensual feasts and fruits of your journey ... Sit near a waterfall and feel the wonder of its vastness ... it's all within you!

5 ★ Use your lucky numbers 7 and 8 whenever you are needing an extra stroke of luck.

6 ★ Magnify and celebrate your devotion, dedication, persistence, your caring nature, your willpower, your inherent wisdom, and your often untapped but intuitively in-touch psyche.

7 ★ Remind yourself of your mission constantly, that is by speaking, breathing and *truly living* your dreams and insights - share them with others instead of keeping them to yourself!

8 ★ Focus your energies on exploring your inner depths, and transforming yourself through your high-minded ideals - which are strongly accessible to the acutely striving, aspiring and determined Capricornian

mind. Connect with your deep imagination and inborn creativity through any means possible.

9 ★ Use your innate powers of steadfastness and financial acumen to visualise and draw that which you desire towards you. If you can develop simple faith in the positive outcome of events, you can easily use your oft-neglected intuition to great creative effect.

10 ★ Tap into and utilise your ability to guide, advice, help, and elevate others through sharing your emotions, spirit and soul. But to do that, you'll need to bring your feelings closer to the surface and show a bit of vulnerability.

11 ★ View your pragmatic, solid, structured and highly organised nature as strengths and call forth the powers of your incredibly gifted, unique self. Be who you *really* are, without reservation or apology, and the rest will fall into place.

12 ★ Become the 'Mountain Path Guide Enlightener' of others - and yourself - that you were born to be!

13 ★ Once you have mastered purer compassion for others, and become more in touch with your deeper, tender self, learn to share the resulting abundance, insights and knowledge with others so they too can walk the Higher Path!

HAVE YOU PACKED YOUR MAGICAL BAG FOR THE JOURNEY?

If you wish to increase and draw more luck, love and abundance into your life, a power pack is essential. For Capricornians, I would recommend carrying or wearing the following items on you on your travels. Then just sit back and watch as magic pours into your experiences and realities, both inner and outer!

★ One of each of the following gemstones: Garnet, Turquoise, Smoky Quartz, Jet, Blue Sapphire
★ Tarot cards The Devil and The World
★ A goose in any form (use your imagination!)
★ Something made of lead
★ A cat symbol in any form
★ A postcard or image from a cool, dry place (representing your Melancholic disposition). Bon Voyage!
★ A postcard from the future to yourself, proclaiming, 'Wish You Were Here!'

A FINAL WORD ★ TAPPING INTO THE MAGIC OF CAPRICORN

There is something inherently magical about Capricorn, the steady-footed Sea-Goat. Blessed with an unwavering ambition, unrivalled determination, and unequalled self-discipline, they truly are the Magical Mountain-Climbers of the zodiac, affecting everyone around them with their power and sense of duty, responsibility, sensuality and calm efficiency.

Nothing is wishy-washy about you. The cosmos has endowed you with the precious and important gifts of strength, authority, leadership, resilience, resourcefulness, perseverance, and an enviable quality of endurance that outlasts all around you. You are the wise old soul of the zodiacal experience, and have much to teach and share with others - if you let down your cool façade and let other people in. Accomplished, pragmatic and prudent, you are likely to be successful in any endeavour upon which you set your heart, head or capable hooves. Overall, you are the stoic tower of strength that others can rely upon at all times and under any circumstances. Your stability and steadiness in times of crisis and calamity are among your finest qualities. Whether you are fully cognisant of it or not, a magical reservoir of energy is available to you to tap into whenever it is needed.

Finally, to attune yourself to luck, harmony and success, Capricornians should wear, eat, inhale, meditate upon, create, design, and dance with any or all of the suggested luck-enhancers for your Sun sign to receive the most beneficial astral vibrations these 'boosters' can offer you. Wearing, decorating and working with the amazing powers of all your lucky guides, animals, crystals, colours, woods, cards, herbs, foods, places, talismans, planetary influences, charms, numbers, and other magical tips contained within the words of this very book, will bring you greater abundance, love, magic, energy, happiness and personal power, and attract all manner of things to you like bees to sweet flowers. This, my Capricornian friends, I promise you - and Aquarians *never* lie.

Good luck on the rest of your amazing life journey, and may the LUCK be with you!

Lani is also available for personal Astrology, Numerology, Aura * & Tarot reading consultations, via post, email, Skype and in-person.

Please email lalana76@bigpond.com for more information.

In-person only

Facebook Page ★ Astrology Magic

Other Books in the **Lucky Astrology** Series

Lucky Astrology ★ Aries
Lucky Astrology ★ Taurus
Lucky Astrology ★ Gemini
Lucky Astrology ★ Cancer
Lucky Astrology ★ Leo
Lucky Astrology ★ Virgo
Lucky Astrology ★ Libra
Lucky Astrology ★ Scorpio
Lucky Astrology ★ Sagittarius
Lucky Astrology ★ Aquarius
Lucky Astrology ★ Pisces

Order your copies now, from White Light Publishing House, at www.whitelightpublishingau.com

www.ingramcontent.com/pod-product-compliance
Lightning Source LLC
Chambersburg PA
CBHW071154300426
44113CB00009B/1200